Whimsical Whirligigs and How to Make Them

Anders S. Lunde

DOVER PUBLICATIONS, INC.
Mineola, New York

Copyright

Bibliographical Note

This Dover edition, first published in 2000, is an unabridged republication of *Whirligigs for Children Young and Old* originally published by the Chilton Book Company, Radnor, Pennsylvania, in 1992.

Library of Congress Cataloging-in-Publication Data

Lunde, Anders S.
Whimsical whirligigs and how to make them / Anders S. Lunde.
p. cm.
Reprint. Originally published: Radnor, PA : Chilton Book Co., 1992.
ISBN-13: 978-0-486-41233-7
ISBN-10: 0-486-41233-4
1. Wooden toy making. 2. Whirligigs. I. Title.

TT174.5. W6 L8637 2000
745.592—dc21

00-031390

Manufactured in the United States by LSC Communications
41233411 2020
www.doverpublications.com

To creative children everywhere and their teachers

In remembrance of Tony

Contents

Foreword

In July 1988 I led a workshop on whirligig-making at the Forty-First Annual Seminar in American Culture at the New York State Historical Association in Cooperstown, New York. During this exciting week, a number of people approached me about using whirligigs in children's workshops and in teaching history. They requested that I convert some of my more complex whirligig designs so that they could be made by children. While pre- and early teenage children could use simple saws (like a coping saw) and could glue things together, they may have difficulty using sharp knives for extensive woodcarving. After spending some time examining standard whirligigs and new designs, I realized that it was possible to make authentic whirligigs using simple construction techniques. When I arrived back at my workshop I began to design whirligigs for children and realized that the designs would be fun for children young and old.

This book covers both simplistic designs and more complicated patterns. Most of the whirligigs in the first part of the book (the Vane through Mary in Her Garden) were designed with young children in mind. Whirligigs in the second part of the book were created for older youth and adults. The first two chapters are important reading for all ages because they discuss the tools and materials used in all whirligig construction. Part II lists advanced methods for more complex whirligigs.

Just remember, whirligigs are fun to watch but they are even more fun to make!

Whimsical Whirligigs
and
How to Make Them

Chapter 1
An Introduction to Whirligigs

What Is a Whirligig?

A whirligig is something that turns and spins in the wind. In some places it is called a wind toy, in other places a windmill, and in still other places a wind machine. Whirligigs are fun, and can be made to represent just about anything—birds, pigs, dogs, cats, whales, codfish, ships, planes, people—you name it. A whirligig works in the wind, all by itself. It doesn't need a motor or an engine or any other power. It uses wind power. Once you make one and leave it out in the wind, the wind will take care of it!

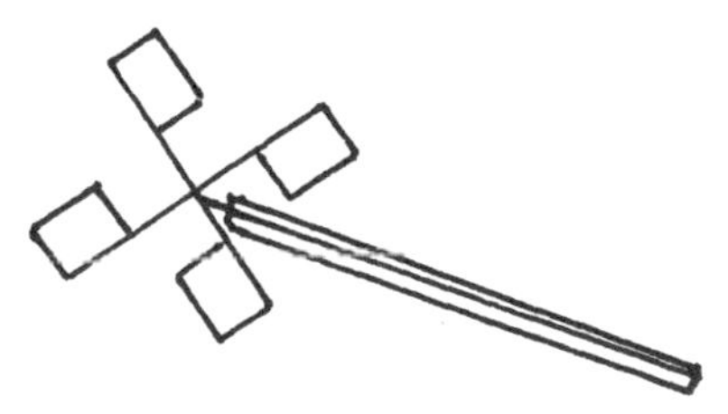

The word *whirligig* comes to us through the English language. Many years ago in England it was spelled *whirlegogge, whyrlegygge,* and *worlegyg*. Before that, it was two separate words the Vikings brought to England. One was *whirl,* meaning "to spin and turn around." The other word was *gig,* which meant "to turn fast." Combine them and you have something that spins and turns at the same time. Most whirligigs turn horizontally (sideways and around) and at the same time move vertically (up and down). Take the simple bird whirligig, for example. It turns its body on a pivot or spindle horizontally and waves its wings vertically.

Whirligigs are very old. We know that children played with them over 500 years ago in Europe. Their whirligigs were quite simple, mostly consisting of propellers on sticks. One hundred years ago in our country, whirligigs were very popular and there were lots of whirligig makers.

Almost every yard had a whirligig, and your great-grandfather probably made a whirligig or two just for fun. Today, there are few whirligig makers, and it is said that making whirligigs is a lost art. Once you have made a whirligig and become a whirligig maker, you will be one in a million!

Whirligigs look simple to make, and they are simple if you know what makes them work. Whirligig making, like every craft, has its secrets, but once you know these secrets, making them is easy.

The Whirligigs in This Book

The whirligigs in this book are real whirligigs and can be made by anyone. They are easy to make and they will work if they are made according to the instructions. They don't cost much either, because only a couple of pieces of wood and a few tools, plus a nail and screw or two, are needed.

But before I begin, let me tell you about the main types of popular whirligigs and which ones are in the book. Perhaps the oldest type is the *simple vane,* which always faces the wind with a propeller in front.

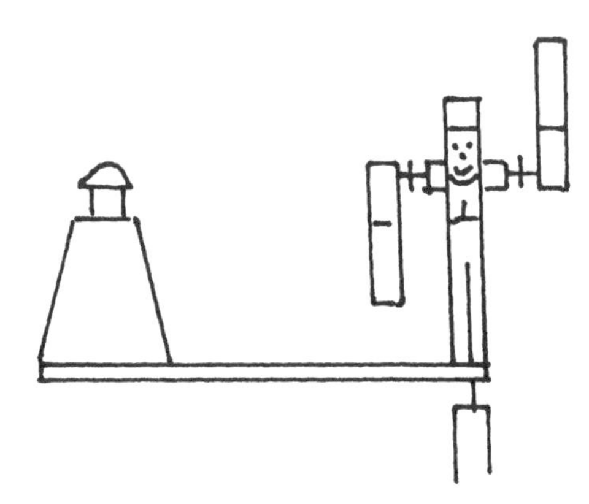

Among the oldest American whirligigs are the *arm-waving* type, often featuring soldiers waving swords and sailors waving flags. Examples included here are a Toy Soldier, Happy Sailor, Doctor Doolittle, Smiling Lady, and Pinocchio. They are unusual and fun to watch in action. Sometimes these models stand alone and sometimes they have a tail attached to keep them sideways in the wind, which allows their arms to turn correctly. The Happy Sailor has this attachment just to show you how it works.

Then there is the *winged* type. These models are usually birds, like the Coo-Coo Bird, but we have included the Guardian Angel to show that not only birds have wings. Using the same technique used in these two types, we have added the Flying Elephant to show that, with a little imagination, anything is possible—even a flying pig!

Once in a while you may find a *weathervane whirligig*. This type points into the wind, just like a weathervane. The difference is that the whirligig has something turning on it, usually a propeller of some sort. The codfish weathervanes of New England can be turned into whirligigs that way. The Cruise Ship whirligig turns into the wind and this turns the propeller at the stern. Airplane whirligigs once were very popular; their rudders kept them turned into the wind, which then turned their propellers. The two types of clowns are weathervanes of a sort because they are made to go sideways into the wind; they are balanced on one side of the body.

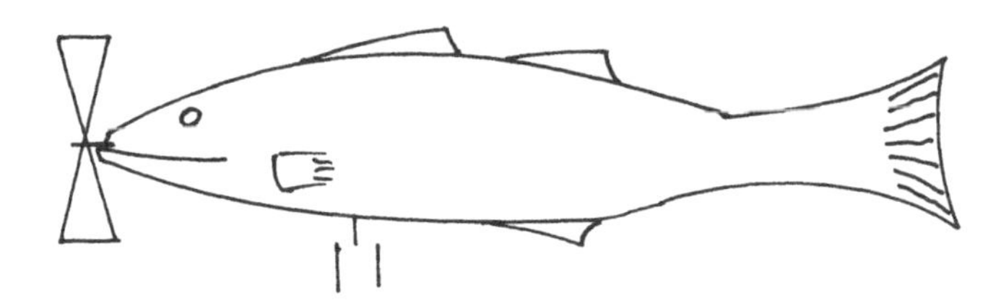

Last but not least is the *mechanical whirligig*. This is the type that most people think of when they think of whirligigs. The mechanical variety has a propeller on it that makes a driveshaft turn and makes other things move as well. Sometimes mechanical whirligigs are very complicated and take a long time to make. The most common American mechanical whirligigs are the Wood Chopper, the Man Sawing Wood, the Woman Churning Butter, the Mule Kicking the Farmer, and other subjects that deal with life in the country. Chapter 6 of this book contains three easy-to-make mechanical whirligigs: Danny the Dinosaur, David the Wood Chopper, and Mary in Her Garden.

For older persons, or those experienced in craft work, Part II also contains advanced methods for whirligig construction and instructions for making more complicated mechanical whirligigs, including the Fisher in the Boat, Clashing Knights, and the Winning Race Car, among others.

The Parts of a Whirligig

Most whirligigs have the same basic parts, and the illustration shows what their names are and where they are located. The main part is called the *body* and this is where the action is centered. At the bottom is the *pivot point* (P), where the body will be balanced. It is here that a *socket* for the *spindle* is drilled. The socket often has a metal *socket liner*. At the bottom of the socket is a *cap*. The cap prevents the spindle from cutting through the body.

Located on the body is the *hub* (H). This is where the axle will go through and the arms or wings will be attached. Sometimes a *tail* or *rudder* is attached to the whirligig by means of an extension; the purpose of the rudder is to keep the whirligig aimed correctly into the wind.

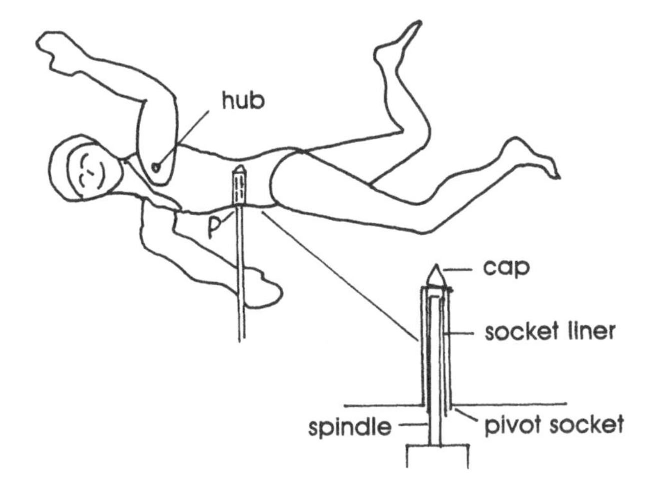

In the mechanical whirligig there is a *base* or *platform* on which the action takes place. There is a *camshaft* held in position by *brackets* of some kind. In Danny the Dinosaur the *body* is a dinosaur, attached to the *cam* by means of a *connecting rod* or *wire*. The camshaft (or *driveshaft*) is turned by a *wind propeller*.

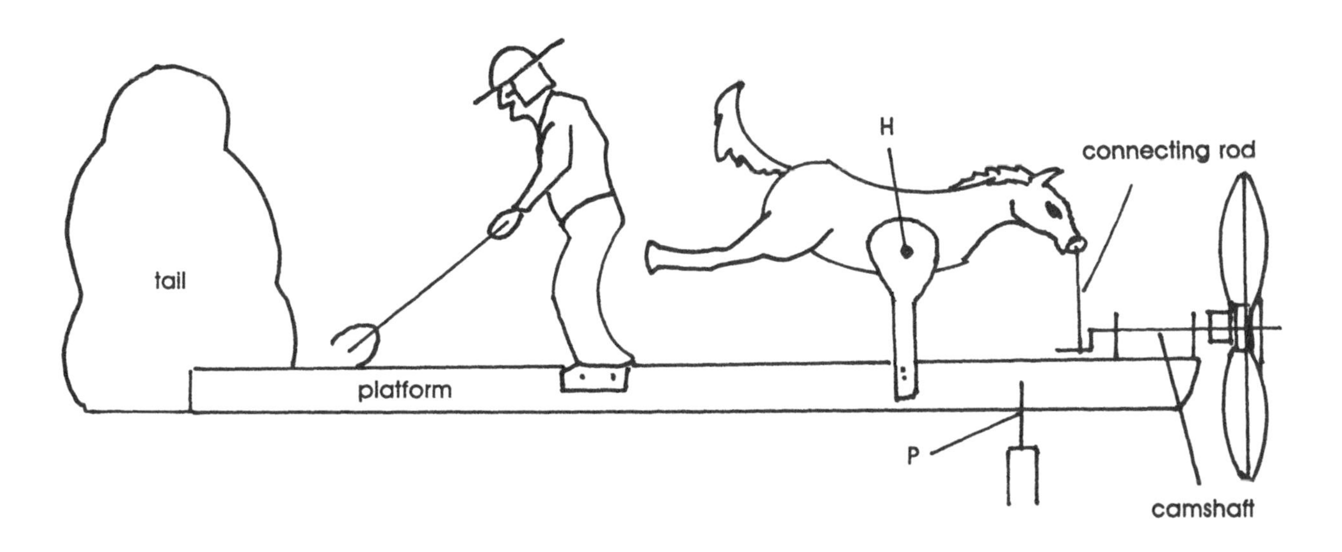

What You Need to Make a Whirligig

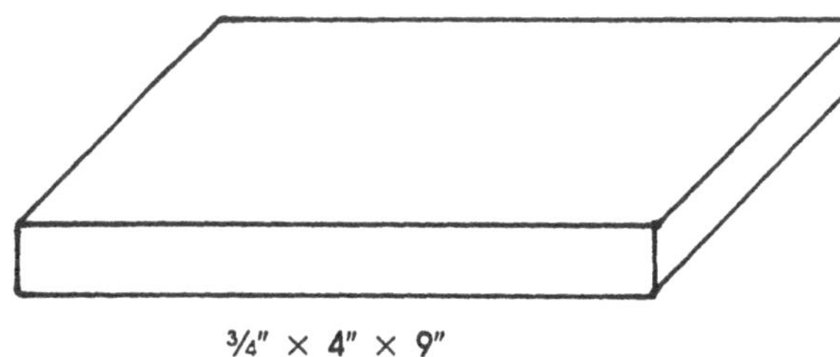

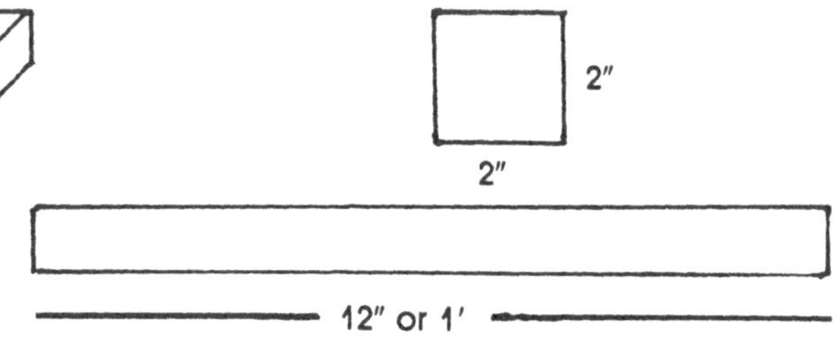

Wood

The whirligigs that were made in America 100 to 200 years ago were made of wood. The whirligigs in this book are made of regular, three-quarter-inch-thick (¾") lumber. In the lumberyard, this is called one-inch (1") lumber because that is how it originally was cut. It is smoothed down on the top and bottom sides, or planed down on a machine, and the actual measurement of the thickness of the wood becomes ¾". This is a common thickness of regular lumber.

I used pine for these whirligigs. Pine is a soft wood that is easily cut and shaped. If you buy first-grade pine, it will be more expensive than regular pine but it will not have any knots in it. I buy shelving pine, which has knots but is much cheaper and is good wood with which to work. You always can cut around the knots. Look the boards over carefully and buy the one that has the fewest knots!

The sizes of the main block of wood used for *figures* are given with each drawing. The piece for the soldier, for example, is ¾" × 2" × 10". That means that the block is three-quarters of an inch (¾") thick, two inches (2") wide, and ten inches (10") long.

Other pieces of wood are described accordingly. *Shoulder* pieces are ¾" × 1" × 2", which means that they are ¾" thick, 1" wide, and 2" long. *Arm* pieces are ⅛" × ¾" × 3", which means that they are ⅛" thick, ¾" wide, and 3" long. It won't take you long to figure out the sizes. You should always have a standard rule or ruler around to help you with the measurements.

Dowels are used for legs and axles. A dowel is a round wooden rod usually made of a hardwood like oak. It comes in lengths of three feet (3') and is obtainable in hardware stores or lumberyards. (I found some in a drugstore last week!) Whirligigs in this book use dowels that are 3/16" and ¼" in diameter. Check your ruler and see if you can find what 3/16" and ¼" look like.

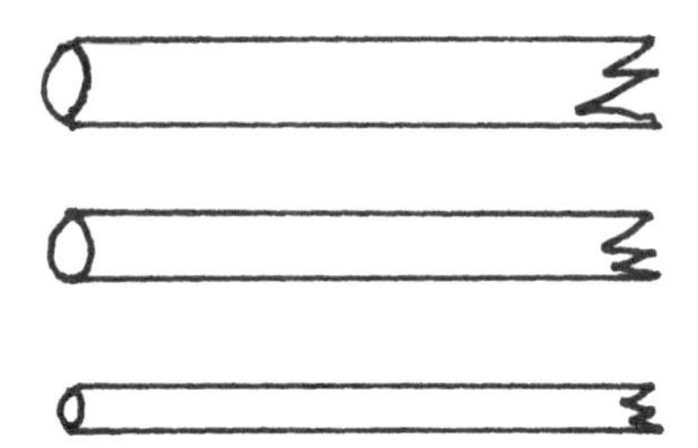

There were no lumberyards or hardware stores around 150 years ago. When people wanted to make whirligigs they looked around the house or barn for scrap wood. Maybe you can find some wood that you can use for your whirligig.

Other Materials

As for hardware, you will need screws, washers, and brass tubing. These will be described and illustrated with each model, but a few general items are listed below that can be obtained in a hardware store or lumberyard.

Nails

For *spindles,* on which the whirligig turns, you will need 16- or 20-penny regular nails (written 16d and 20d). You can make a fine spindle by cutting off the heads of these nails and filing down the rough edges. A 16d nail will fit into a 3/16" pivot socket, and a 20d nail into the ⅜" or ¼" pivot socket of the large mechanical whirligigs.

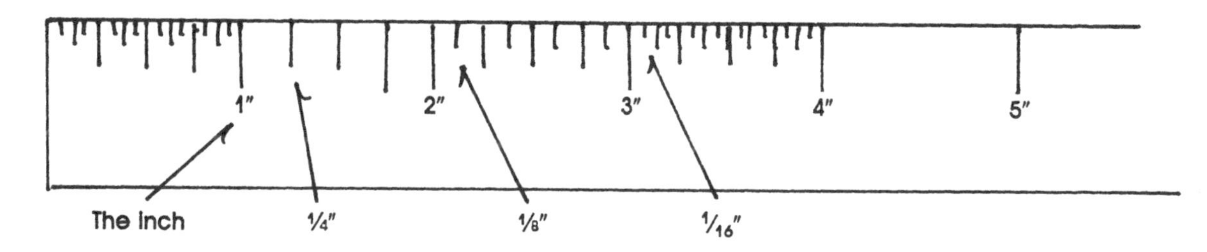

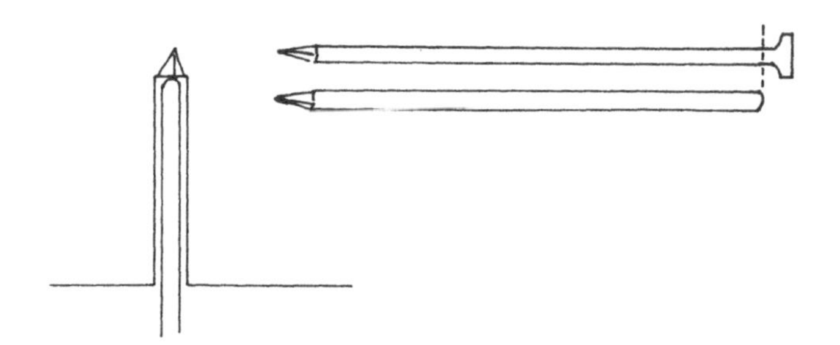

Screws and Washers

The usual screw referred to will be the No. 6 round-headed brass screw, which is $1\frac{1}{4}$" long. The washers for this screw will be brass No. 6 or No. 8. For the Cruise Ship propeller a No. 4 screw can be used. For the $\frac{3}{16}$" dowel/axles, use $\frac{3}{16}$" washers; for the $\frac{1}{4}$" dowel/axles, use $\frac{1}{4}$" brass washers.

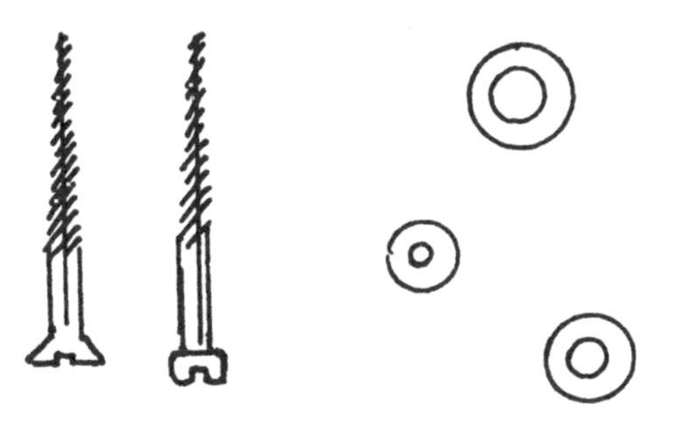

To make sure the aperture (hole) is large enough for the dowel to move freely, take a piece of dowel with you and test the washers in the store. Sometimes washers can be too tight and the next larger size will work better. You can use steel screws and washers, which are cheaper than the brass ones. The problem is that they rust quickly outdoors, although you can paint over them and they will be fine.

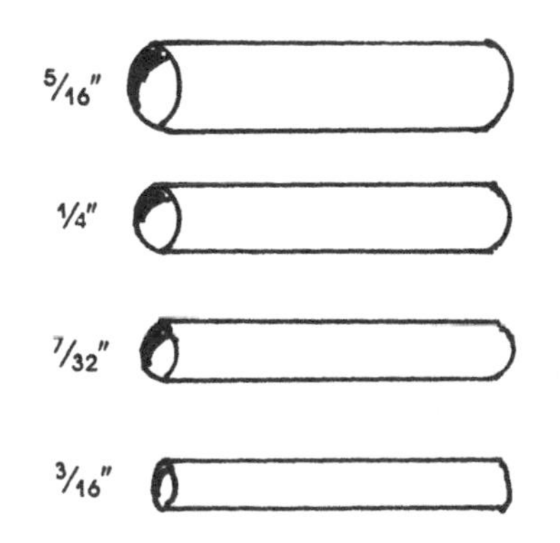

Brass Tubing

You don't need brass tubing to make any of these whirligigs work, although tubing reduces wear and tear and makes axle movement easier. So if you have a hobby shop or hardware store near you that has tubing for sale, it is advisable to get some. Tubing comes in one-foot sections and is inexpensive. The following list outlines sizes of tubing used in this book.

$\frac{5}{16}$" tubing is used for the $\frac{1}{4}$" axles.
$\frac{1}{4}$" tubing is used for the $\frac{3}{16}$" dowel axles.
$\frac{7}{32}$" tubing for lining small pivot sockets.
$\frac{3}{16}$" tubing is used for No. 6 screws.

If you use tubing, you should have a tubing cutter. This is a small hand-held machine that cuts the tube when rotated around the diameter of the tube. You can get a cheap tubing cutter in hobby shops and more expensive ones in hardware stores. Tubing also can be cut using a saw with a metal-cutting blade. If you have trouble cutting tubing, or any metal, ask for help.

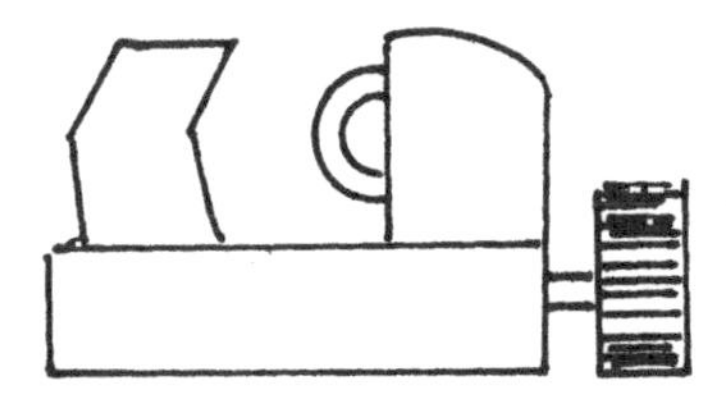

Glue

To hold wooden parts together, you will need glue. The best glue for whirligigs is yellow carpenter's glue. It comes in plastic bottles; get the small size.

Paint

Any kind of paint will do. A good acrylic-latex paint dries faster, is easy to use, and allows quick cleanup with water. Oil paint is excellent but takes a long time to dry. Give whirligigs at least two coats of paint.

Hobby stores have artist's acrylic paint in many bright colors. When I use these, I then cover them with polyurethane varnish, which comes as paint or a spray. Follow the directions carefully. If you use the spray, apply it outdoors. The varnish will protect the paint and the whirligig.

Tools

Some ordinary tools will be needed to make the whirligigs in this book, and you may find them around the house. Let's start with a *pencil,* which may be called a "tool."

Ruler

You will need a simple ruler a foot (1' or 12") long to make careful measurements. Don't forget that when you work with wood, inches are written " and feet are written '.

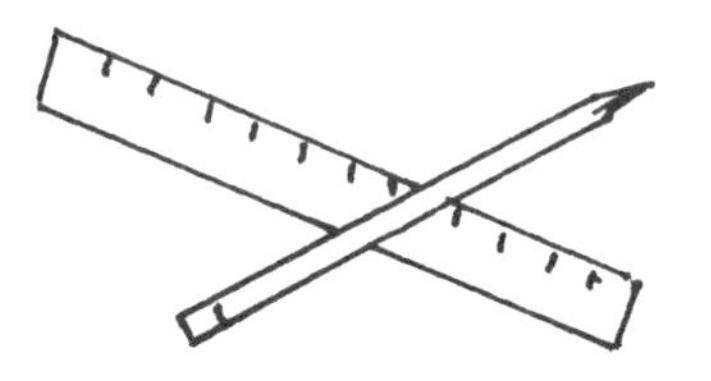

Vise

To hold the wood to be sawed or drilled, you will need a small vise. I use one with 4″ jaws that does well. Sometimes I use my worktable; the top is a big clamp. Of course, a large vise will do as well.

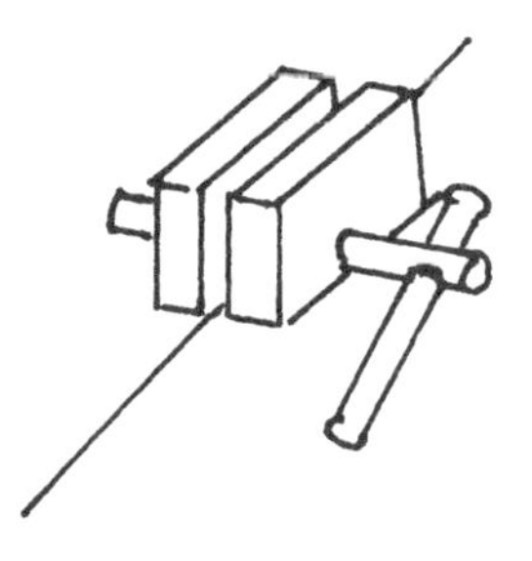

Coping Saw

This is a small saw with a thin blade that can saw straight or in curves. The figures and other parts of the bodies and objects shown in this book can be cut out with a coping saw. This saw is sharp enough to cut rapidly through pine $\frac{3}{4}$″ thick. Also, because of its thin blade, it can cut curves and corners in the wood. Don't push too hard; let the saw blade do the work. Keep the blade straight. If you bend or twist it, it may break. Keep a steady back and forth motion when sawing.

Using a coping saw to cut out the Signaling Scout whirligig body.

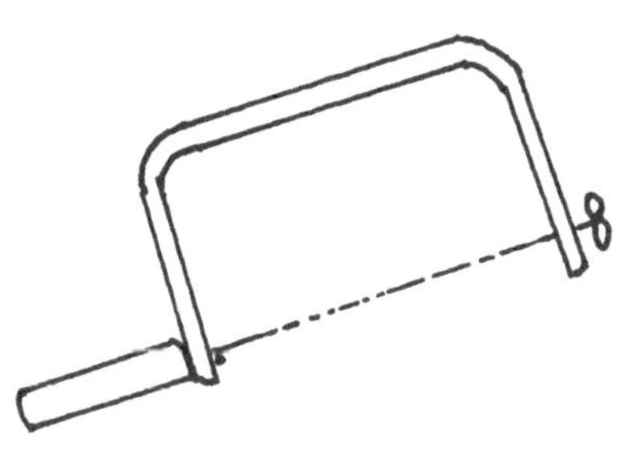

Backsaw

A backsaw has a steel top edge that holds the saw blade stiff and therefore is very good for making straight cuts across the wood. If you do not have a backsaw, a small regular crosscut saw will do the job.

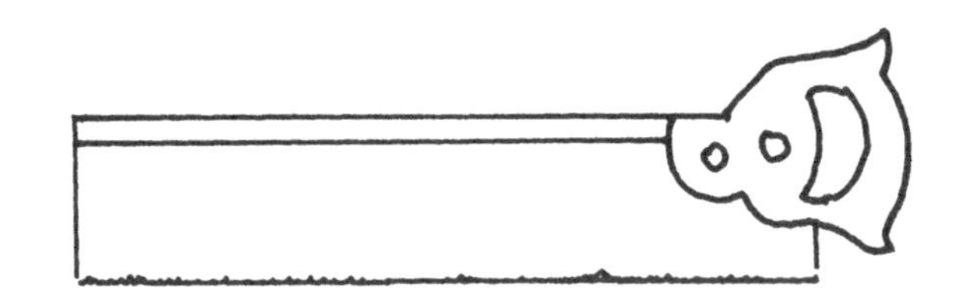

Hacksaw

This is a metal-cutting saw. It will cut the nails used as spindles, and cut off the points for caps. It also can be used for cutting brass tubing. Don't press down too hard; let the saw do the work, especially with the tubing. You may need help if you have never used a hacksaw before.

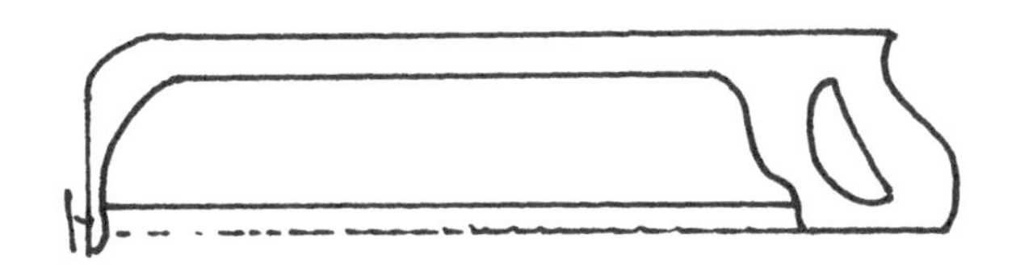

Hand Drill and Bits

To drill out the holes you will need a hand drill or drills that can use different-sized bits. Bits are the exchangeable cutting parts that make holes. They are usually packaged in cases that hold a dozen bits ranging in diameter from $\frac{1}{16}$″ to $\frac{1}{4}$″.

Don't let the fractions confuse you. They confuse me sometimes, and I have made a measurement table for my workshop. The table shows me the relation between $\frac{7}{64}$″ and $\frac{1}{8}$″, for example, which is $\frac{1}{64}$″ different.

Table 1

							1/8				
			1/16				2/16				3/16
	1/32		2/32		3/32		4/32		5/32		6/32
1/64	2/64	3/64	4/64	5/64	6/64	7/64	8/64	9/64	10/64	11/64	12/64

Some of the bits used most frequently in our work are:

1/16—for making small "pilot holes" to guide larger bits
7/64—for drilling holes in the centers of some hubs, to permit threaded 1/8" rods to go through
1/8—for making some axle holes
3/16—for tubing to hold 1/8" axles
7/32—for tubing to line most small pivot sockets

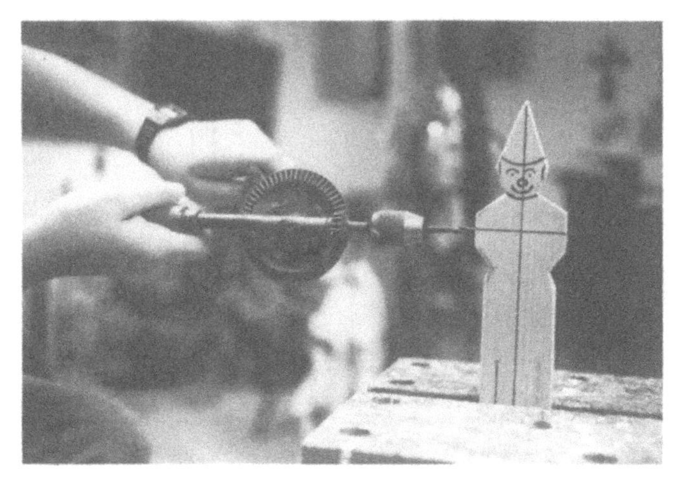

A hand drill is used to create a hub hole for the Juggling Clown.

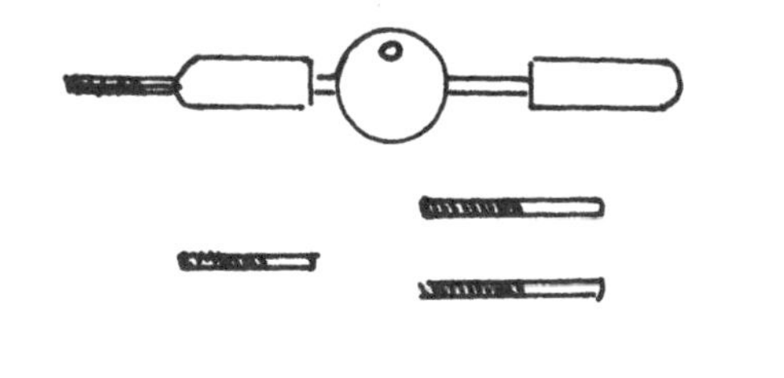

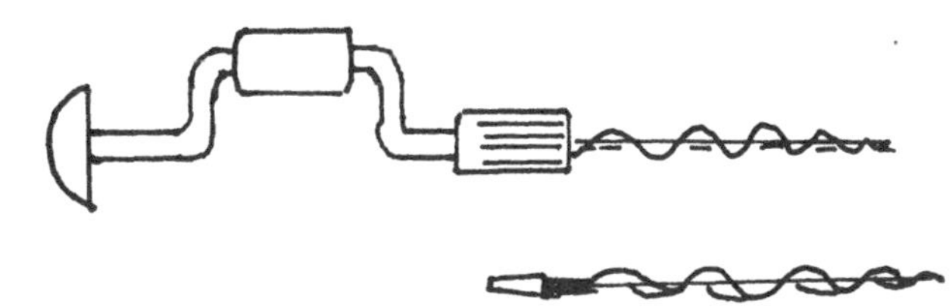

With my table I can quickly and easily see that 8/64" equals 4/32" equals 2/16" equals 1/8". You can work this out for yourself on the above chart and continue it, if you like numbers. Of course, not all of these are used for any single whirligig.

Some holes will be larger than 1/4", and for those you will need a brace and bit, a larger tool with a swing handle and larger auger bits. In this book reference is made to a 5/16" hub hole for a 1/4" axle, a 3/8" pivot socket hole for large whirligigs, and a 3/4" hole for some whirligig stands. These would require the use of a brace and bit.

Files

You should have a wood file to smooth over the edges of the wood after you have cut it. You also should have a metal file to round off the tops of the spindles.

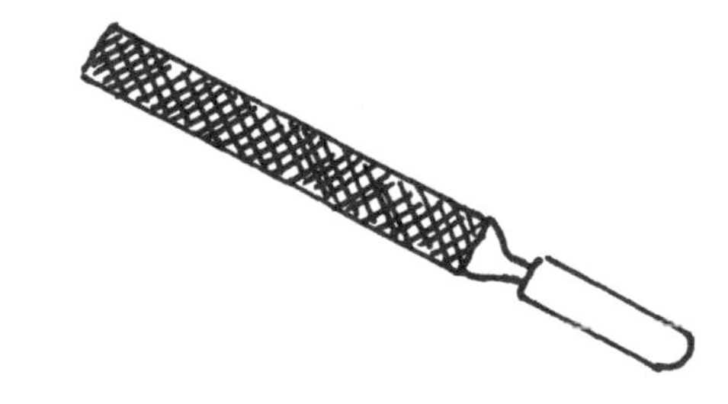

Sandpaper

When the parts are cut out with a saw and are filed down, finish smoothing them with sandpaper. Sandpaper comes in different grades of coarseness. The very fine sandpaper has high numbers and the very rough has low numbers. Don't worry about this; just select a medium rough and a medium fine sandpaper.

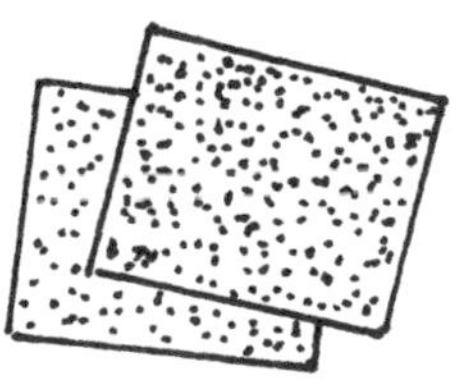

Other Carpenter's Tools

You will need a hammer to tap pieces of wood into wing or propeller slots or to nail a spindle in a post. A small screwdriver is useful in making several of the models. You also will need small clamps to hold glued parts together. Use C-clamps and spring clamps for this purpose. A pair of pliers also is useful.

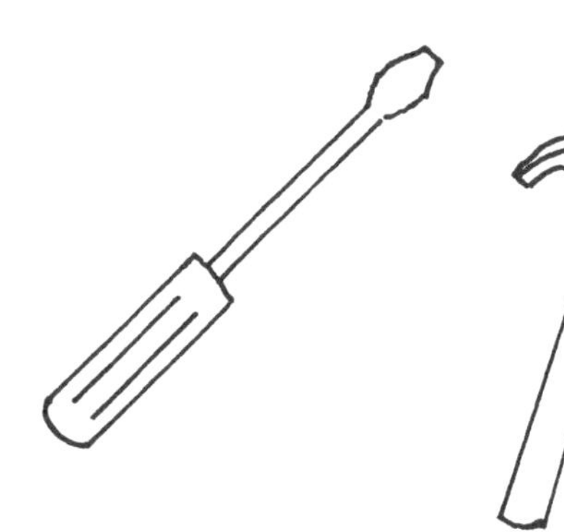

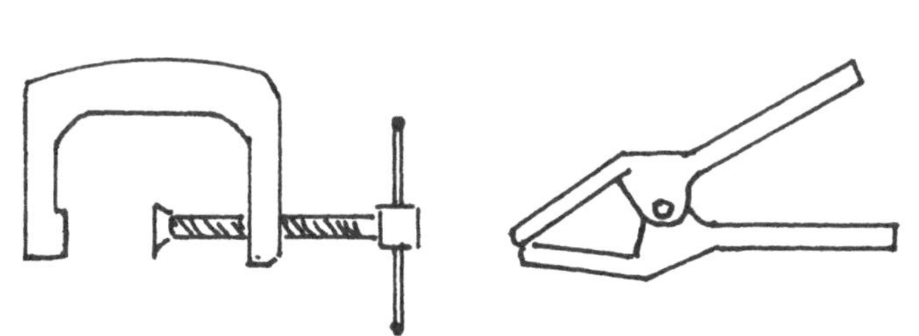

Mounting the Whirligig

Making a Stand

When you are in the middle of the job and have the main body completed, with holes drilled and the pivot socket ready, you should make a stand for the whirligig. This will make it easier to complete the work. The standing whirligigs, like the arm-waving types (Pinocchio and the Happy Sailor, for example) need only a simple stand. First cut the base, which can be $\frac{3}{4}''$ × 4″ × 4″. Drill a hole in the middle that will hold a 16d nail snugly. Then cut off the point of the nail (with a hacksaw), file it smooth, and insert it from the bottom. You may have to trim the wood at the bottom to hold the head of the nail so the stand doesn't wiggle. (See Stand A.)

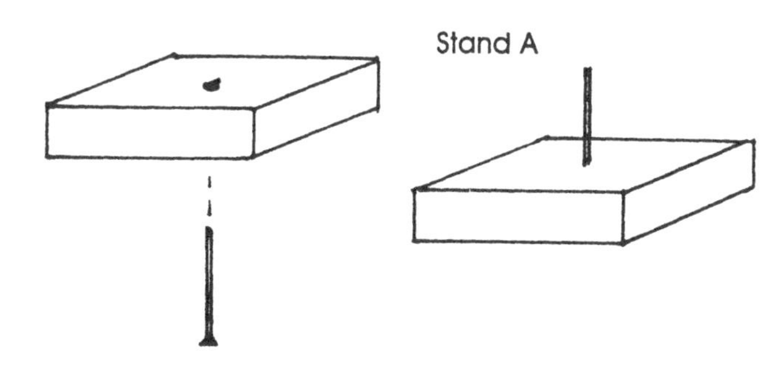

For the Coo-Coo Bird, Guardian Angel, Cruise Ship, and others, you will need a higher spindle to clear the wings and propellers. Make a base 5″ × 5″. Through the middle drill a hole large enough for a $1\frac{1}{4}''$ or $1\frac{1}{2}''$ flat-headed screw to pass through. Then make a small post $\frac{3}{4}''$ × $\frac{3}{4}''$ × 4″ and screw that to the base, with glue added. It is advisable to drill a small "pilot" hole in the bottom of the post before screwing it to the base to prevent the post from splitting. Use the $\frac{1}{16}''$ bit for this. Drill a hole in the top of the post and insert a 16d nail with the head cut off for a spindle. (See Stand B.)

You also can drill a $\frac{3}{4}''$ hole in the center of the base and glue a $4\frac{1}{2}''$ long piece of $\frac{3}{4}''$ dowel in it. Drill a hole in the top of the dowel for the 16d nail, which will act as a spindle. (See Stand C.)

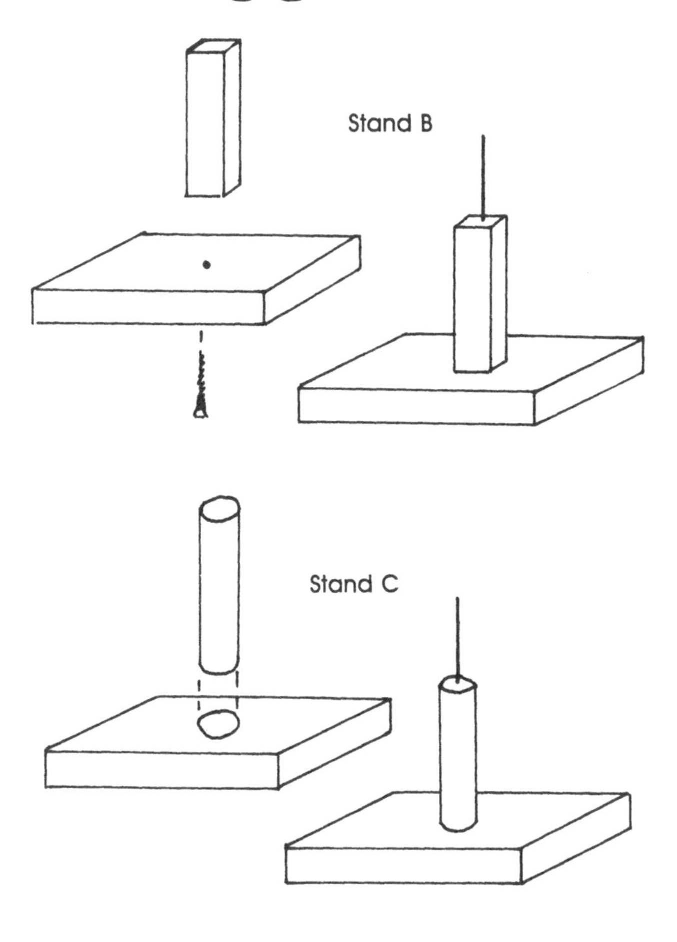

For the small mechanical whirligigs (see Chapter 6), make the bases $4\frac{1}{2}''$ × $4\frac{1}{2}''$ square. Then drill $\frac{3}{4}''$ holes in the center, as done previously. Cut 2″ dowel pieces and glue them in the hole. Drill a hole in the top for the spindle. Another small mechanical whirligig base is a piece of so-called 2″ × 4″ (which actually measures $1\frac{1}{2}''$ × $3\frac{1}{2}''$). Cut a piece of $3\frac{1}{2}''$ long and drill the center with a $\frac{3}{4}''$ bit. Because a 2″ × 4″ is heavier, it will be very steady. (See Stand D.)

For the larger mechanical whirligigs with large propellers (see Chapter 8), a wider base (7″ × 7″ to 9″ × 9″) and a higher dowel or support (6″ or 7″) will be

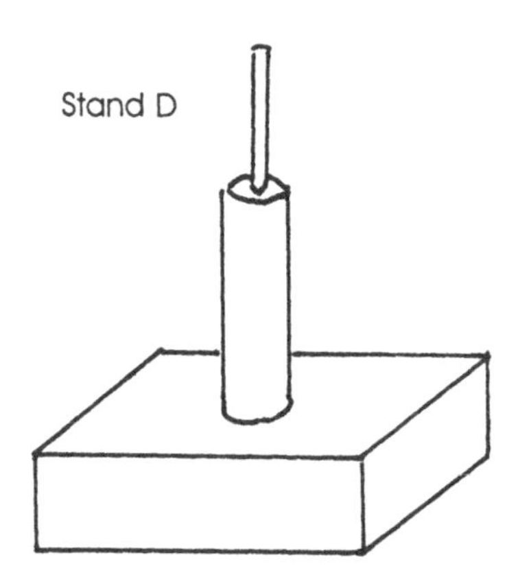

required. The spindle for these whirligigs will be a 20d nail with the head cut off and rounded.

If any stand tips over with the whirligig on it, just nail another wider piece of wood, any thickness, underneath.

Mounting the Whirligig Outside

When the whirligig is finished and painted, you will want to have it work outside. Select a breezy place and mount the whirligig on a post, pole, or stake using a 16d or a 20d nail as a spindle. You also can use a small stick nailed to a fence or other wooden post. The pole doesn't have to be fancy as long as it holds the whirligig securely. For some years on Cape Cod I had whirligigs mounted on broomsticks poked into the sand.

For better performance, put a steel BB in the socket; this will keep the whirligig turning easily.

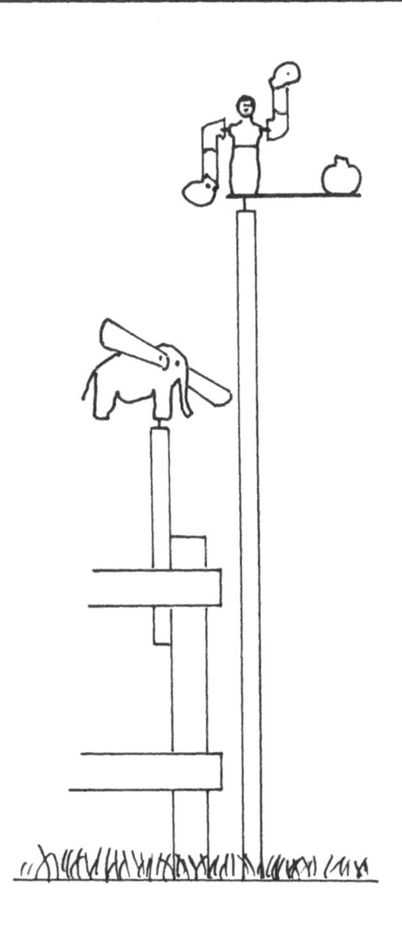

The true test of the whirligig and of your skill in making it comes when the wind strikes it and it spins its arms, turns its wings, or moves the propeller. Then you will experience the thrill of achievement and the excitement of seeing the whirligig work.

When You Need Help

Ask questions. You may have trouble with measurements, with recognizing the correct tools, with getting the right wood, with cutting it, and so on. My advice to you is to ask questions and ask for help. Don't be shy. Members of your family and your friends will be glad to help, as will people in hardware stores, hobby shops, and lumberyards—especially if you ask the right questions.

Get the right wood. First, know exactly what you want and the questions you want to ask. Write questions down on paper. Go to the lumberyard or wood shop, tell the clerk what you are making, and then tell him what you need. Show him the paper. You may have written "Piece of pine: $\frac{3}{4}''$ × 4″ × 12″ or larger." He will know exactly what you need and may find you a leftover piece. Many stores have scrap bins in which you can browse to find what you want. You also can take this book with you and show the store clerk the Materials List featured with each whirligig project. He or she will help you find what you need.

You also may have trouble sawing the basic pieces. For example, the platform pieces are made of wood $\frac{3}{4}''$ × $\frac{3}{4}''$ square. Most thin pieces for propellers and such are $\frac{1}{8}''$ thick. Cutting out these pieces with a handsaw is very difficult. If your family or friends do not have a table saw, go to the lumberyard or wood shop. Ask them to saw you some short lengths of pine $\frac{3}{4}''$ square or to cut some pine $\frac{1}{8}''$ thick and 2″ wide. There will be a charge for machine work, but it will not amount to much. *Always ask the cost before you tell the yard to go ahead.*

Use the right tools. Most households have a collection of tools of some sort, and you can begin by using those tools. If you don't have some of the basic tools suggested in this book, you should begin to collect them for yourself. Ask for them for your birthday! Make a toolbox and keep your own tools in it. Some tools you may only need once, like the brace and bit for drilling holes that are $\frac{5}{16}$" in diameter. See if you can't borrow such tools. Again, if you are not sure of the tool mentioned in the book, don't be afraid to ask somebody about it, so you don't make a mistake. *If you are not sure about how to use the tools, ask somebody.* You will save a lot of time by asking people who know.

Part I

Simple Whirligigs

Chapter 2
Basic Whirligigs

There is nothing more simple than a vane whirligig—unless it is a pinwheel, which is also a whirligig and a very old one at that. Hundreds of years ago children ran through the streets of Europe with small (usually four-bladed) propellers on the end of long sticks. When you add a rudder and balance this kind of stick on a pole or stake in the ground, it becomes a vane whirligig.

The Simple Vane Whirligig

The word *vane* comes from an old English word meaning "banner," and perhaps you can see in your imagination all kinds of flags and banners waving from the turrets of castles, blown by the wind. Vanes were used to show wind direction. When you put a propeller on it, a vane becomes a whirligig.

It is fun to make a simple vane whirligig, and you can have it spinning in the wind in a matter of minutes.

Materials

Platform	$\frac{3}{4}$″ × $\frac{3}{4}$″ × 24″
or	1″ × 1″ × 24″
Tail	$\frac{1}{8}$″ × 3″ × 5″
or	thin metal
Propeller (hub)	$\frac{3}{4}$″ × $1\frac{1}{4}$″ × $1\frac{1}{4}$″
Blades (2)	$\frac{1}{8}$″ × $\frac{3}{4}$″ × 4″
Spindle	a 6d or 8d nail
Washers (2)	$\frac{3}{16}$″ or $\frac{1}{4}$″

Procedure

1. The *platform* can be made of any piece of wood approximately 1″ square. An old broomstick will do fine. Saw it to a 2′ length. Drill a small hole (with a $\frac{3}{16}$″ bit) big enough for a nail to go through 7″ from the front end. The spindle will go there. At the back end saw a slot wide enough for the tail. If you are using wood, you will have to make two cuts with a coping saw to make the slot wide enough. If you are using metal, one saw cut should be enough.

   Drill a small pilot hole at the front for a small nail (like a 4d box nail) to hold the propeller. This will prevent the wood from splitting when the propeller is attached. Round off the front of the stick.

2. After you have decided on the shape of the *tail* or *rudder,* draw it on the wood or metal and cut it out. You usually can make larger tails with metal. Aluminum sheathing is very good and can be purchased in any hardware store. It comes in pieces 4″ × 7″ or in 6″ wide rolls. Glue the rudder in place if it is made of wood; metal will slide easily into the slot. In any case, secure the rudder with two small nails. Drill pilot holes so the wood does not split.

3. Make the two-bladed *propeller* as shown in the vane propeller illustration. Saw out a square hub ($\frac{3}{4}$″ × $1\frac{1}{4}$″ × $1\frac{1}{4}$″) and drill a hole in the center. At the same time cut out two wooden blades $\frac{1}{8}$″ × $\frac{3}{4}$″ × 4″. Then, on opposite sides of the hub, measure off two slots that are at a 45-degree angle. Make sure the slots

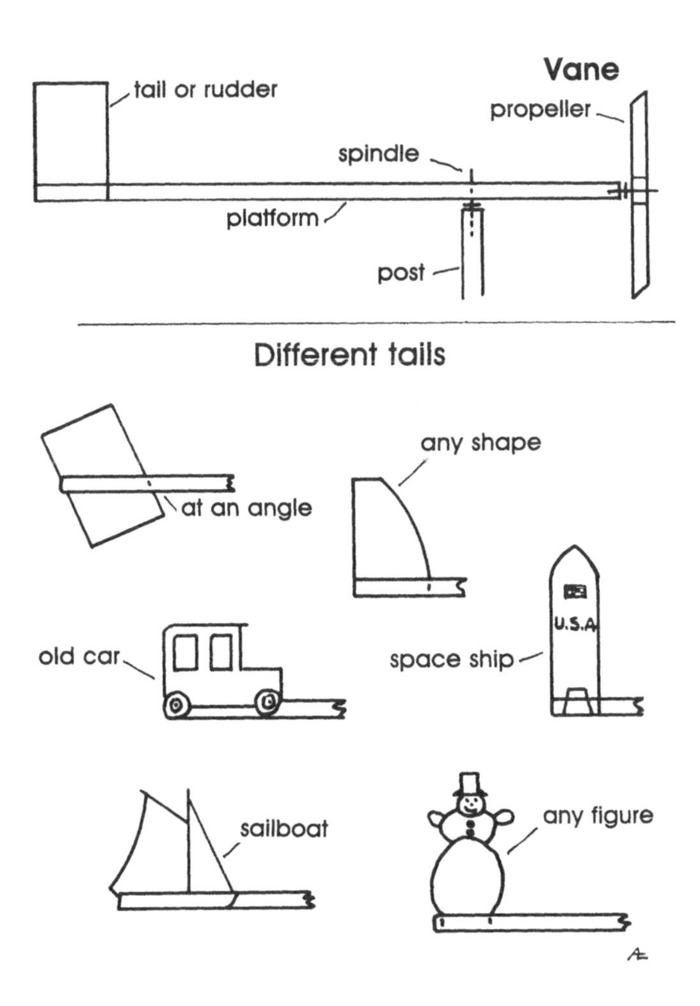

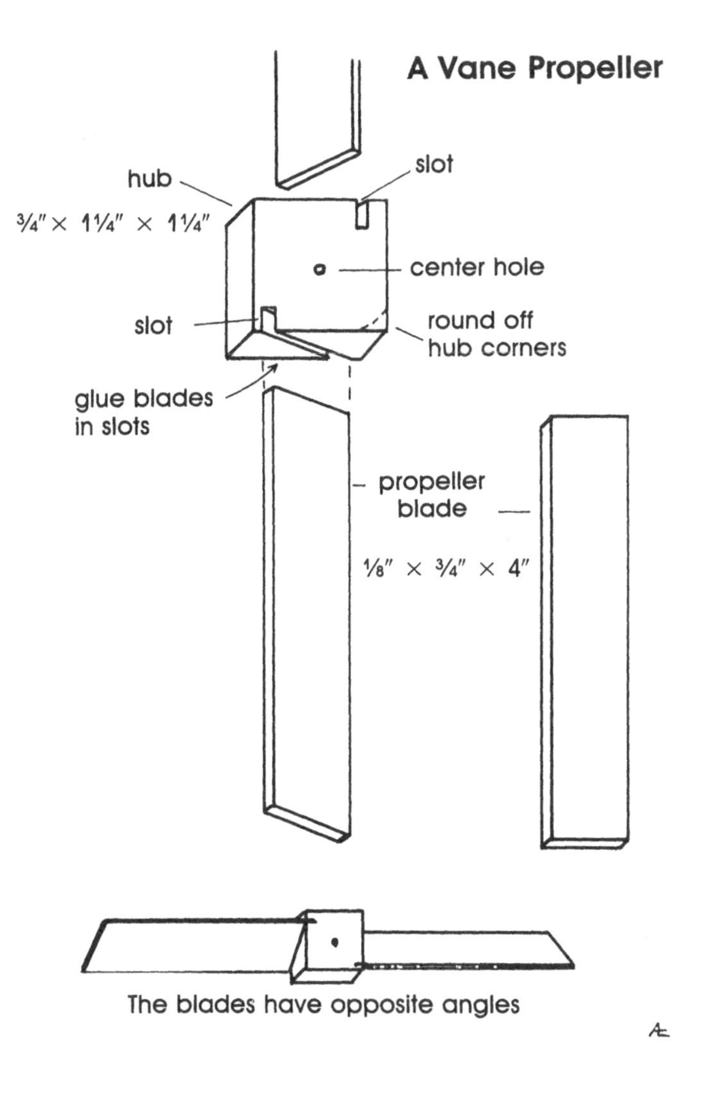

The blades have opposite angles

will go through the middle of the side so the blades won't look lopsided when you are through. Cut the slots ¼" deep and as wide as the blades. You can round off the hub with a file before you glue the blades in position. Attach the propeller to the platform with a nail and washer.

4. Mount the vane whirligig on a post outdoors in a windy location. Drive a finishing nail, or one with the head removed, into the top of the post and set your whirligig on it with some kind of washer underneath. The headless nail will permit the easy removal of the whirligig from the post for repairs or painting. As soon as it is in place, the vane whirligig should begin to turn and spin at once.

Once I had about five different vane whirligigs turning in my yard. They were fascinating to look at and I enjoyed just having them around. They turned day and night, in rain or shine, for years.

Chapter 3
Arm-Waving Whirligigs

Most arm-waving whirligigs are human figures that stand upright, but the same principles apply to other whirligigs, such as the winged ones. If you learn to make an arm-waver, you can easily make a winged whirligig. Parts of the arm-waving whirligig include the body, the pivot point, the pivot socket, the hub, the hub pieces, and the shoulder and arm pieces.

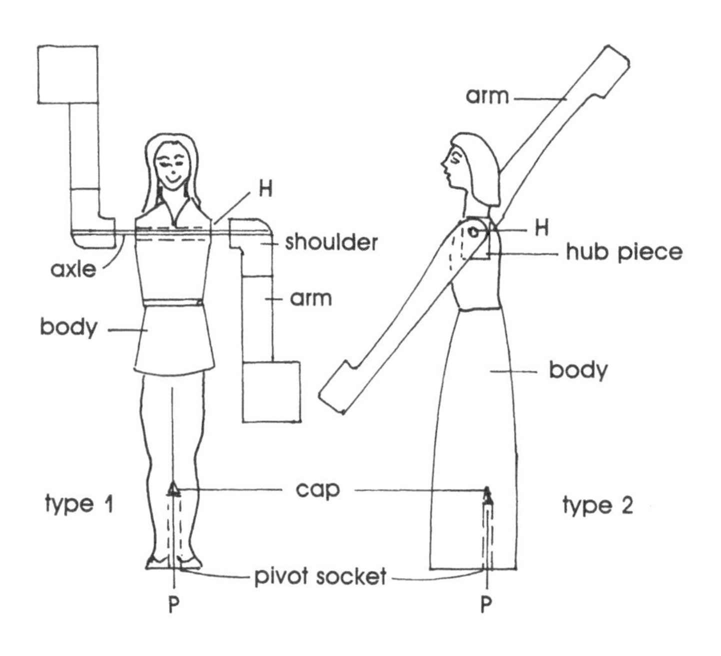

The *body* or figure design is basic to the whirligig, and we will start with that so you can understand the models in this book and learn how to design them yourself. The body is a piece of wood on which you draw your design, as in the case of the Toy Soldier. After you have marked all the parts, you will drill the holes and cut out the body outline.

The *pivot point* (P) is the place where the whirligig turns. A pivot socket of about 1″ to 1½″ long is drilled there; it is the hole where the support pin or spindle will hold the whirligig in position. The *hub* (H) is the place where the propeller will be mounted through the body. The hub hole must be just in front of (or back of) the vertical line of the pivot socket. The relationship between the pivot and the hub is very important. If the pivot and hub are too far apart on an arm-waver, the body will turn into the wind and stop turning the arms. If the hub is right over the pivot point, the body may spin too much. When the holes are in the right place, the body will remain sideways to the wind and keep waving its arms. The Signaling Scout is an excellent example. I made him with two pivot sockets. If you make him you will see that he acts differently depending upon which socket is used.

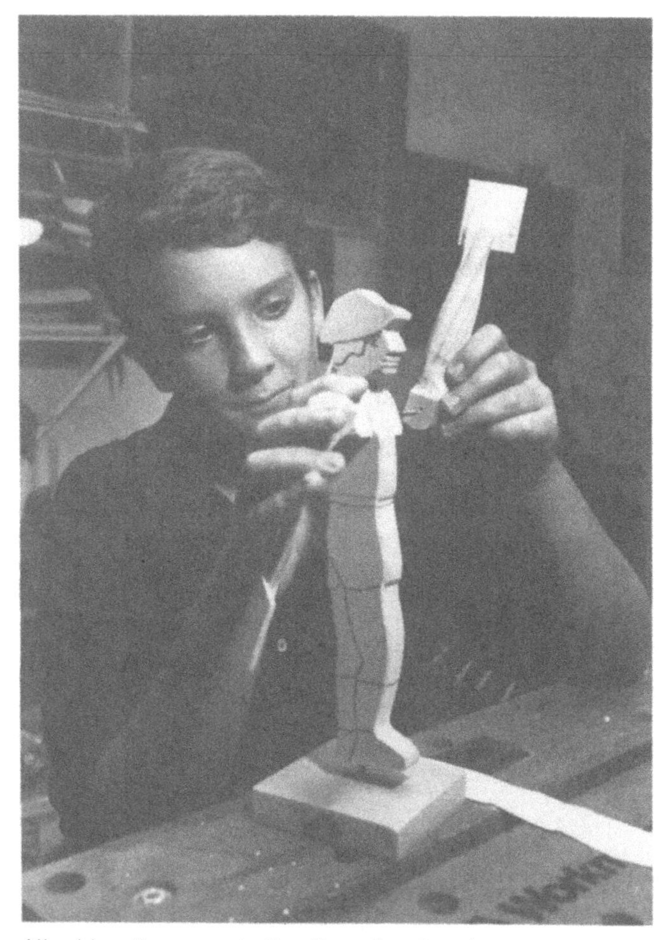

Attaching the arms to the Signaling Scout.

The *pivot socket* hole is made with a $\frac{7}{32}''$ bit (or other size), and lined with brass tubing of the same size. A *metal cap* is placed in the base of the socket to prevent the spindle from boring up through the body. I find that the cutoff point of a 16d nail slides easily into the tubing and can be driven in with a nail and hammer.

To make sure that the arms move away from the body, *hub pieces* are glued to the body at the hub. Wood pieces $\frac{5}{8}'' \times \frac{5}{8}'' \times 1''$ are big enough for this job. Drill the hub hole in the body and holes through the hub pieces. Often this hole is $\frac{1}{4}''$ in diameter; it can be lined with brass tubing to save wear. The tubing also will make it easier to line up the holes. Glue the hub pieces to the body with a C-clamp.

The *arms and shoulders* come next. The first thing to understand is that the arms are the two blades of a propeller. On a bird, the same construction is called a "split wing" propeller. Instead of a regular two-bladed propeller joined at a hub in the middle, the arm-waver propeller blades are separated at the hub by a long axle. If the blades have opposite angles (turned in different directions), they will spin in the wind.

The *axle* will be a $\frac{3}{16}''$ or $\frac{1}{4}''$ diameter piece of hardwood dowel, depending on the model. The length of the dowel will be approximately $4\frac{1}{2}''$. It is best to cut the dowel a little longer so that enough room will be left for the washers and to assure free movement of the arms.

The following illustration shows how to make the arms for the arm-waving whirligigs.

Making Arms for Arm-Wavers

Materials

Shoulder pieces (2)	$\frac{3}{4}'' \times 1'' \times 1\frac{1}{2}''$
Blades (2)	$\frac{1}{8}'' \times \frac{3}{4}'' \times 4\frac{1}{2}''$

Procedure

1. The *shoulder piece* measures $\frac{3}{4}'' \times 1'' \times 1\frac{1}{2}''$. Drill a $\frac{3}{16}''$ hole through the middle of the piece $\frac{1}{2}''$ from the top. For accuracy, drill halfway in from both sides.
2. Cut out a section $\frac{1}{4}'' \times \frac{1}{2}''$ from the inside of the shoulder piece.
3. Cut out the *arm blade* ($\frac{1}{8}'' \times \frac{3}{4}'' \times 4\frac{1}{2}''$). You will need to know its exact width for Step 4.
4. Cut out the blade slot at the bottom of the shoulder piece. It is $\frac{1}{2}''$ deep and only as wide as the arm blade. It is better to cut it small instead of too wide.
5. Glue the arm blade in the slot. If it is loose, wedge it in with slips of wood. When dry, round off the shoulder with a file.

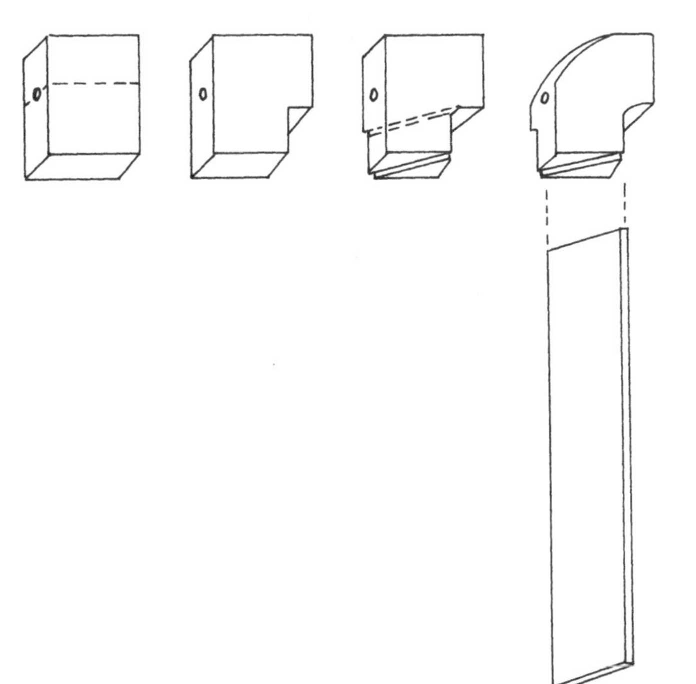

Toy Soldier

You may have heard of the headless horseman from "The Legend of Sleepy Hollow." It was written by Washington Irving and published in 1815. In it there is a description of Balt Van Tassel sitting on his porch, looking over to his barn. There on the peak of the roof is a little wooden soldier armed with a sword in his hand "valiantly fighting the wind." That is one of the few direct references to whirligigs in early American literature.

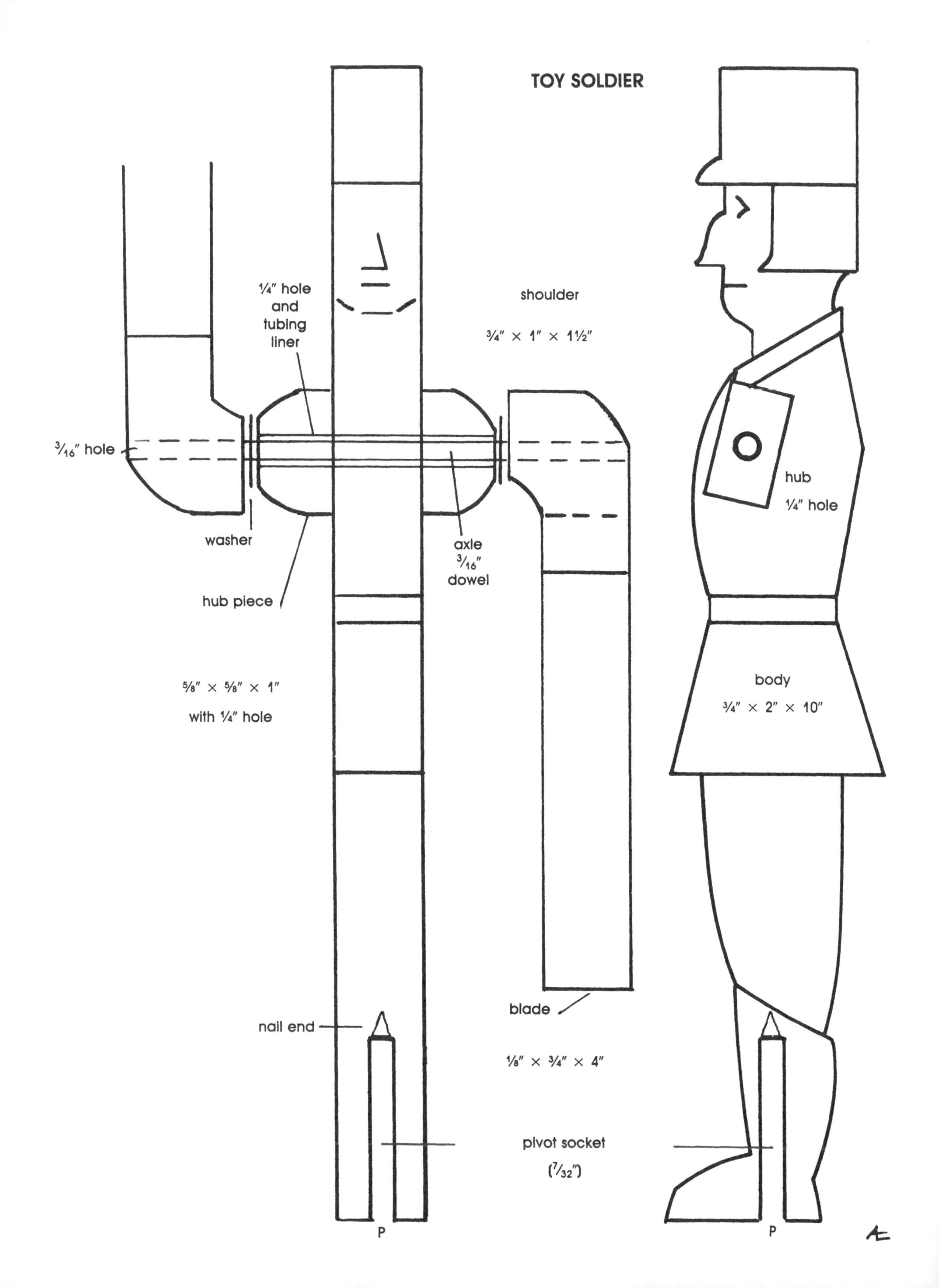
TOY SOLDIER
¼″ hole
and
tubing
liner
shoulder
¾″ × 1″ × 1½″
³⁄₁₆″ hole
hub
¼″ hole
washer
axle
³⁄₁₆″
dowel
hub piece
⅝″ × ⅝″ × 1″
with ¼″ hole
body
¾″ × 2″ × 10″
blade
nail end
⅛″ × ¾″ × 4″
pivot socket
(⁷⁄₃₂″)
P
P

Materials

Figure	$\frac{3}{4}$" × 2" × 10"
Arms	
shoulders (2)	$\frac{3}{4}$" × 1" × $1\frac{1}{2}$"
blades (2)	$\frac{1}{8}$" × $\frac{3}{4}$" × 4"
Hub Pieces (2)	$\frac{5}{8}$" × $\frac{5}{8}$" × 1"
Axle	$\frac{3}{16}$" dowel, $4\frac{1}{2}$" long
Metal liners (if used)	
pivot socket	$\frac{7}{32}$" brass tubing, 2" long
hub hole	$\frac{1}{4}$" tubing, 2" long
Washers (2)	$\frac{1}{4}$" brass

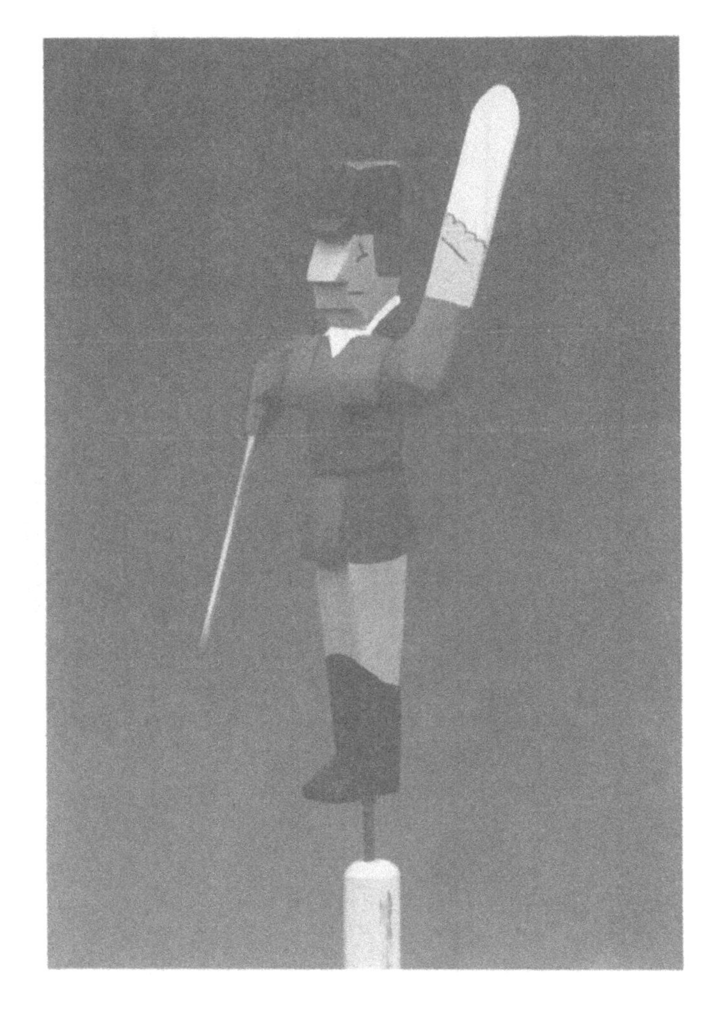

Procedure

1. Trace the pattern of the *figure* on the wood and cut it out. File or sand it smooth. With a pencil mark out where the pivot point (P) and the hub (H) are located. Drill a pivot socket hole $1\frac{1}{2}$" deep with a $\frac{7}{32}$" bit and a hub hole through H with a $\frac{1}{4}$" bit. If you have a piece of $\frac{7}{32}$" brass tubing, cut a piece for the socket liner and insert it. Put a cap in the socket hole; the cutoff point of a 16d nail or a small screw will do.

2. Cut out the *hub pieces* and carefully drill $\frac{1}{4}$" holes through them. Glue them over the hub hole in the figure. If you have $\frac{1}{4}$" brass tubing, cut a piece to go through the body and hub pieces as a hub liner, and glue the pieces with the liner in place. Use a C-clamp to hold everything firmly.

3. Cut out the two *shoulder pieces* of the arms and shape them as shown in the illustration. First, drill holes through the upper part with a $\frac{3}{16}$" bit. Then on the bottom mark the angles for the blade slots, remembering that the propeller blades must slant opposite each other when they are in position on the figure.

4. Cut out the *blades* and then cut out the blade slots to fit the blade ends. Glue the blades in the slots. After the glue dries, shape the shoulders. Put a temporary axle in the hub holes and test the balance of the arms. Trim them until they balance.

5. Glue the *axle* into one arm first, then insert the axle into the hub with a washer. Glue the other arm, with washer in place, on the other side of the figure. The arms should be directly opposite each other.

Suggested Colors

Jacket: red, boots: black or brown, pants: blue, hat: black, swords (arms): silver.

Doctor Doolittle

Doctor Doolittle loved animals and could speak with them. He also founded a post office and created his own stamps. This whirligig should have an animal in it, and I think one will fit on his hat (after you have finished making the figure). Draw a small figure of either a monkey or a parrot. Cut one of them out of thin wood or plywood and mount it in a slot on his hat. Then he will look right. I made the blades wide enough to let you draw a stamp on each of them if you like. Old whirligig makers made arms in a similar way: They put shovels or milk pails in farmer's hands signaling flags in sailor's hands, and so on. So Doctor Doolittle can wave his stamps around!

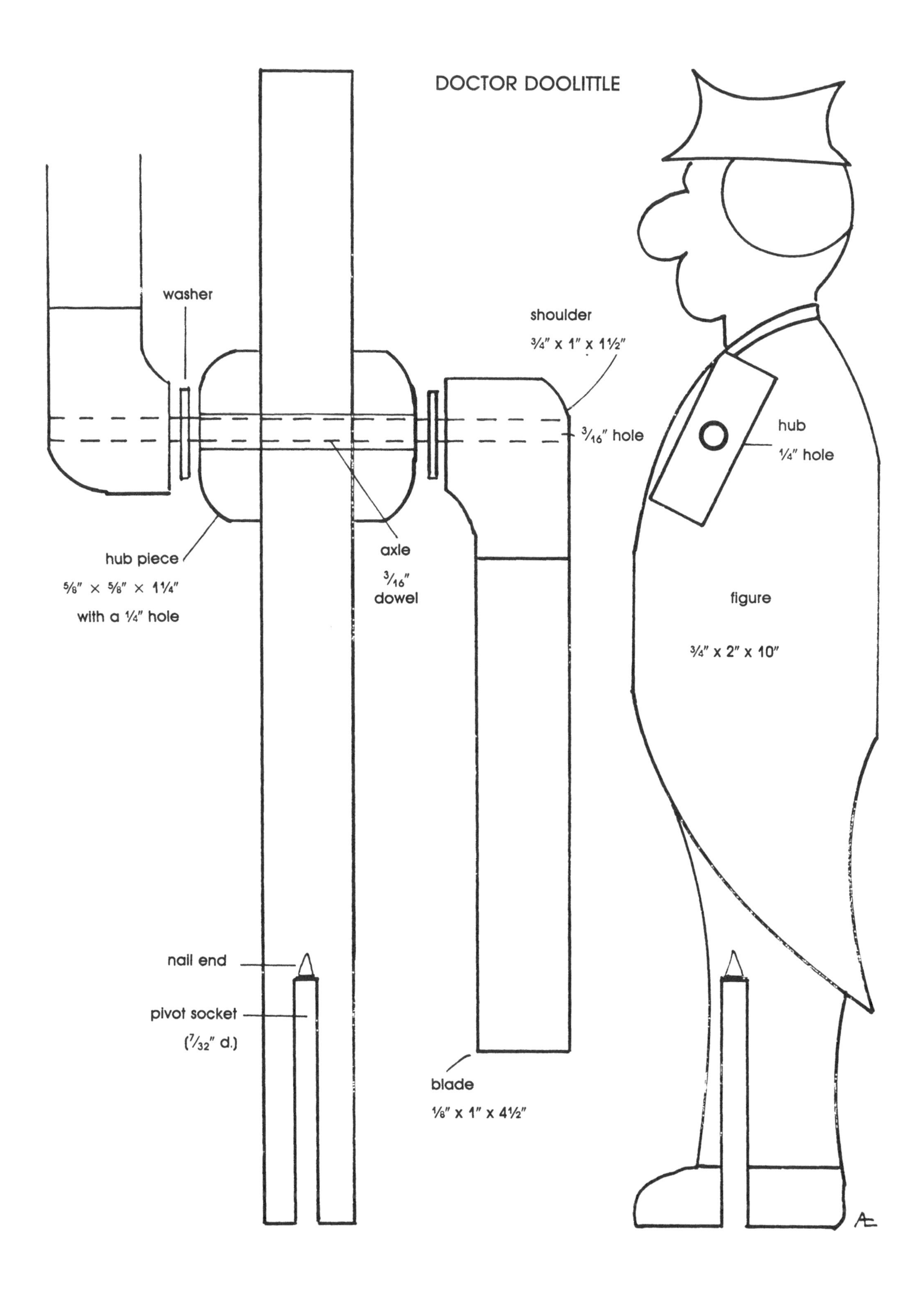
DOCTOR DOOLITTLE
washer
shoulder
¾" x 1" x 1½"
⅜₁₆" hole
hub
¼" hole
hub piece
⅝" × ⅝" × 1¼"
with a ¼" hole
axle
³⁄₁₆"
dowel
figure
¾" x 2" x 10"
nail end
pivot socket
(⁷⁄₃₂" d.)
blade
⅛" x 1" x 4½"

Materials

Figure	$\frac{3}{4}'' \times 2'' \times 10''$
Arms	
shoulders (2)	$\frac{3}{4}'' \times 1'' \times 1\frac{1}{2}''$
blades (2)	$\frac{1}{8}'' \times 1'' \times 4\frac{1}{2}''$
Hub pieces (2)	$\frac{5}{8}'' \times \frac{5}{8}'' \times 1\frac{1}{4}''$
Axle	$\frac{3}{16}''$ dowel, 4″ long
Metal	
pivot socket	$\frac{7}{32}''$ brass tubing, 2″ long
hub liner	$\frac{1}{4}''$ brass tubing, $2\frac{1}{4}''$ long
Washers (2)	$\frac{1}{4}''$ brass washer

Procedure

1. The Doctor Doolittle whirligig is made just like the Toy Soldier. After the *figure* is traced and cut out, file and sand it smooth. Mark the location of the pivot socket (P) and the hub (H). Drill the socket $1\frac{1}{2}''$ deep with a $\frac{7}{32}''$ bit and line it with tubing if you have it. Place a cap (point of a 16d nail, smoothed off) in the bottom of the socket. Drill the hub hole with a $\frac{1}{4}''$ bit.
2. Cut out the *hub pieces* and drill a $\frac{1}{4}''$ hole through them. Glue them over the hub hole with $\frac{1}{4}''$ tubing in place as a liner. Hold the pieces firmly with a C-clamp until the glue dries.
3. Cut out the two *shoulder pieces* of the arms and shape them as shown in the illustration. Drill $\frac{3}{16}''$ holes through the upper shoulder. On the bottom mark the angles for the blade slots; remember that the blades must slant opposite each other when on the body.
4. Cut out the *blades,* then cut out the blade slots in the shoulder pieces. Glue the blades in the slots. After the blades dry, shape the shoulders. Put a temporary axle in the hub holes and test the balance of the arms. Trim them until they balance. If you want to design a stamp on the end of the arms, do so now. At this point you also can paint the arms separately from the body. When everything is completed, glue one end of the axle into the hub (with a washer) and insert it through the body. Attach the other blade carefully (with a washer) and make sure the blades are in a straight line. If the arms droop they won't turn.

Suggested Colors

Doctor Doolittle's hair: white, coat: bluc, hat: black, pants: gray, shoes: black.

Pinocchio

The popular story of the boy whose nose became longer when he told lies is probably familiar to you. How long is your nose? The nose in my model is about 1″ long, but you can make Pinocchio's nose as long as you like. If you want to make it longer, make the front of his face flat and drill a $\frac{1}{4}''$ hole where the nose is located. Then cut a $\frac{1}{4}''$ diameter dowel any length you like and glue it in place. You can shape it a bit if you like, but whatever you do, people will think it looks funny and laugh at poor Pinocchio, just as in the story.

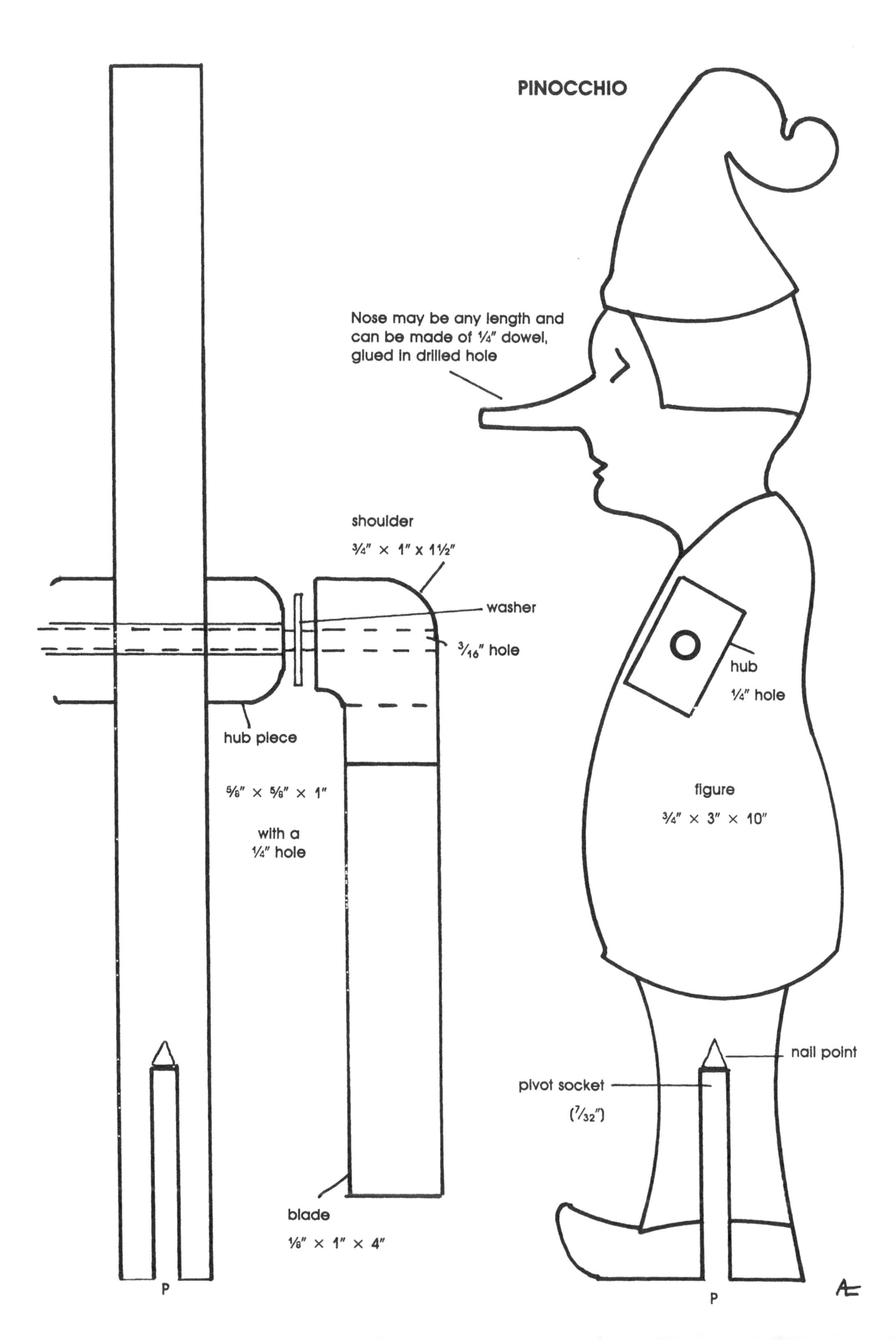
PINOCCHIO
Nose may be any length and can be made of ¼″ dowel, glued in drilled hole
shoulder
¾″ × 1″ x 1½″
washer
³⁄₁₆″ hole
hub
¼″ hole
hub piece
⅝″ × ⅝″ × 1″
with a
¼″ hole
figure
¾″ × 3″ × 10″
nail point
pivot socket
(⁷⁄₃₂″)
blade
⅛″ × 1″ × 4″
P
P

Materials

Figure	$\frac{3}{4}'' \times 3'' \times 10''$
Arms	
shoulders (2)	$\frac{3}{4}'' \times 1'' \times 1\frac{1}{2}''$
blades (2)	$\frac{1}{8}'' \times 1'' \times 4''$
Hub pieces (2)	$\frac{5}{8}'' \times \frac{5}{8}'' \times 1''$
Axle	$\frac{3}{16}''$ dowel, $4\frac{1}{2}''$ long
Metal	
socket liner	$\frac{7}{32}''$ brass tubing, 2″ long
hub liner	$\frac{1}{4}''$ brass tubing, $2\frac{1}{4}''$ long
Washers (2)	$\frac{1}{4}''$ brass washers

Procedure

1. Trace the pattern on the woodblock and cut out the *figure*. File or sand it smooth and, with a pencil, mark the location of the pivot point (P) and hub (H).

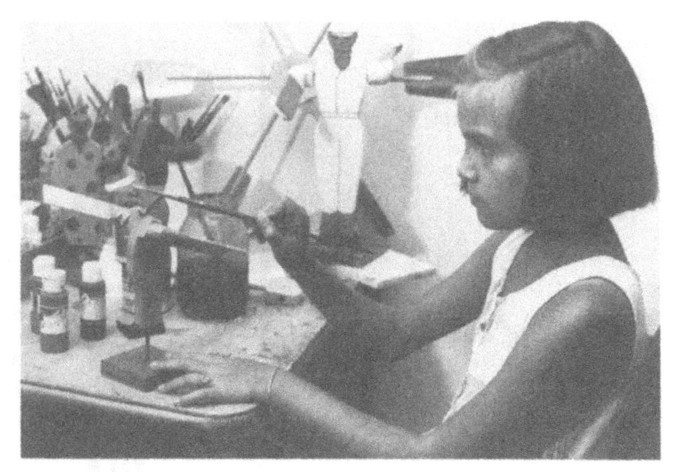

Painting Pinocchio.

Drill the $\frac{7}{32}''$ hole for the pivot socket and the $\frac{1}{4}''$ hole for the hub. Line the pivot socket with $\frac{7}{32}''$ brass tubing and put a metal cap in the base.

2. Cut out the *hub pieces* and drill $\frac{1}{4}''$ holes through them. Then cut out a piece of $\frac{1}{4}''$ brass tubing and line the hub with it, gluing the hub pieces at the same time. A C-clamp will do the job.
3. Cut out the two *shoulder pieces* of the arms and shape them as shown in the illustration. Drill $\frac{3}{16}''$ holes through the upper part. On the lower part draw the angles for the blade slots, remembering that the propeller blades must slant in opposite ways when they are in position on the figure.
4. Cut out the arm *blades* and use them to measure the width of the slots; then cut the slots. Glue the blades in place. After the glue dries, shape the shoulders. Put a temporary axle in the hub holes and test the balance of the arms. If they are out of balance, file down the heavier arm until the arms balance.
5. Glue one of the arms to the *axle* and put the axle through the hub with a washer in place. Before attaching the other arm, make sure you get both arms in a straight line. Otherwise, the arms won't turn right.

Suggested Colors

Hat: red, jacket: blue, pants: yellow, shoes: brown or black, hair: brown or black.

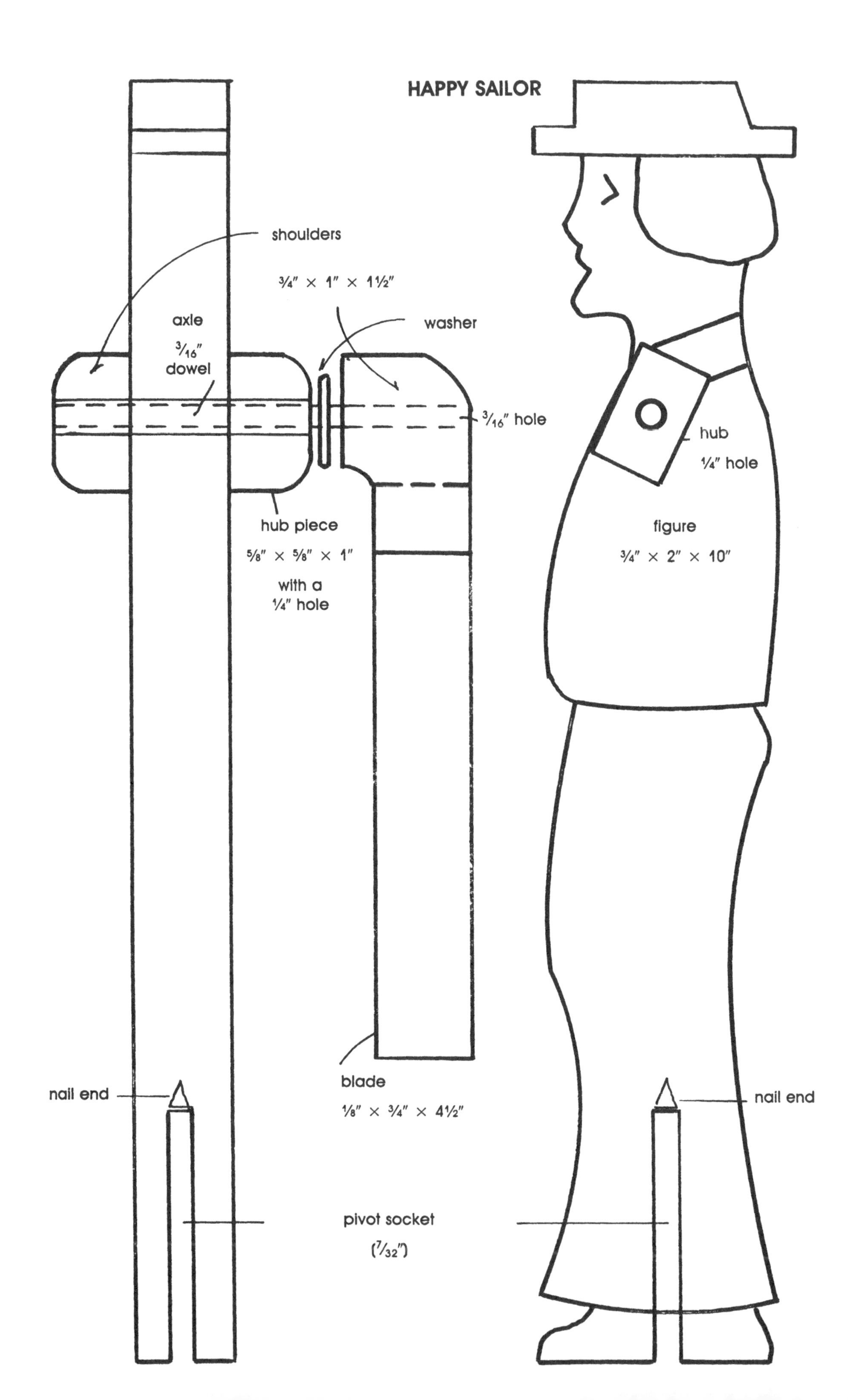
HAPPY SAILOR
shoulders
3/4″ × 1″ × 1½″
axle
3/16″
dowel
washer
3/16″ hole
hub
1/4″ hole
hub piece
5/8″ × 5/8″ × 1″
with a
1/4″ hole
figure
3/4″ × 2″ × 10″
blade
1/8″ × 3/4″ × 4½″
nail end
nail end
pivot socket
(7/32″)

Happy Sailor

Sailor whirligigs have been around for many years and you can tell how old they are by their uniforms. Sailors put tar in their hair during the War of 1812 (sailors were called "tars" in those days), and they wore hard hats during the Civil War. Bell-bottomed trousers are still in fashion after all these years, but sailor's hats are different today. The clothes in this model would date it around 1850 or 1860. Many of the older whirligigs show sailors waving signal flags. We will show you how to add flags to this one.

Materials

Figure	$\frac{3}{4}$" × 2" × 10"
Arms	
shoulders (2)	$\frac{3}{4}$" × 1" × $1\frac{1}{2}$"
blades (2)	$\frac{1}{8}$" × $\frac{3}{4}$" × $4\frac{1}{2}$"
flags (2)	$\frac{1}{8}$" × $1\frac{1}{4}$" × $1\frac{1}{4}$"
Hub pieces (2)	$\frac{5}{8}$" × $\frac{5}{8}$" × 1"
Axle	$\frac{3}{16}$" dowel, 5" long
Metal	
socket liner	$\frac{7}{32}$" brass tubing, 2" long
hub liner	$\frac{1}{4}$" brass tubing, 4" long
Washers (2)	$\frac{1}{4}$" brass washers

Procedure

1. Trace the pattern on the woodblock and cut out the *figure*. File or sand it smooth. With a pencil locate the pivot point (P) and the hub (H). Drill the pivot socket hole with a $\frac{7}{32}$" bit and the hub hole (H) with a $\frac{1}{4}$" bit. Line the pivot socket with $\frac{7}{32}$" brass tubing and put a metal cap in the base. This can be a screw or the cutoff point of a 16d nail.
2. Cut out the *hub pieces* and drill them with a $\frac{1}{4}$" bit. Glue them over the hub hole of the figure. If you have $\frac{1}{4}$" brass tubing, cut a piece for the hub liner. Glue the hub pieces to the body with the liner inside, using a C-clamp to hold the pieces firm.
3. Cut out the *shoulder pieces* and shape them as shown in the illustration. Drill a $\frac{3}{16}$" hole through the upper part. Draw the angles for the blade slots on the lower part. Hold the shoulders against the body to make sure the angles are right.
4. Cut out the arm *blades*, and use their width in measuring the cut of the slots. Then glue them in the slots. If you want to add signal flags (as shown in the Signaling Scout), cut them out and glue them to the ends of the arms with the flags extending out from the body. Otherwise the flags may strike the body as the arms turn. When the flags are secure, thin them down a little so they will be lighter. Then balance the arms by putting them on a temporary axle; if one is too heavy, trim it down.
5. When everything is finished, glue one end of the *axle* to the shoulder (with a washer in place), run the axle through the body, and glue on the other shoulder (with a washer in place). Make sure the arms are straight across or they won't turn.

Suggested Colors

Pants: white, jacket: blue, hat: black, collar: white, flags: white and red diagonals.

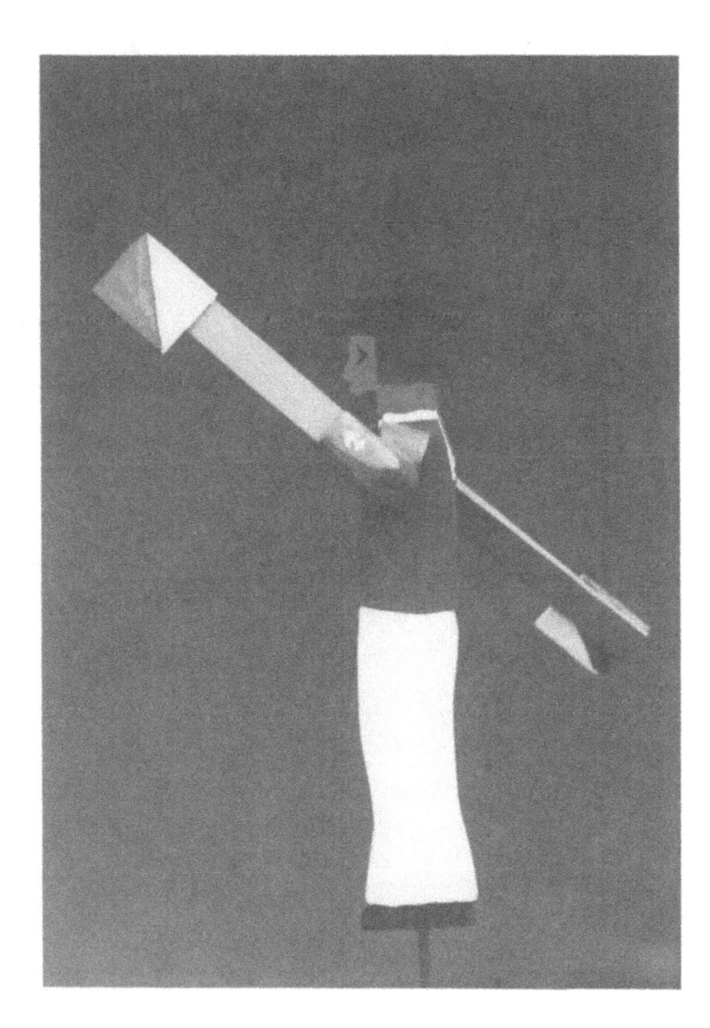

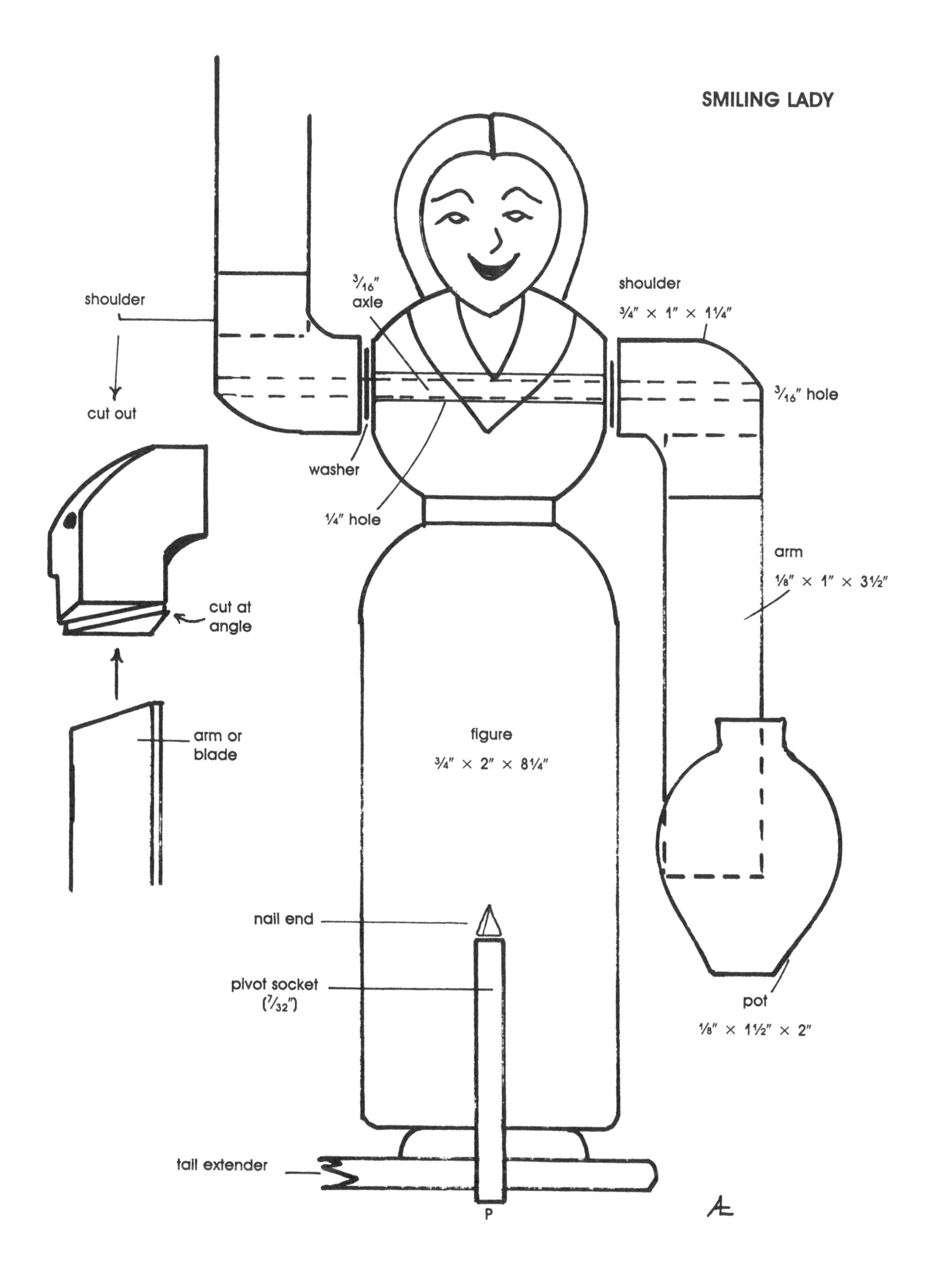
SMILING LADY
shoulder
cut out
3/16″
axle
shoulder
3/4″ × 1″ × 1 1/4″
3/16″ hole
washer
1/4″ hole
arm
1/8″ × 1″ × 3 1/2″
cut at
angle
arm or
blade
figure
3/4″ × 2″ × 8 1/4″
nail end
pivot socket
(7/32″)
pot
1/8″ × 1 1/2″ × 2″
tail extender
P
AL

Smiling Lady

Some arm-waving whirligigs are designed to work correctly under any conditions. They have no problem with the relationship between the hub (H) and the pivot point (P). That is because they are steered into the wind by means of a tail or rudder. The Smiling Lady shows how to make this foolproof type of whirligig.

Materials

Figure	$\frac{3}{4}'' \times 2'' \times 8\frac{1}{4}''$
Arms	
shoulders (2)	$\frac{3}{4}'' \times 1'' \times 1\frac{1}{4}''$
blades (2)	$\frac{1}{8}'' \times 1'' \times 3\frac{1}{2}''$
Axle	$\frac{3}{16}''$ dowel, 5″ long
Pot (2)	$\frac{1}{8}'' \times 1\frac{1}{2}'' \times 2''$
Tail or rudder	$\frac{1}{4}'' \times 2'' \times 3''$
Tail extender	$\frac{1}{4}'' \times 1\frac{3}{8}'' \times 10''$
Metal	
socket liner	$\frac{7}{32}''$ brass tubing, 2″ long
hub liner	$\frac{1}{4}''$ brass tubing, 2″ long
Washers (2)	$\frac{1}{4}''$ brass washers

Procedure

1. Trace the pattern of the *figure* and cut it out. Sand it smooth. Locate the pivot point and the hub and drill the pivot socket hole ($\frac{7}{32}''$) and the hub hole ($\frac{1}{4}''$). Line the pivot socket with brass tubing; but leave at least $\frac{1}{4}''$ of the brass tubing sticking out of the bottom. This will fit into the tail extender (see the illustration). Put a cap in the base of the socket.
2. Cut out the *shoulder pieces* of the arm. Drill $\frac{3}{16}''$ holes through the upper shoulders and shape them. Then, on the lower part, mark the angles for the blade slots and remember that the arms will be a propeller when finished, with opposite blades.
3. Cut out the arm *blades;* then cut out the blade slots in the shoulder pieces to fit the blade ends. Glue the blades in the slots. When the glue is dry, put the arms in a temporary axle and test them for balance. Trim them with a file and sandpaper until they balance perfectly.
4. If you want to show the lady holding something like a flowerpot, it can be drawn at the bottom of the blades. Or you can cut out very thin *wooden pots* and glue them on the ends of the blades, as shown in the drawing.
5. Cut out the *tail rudder* and the *tail extender*. Cut a slot in the tail extender for the rudder. Hold the figure in position on the tail extender and mark the location of the pivot socket. Drill a $\frac{7}{32}''$ hole in the extender where the pivot socket will go through. Glue the rudder in position. (You can make the rudder look like a flowerpot, too.) Then put the lady in place over the pivot hole and glue/nail her in place with $\frac{3}{4}''$ brads. Before putting her in a final position, check how she is facing. Put the arms in proper position against her body. Think of how the wind will blow against them. If she faces one way, the arms will seem to go backward; if she faces another way, the arms will go forward. Fasten her to the tail extender after you have decided how the arms should go.
6. Attach one arm to the *axle* with glue. Put it in the hub hole with a washer in place. Then line up the other arm and make sure both arms are in a straight line before gluing it to the axle with a washer in position.

When the Smiling Lady is put in the wind, the rudder will point the whirligig sideways into the windstream. Her arms will always turn.

Suggested Colors

Hair: red, blouse: blue, skirt: white or yellow, pots: earthen red, with designs and flowers.

A Tail Extender

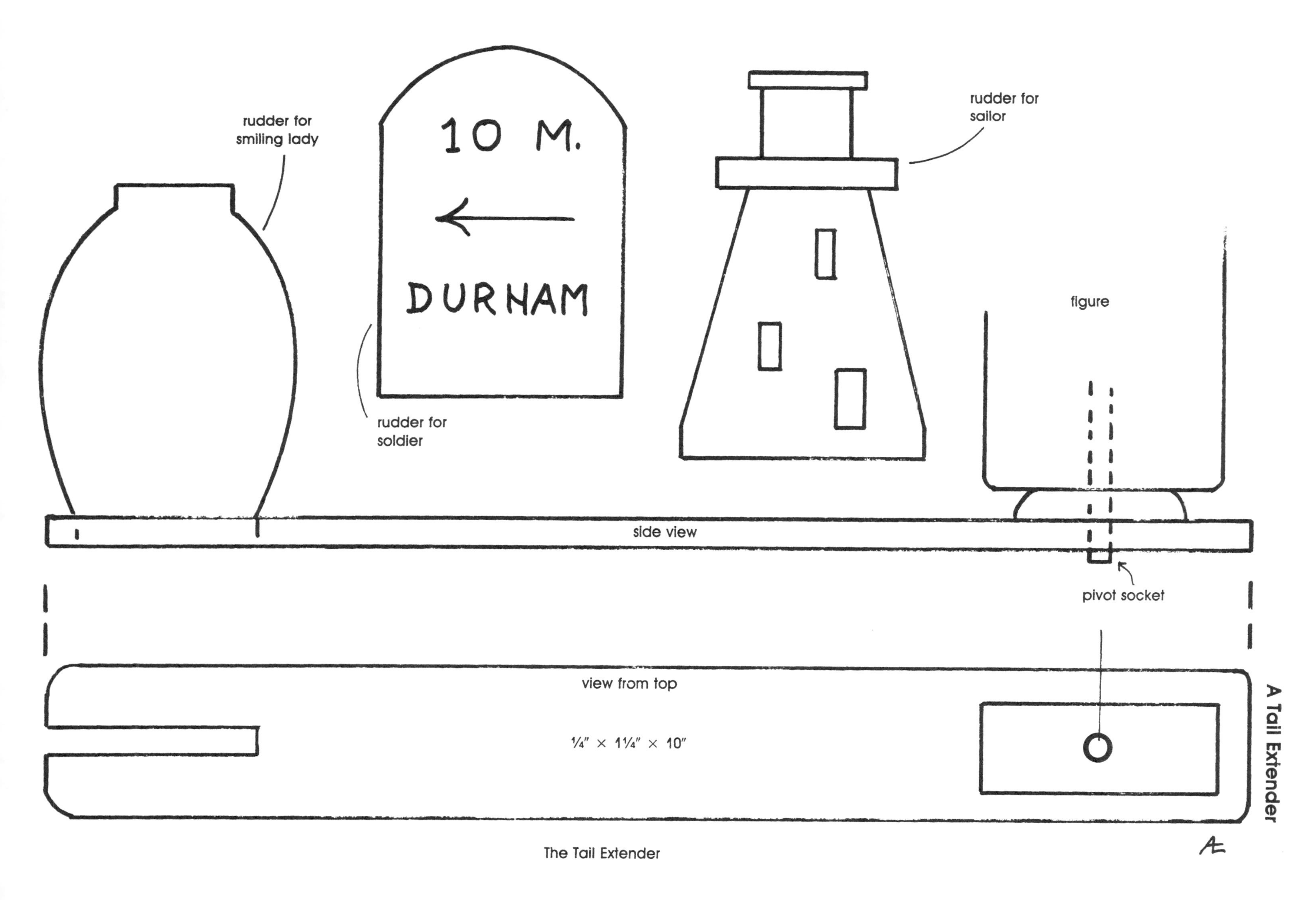

The Tail Extender

When Arm-Wavers Don't Work

Sometimes standing whirligigs, like the Toy Soldier, don't work quite right. They seem to be off-balance. They either turn toward the wind or away from it, and the arms stop waving. The perfect relationship between the position of the pivot point (P) and the hub (H) simply has not been achieved. *But don't worry!* You have not wasted your time and your whirligig is not a failure! You can always add a rudder or tail to an improperly balanced whirligig and it will work better than ever. Here's how.

First, you can make a rudder and a rudder extension like the one on the Smiling Lady. Just follow the previous directions, position your whirligig on the rudder extension, and it will work fine.

Second, let us suppose you want to be more imaginative and also want to do something more simple. You will need 8″ or 10″ length of ⅛″ or $\frac{3}{16}$″ dowel for an extension and ¼″ × 2″ × 3″ of wood for a rudder.

First, cut out the rudder in the shape you want it to be (sailboat, lighthouse, heart, star, or other) and drill a ½″ deep hole in the side of it. The hole will be the same diameter as the dowel used. Then drill a hole (the size of the dowel) in the side of the figure that will be away from the wind. Remember to test the position of the figure; perhaps you don't want the arms to go backward. Glue one end of the extension into the rudder or tail. Then glue the other end into the figure. This rudder extension will do what the other type does: Keep the whirligig properly pointed into the wind.

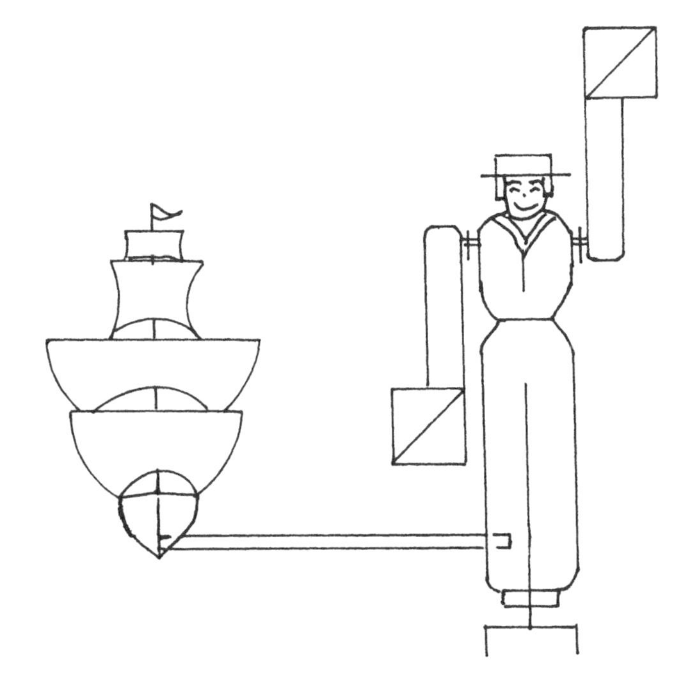

Chapter 4
Winged Whirligigs

Perhaps the most popular whirligigs in America today are the winged whirligigs. You can see all kinds of birds, particularly mallard ducks, spinning around in people's yards. Some are factory made of cheap plastic, but as a woodworker I don't complain because the commercial whirligigs pay tribute to the great American tradition of whirligig making. The tradition has to do with making your own whirligigs by hand with imagination and inventiveness. That's the real fun of whirligigs.

Winged whirligigs are birds, so we have whirligigs of just about every wonderful bird that flies in our country. Canada has some different birds and Mexico and Latin America have many with brilliant colors. All of them can be made into fantastic whirligigs. When I make winged whirligigs, I make them lifesize. Cardinals are about 9″ long, seagulls are about 24″ long, and so on. This makes them seem more real. You also can make fabulous, imaginative birds—and this is what Coo-Coo Bird is all about. It is an example of how bird whirligigs are made, and you can go on and make your own designs from this one.

There are three principal wooden parts to the winged whirligig: the body, the hub base, and the wings. These are described with general instructions on how they are put together.

Body. When you have the body cut out, mark the pivot point (P), which is just back of the balance point (B) of the body. A hole (the pivot socket) will be drilled there for the supporting spindle. The socket may be lined with brass tubing to save wear and tear, and a metal cap should be placed at the socket base. Mark the hub (H), which will be near the top of the body and about $\frac{1}{2}$″ ahead of the pivot point. Once again, the relationship between the hub and the pivot point is what makes the whirligig remain sideways to the wind.

Hub Base. The two hub bases keep the wings from striking the body, and are usually as small as practical. The size largely depends on the size of the wings. Where two separate wings are involved, the hub bases are predrilled with small pilot holes for the hub screws and glued to the body at H. Where split-wings are involved, holes for the axle are drilled through the body and the hub bases. It is usual in such a case for brass tubing to be used as a liner and inserted prior to gluing.

Wings. Whirligigs have two kinds of wings: the double-bladed wing and the split wing. Both are propellers and you have to think of them that way. A propeller works right when the blades are turned at different angles around the hub at the center.

One blade is angled like A and the other is angled opposite it, like B. When looked at from the end, they look like C. As you work on a propeller, think of the wind and how the propeller would turn if you blew on it.

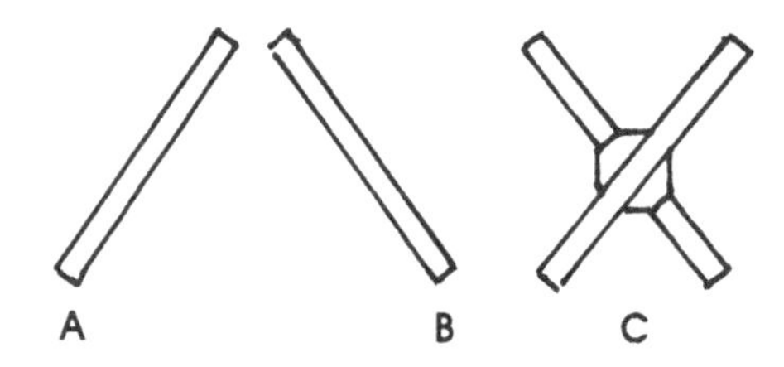

Double-Bladed. In the double-bladed propeller, two blades revolve around a single hub. Note that the two wings must turn in opposite directions when mounted on a bird. The drawing shows a bird whirligig as seen from the front and side.

Split Wings. The split wing is a propeller with two hubs separated by a long axle. The Coo-Coo Bird, the Guardian Angel, and the Flying Elephant, and Carolina Wren have split wings.

Many of the double-bladed propellers for the smaller birds are easiest to make with knives, and the three-piece wings that are included in the book are difficult to make. That is why the split-wing design has been used. Persons who are used to handling sharp knives may wish to make double-bladed propellers for wings on some birds. Such advanced methods are discussed in Chapter 7 under Use of Propellers.

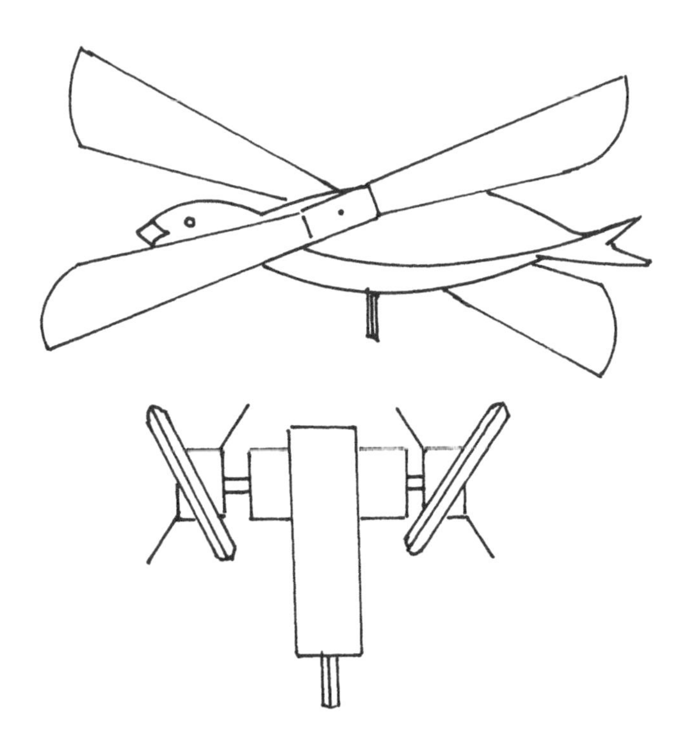

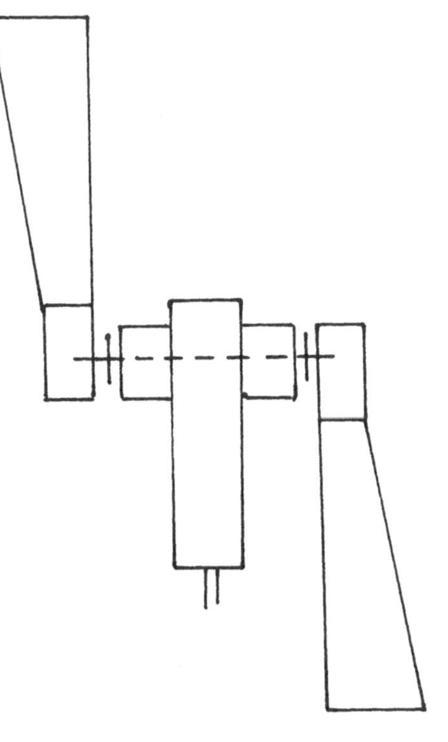

Coo-Coo Bird

The Coo-Coo Bird whirligig is a perfect example of a winged whirligig, and you can make any bird that flies into a whirligig. Maybe, instead of making the Coo-Coo Bird, you would rather make a bird that flies around in your backyard. Just find a good bird book in your home or in the public library and draw your favorite bird. I try to make my birds lifesize, but don't start with 24″ ducks. Try a bird about 9″ or 10″ long, like a cardinal or a robin. Or, if you can't make up your mind, try the Coo-Coo Bird.

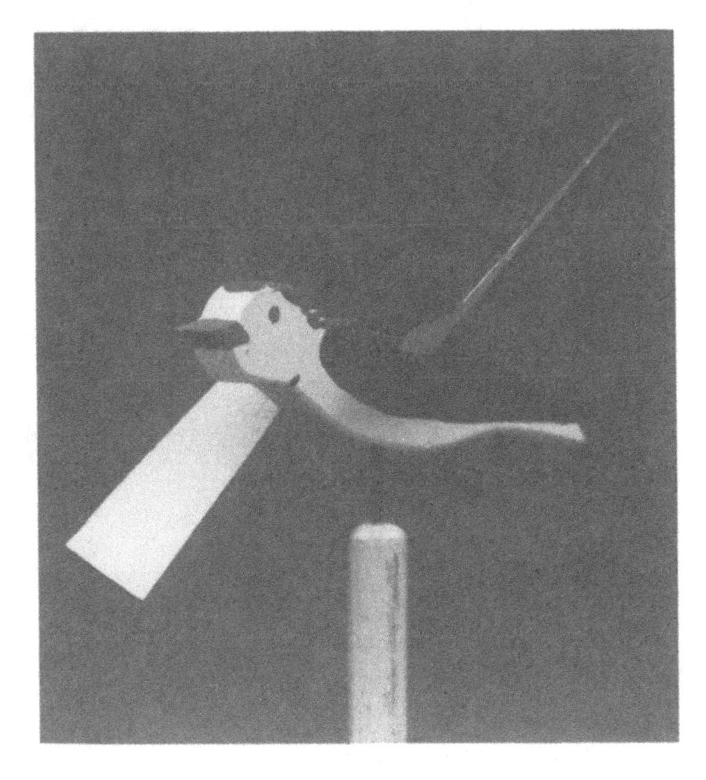

Materials

Body	$\frac{3}{4}$″ × 2″ × 10″
Wing	
hubs (2)	$\frac{3}{4}$″ × $\frac{3}{4}$″ × $1\frac{1}{4}$″
blades (2)	1″ × $1\frac{1}{2}$″ × $4\frac{1}{2}$″
Hub base (2)	$\frac{5}{8}$″ × $\frac{5}{8}$″ × $1\frac{1}{4}$″
Axle	$\frac{1}{4}$″ dowel, $4\frac{1}{2}$″ long
Metal	
pivot socket	$\frac{7}{32}$″ brass tubing, 1″ long
hub	$\frac{5}{16}$″ brass tubing, 2″ long
Washers (2)	$\frac{1}{4}$″ or larger brass washers

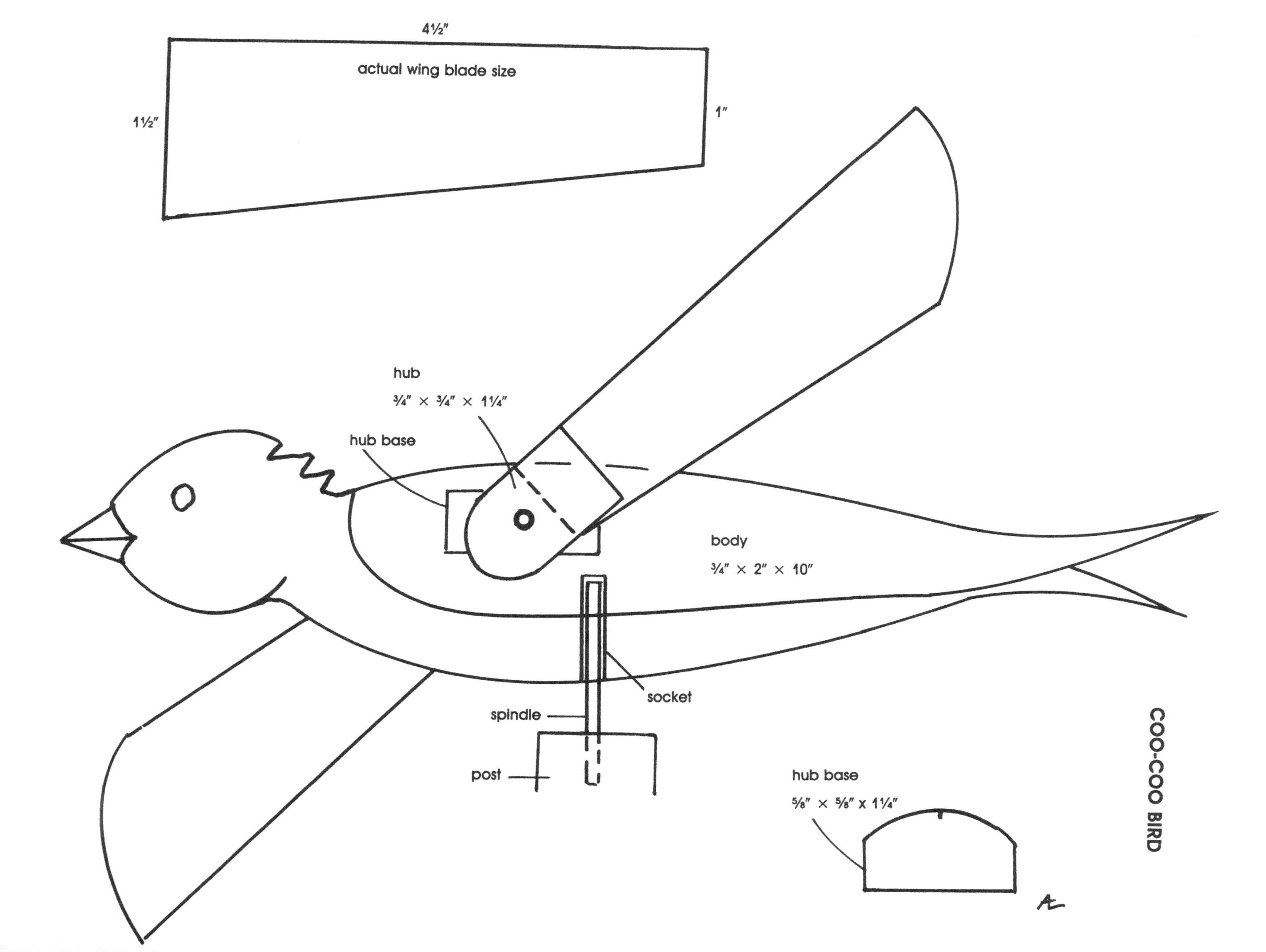
COO-COO BIRD
4½″
actual wing blade size
1½″
1″
hub
¾″ × ¾″ × 1¼″
hub base
body
¾″ × 2″ × 10″
socket
spindle
post
hub base
⅝″ × ⅝″ x 1¼″

Procedure

1. Cut out the bird *body*. Sand it down and mark the positions of the pivot point (P) and the hub (H). Drill the $\frac{7}{32}$" pivot socket hole (P) 1" deep and line it with brass tubing; put a metal cap (the tip of a 16d nail or a BB) in the base of the socket. Drill a $\frac{5}{16}$" hole at H.
2. Cut out the two *hub bases* and drill a $\frac{5}{16}$" hole through them. Round them off and glue them on the body at the hub with a $\frac{5}{16}$" piece of brass tubing for a liner. A C-clamp will hold the pieces until the glue is dry.
3. Make the *wing* parts. Round off one end of the hub bases and mark the other end with an angle for the wing slots. Cut out the wing blades, hold them against the angles to check their widths, and cut out the wing slots. Also check the position of the wings for two things: They must be at correct angles to form a wind propeller; and the straight edge must be inside, next to the bird body. Glue the wing blades to the hubs. When dry, shape them so they look more like wings.
4. Glue the *axle* in one of the hub bases, then pass it through the hub with a washer in place. Before gluing the axle into the other hub, make sure you have the wings in a straight line, otherwise the wings won't work properly. Your whirligig should fly right away. This is a split-wing propeller.

Suggested Colors

As this is an imaginary bird, use bright, crazy colors. On the other hand, if you have a real bird in mind, paint the bird in its natural colors.

More About Double-Bladed Propellers

As mentioned previously, bird whirligigs also fly with separate flashing wings that actually are two propellers turning on the sides of the body. You still have to make the hub bases, but you don't drill holes through the hub of the body or the hub pieces. You have to make two separate propellers, which are designed to turn in opposite directions. That keeps the bird in balance.

Materials

Body	$\frac{3}{4}$" × 3" × 9"
Hub bases (2)	$\frac{3}{4}$" × $\frac{3}{4}$" × $1\frac{1}{4}$"
Propeller:	
wing hub (2)	$\frac{3}{4}$" × $\frac{3}{4}$" × $1\frac{1}{2}$"
wing blades (4)	$\frac{1}{8}$" × $1\frac{1}{4}$" × 4"
Metal	
hub liner	$\frac{3}{16}$" brass tubing
axle (2)	No. 6 round-headed screw, $1\frac{1}{4}$"
Washers (4)	No. 6 brass washers

Procedure

1. After making the *body* (as for the Coo-Coo Bird), make the *hub bases* and drill a small pilot hole through the center for the screw/axles. Then glue the hub bases at H using C-clamps.
2. Cut out the wing parts. Drill a $\frac{3}{16}$" hole through the *wing hubs*. At each end of the wing hubs, draw the diagonals for the wing/blades. Cut out the blade slots.
3. Glue the *wing blades* in the slots. When the glue dries, shape the wings, and perhaps trim the wing hub pieces as well. Make sure that each propeller is balanced. If one end is heavy, file or sand it down until it balances in the center. Also, remember that each one must be a true propeller and have blades at opposite angles. The two propellers also must turn in opposite directions when attached to the body.
4. Attach the *propellers* to the body with screws and washers and make sure they turn easily.

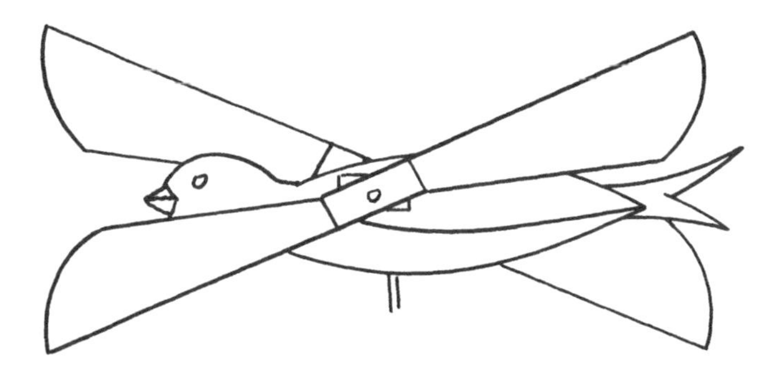

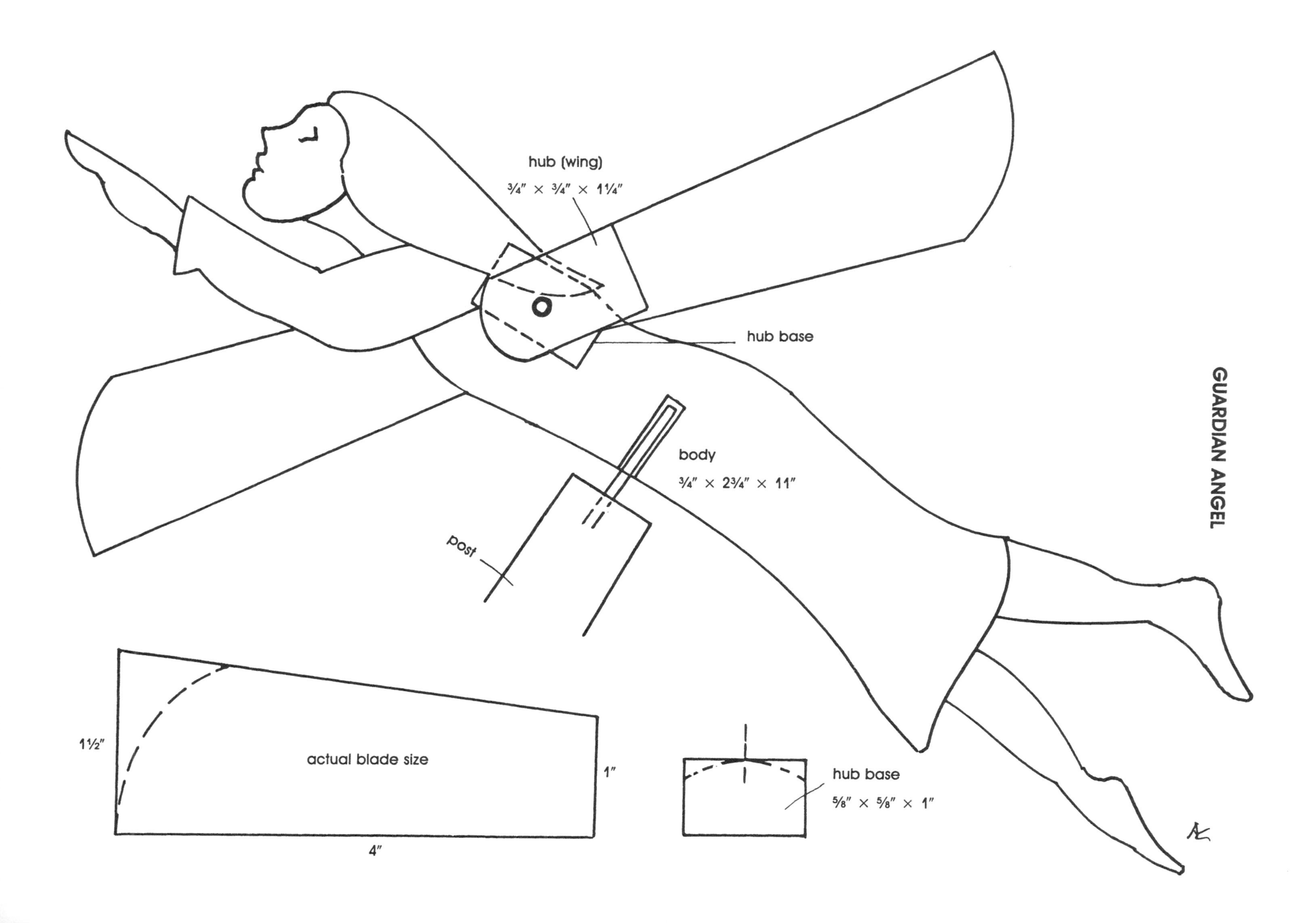
GUARDIAN ANGEL
hub (wing)
3/4" × 3/4" × 1 1/4"
hub base
body
3/4" × 2 3/4" × 11"
post
1 1/2"
actual blade size
1"
4"
hub base
5/8" × 5/8" × 1"

Guardian Angel

Two whirligigs—an angel with wings and an angel holding a flower—can be made with the same body design. The winged angel is a more traditional whirligig while the other is called a weathervane whirligig because it faces the wind and shows wind direction. The flower is a small propeller.

The winged Guardian Angel whirligig is almost like the bird in structure, and the directions for making her are about the same.

Materials

Figure	$\frac{3}{4}$" × $2\frac{3}{4}$" × 11"
Wing	
hubs (2)	$\frac{3}{4}$" × $\frac{3}{4}$" × $1\frac{1}{4}$"
blades (2)	1" × $1\frac{1}{2}$" × 4"
Hub bases (2)	$\frac{5}{8}$" × $\frac{5}{8}$" × 1"
Axle	$\frac{1}{4}$" wood dowel, $4\frac{1}{2}$" long
Metal	
pivot socket	$\frac{7}{32}$" brass tubing, 1" long
hub	$\frac{5}{16}$" brass tubing, 2" long

Procedure

1. Cut out the angel *body*. Sand it and make it smooth. Mark out the location of the pivot point (P) and the hub (H). Drill the $\frac{7}{32}$" pivot socket hole 1" deep and line it with tubing; put in a metal cap (the point of a 16d nail or a BB) in the base of the socket. Drill a $\frac{5}{16}$" hole through the hub (H).
2. Cut out the two *hub bases* and drill a $\frac{5}{16}$" hole through them. Round them off and glue them on the body at the hub with a $\frac{5}{16}$" piece of tubing for a liner. A C-clamp will hold them until the glue is dry.
3. Make the wing parts. On the *hub bases* mark off the hole for the axle and the location of the wing slots, which are $\frac{1}{2}$" deep. Remember to make the wing angles opposite. Hold the hubs in place and check your markings. Drill a $\frac{1}{4}$" hole in the hubs for the axles. Cut out the slots. Cut out the *wing blades*, but make sure of two things before gluing them in the slots. First, they must be at correct angles to form a wind propeller; second, the straight edge of the blade must be on the inside, next to the bird body, or the wings may strike the body in turning. Glue the blades in the hubs.
4. Glue the *axle* in one of the hubs, then pass it through the hub with a washer in place. Before gluing the axle into the other hub, again check the position of the wings.

Suggested Colors

Angel's dress: white, wings: silver or gold.

A Weathervane Whirligig Angel

As I was making the first angel whirligig, I remembered that angels make fine weathervane whirligigs. Use the angel figure for the first angel, but drill the pivot hole a little more forward, as shown in the second drawing.

The weathervane angel whirligig should have a propeller. She can hold one in front of her hands, as shown in the illustration. The propeller can be made so that it looks like a flower with four petals, for example, or even a star. Even a plain propeller will do. This angel will turn into the wind and the star/flower/propeller will turn as well.

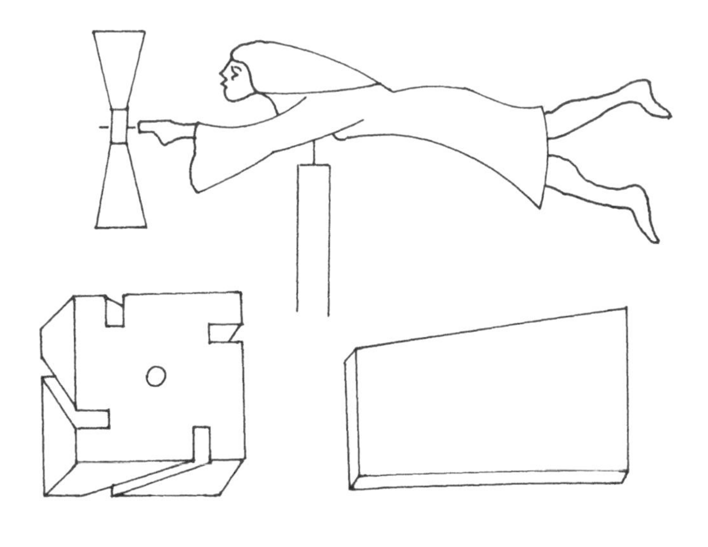

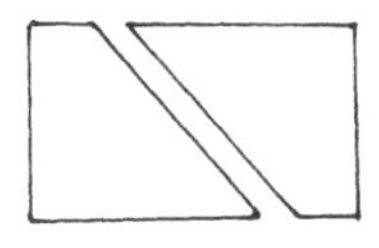

Flying Elephant

The old saying "elephants can't fly" is not quite true. I purposefully didn't give this whirligig a name because I thought you'd like to do that when you made it. I am not sure if it is an Indian elephant or an African elephant, but the bigger ears belong to the African elephant. I also am not sure if this flying creature is a he or she. I will leave that up to you, too.

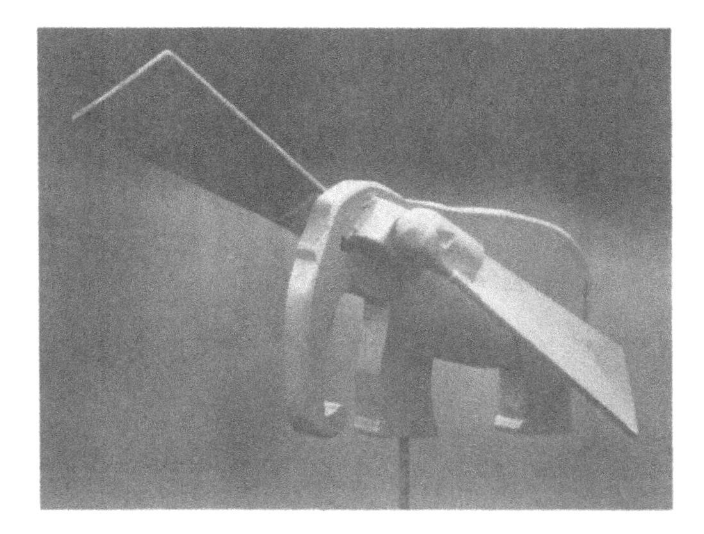

Materials

Body	$\frac{3}{4}'' \times 4'' \times 6''$
Ears	
hub (2)	$\frac{3}{4}'' \times \frac{3}{4}'' \times 1\frac{1}{4}''$
blades (2)	$1'' \times 2'' \times 4''$
Ear base (2)	$\frac{5}{8}'' \times \frac{3}{4}'' \times 1\frac{1}{4}''$
Axle	$\frac{1}{4}''$ dowel, 5″ long
Metal	
socket liner	$\frac{7}{32}''$ brass tubing, 2″ long
hub liner	$\frac{5}{16}''$ brass tubing, 4″ long
Washers (2)	$\frac{1}{4}''$ or larger brass washers

Note: Because you want the trunk and the legs to be strong, be sure the grain of the wood goes along with the length of the trunk and not across it. If it goes across the trunk and legs, they may snap off.

Procedure

1. Draw the pattern very carefully on the woodblock, including the details of the legs and features. Mark the position of the hub (H) and the pivot point (P). Then cut out the *body*. Drill a $\frac{7}{32}''$ hole for the pivot

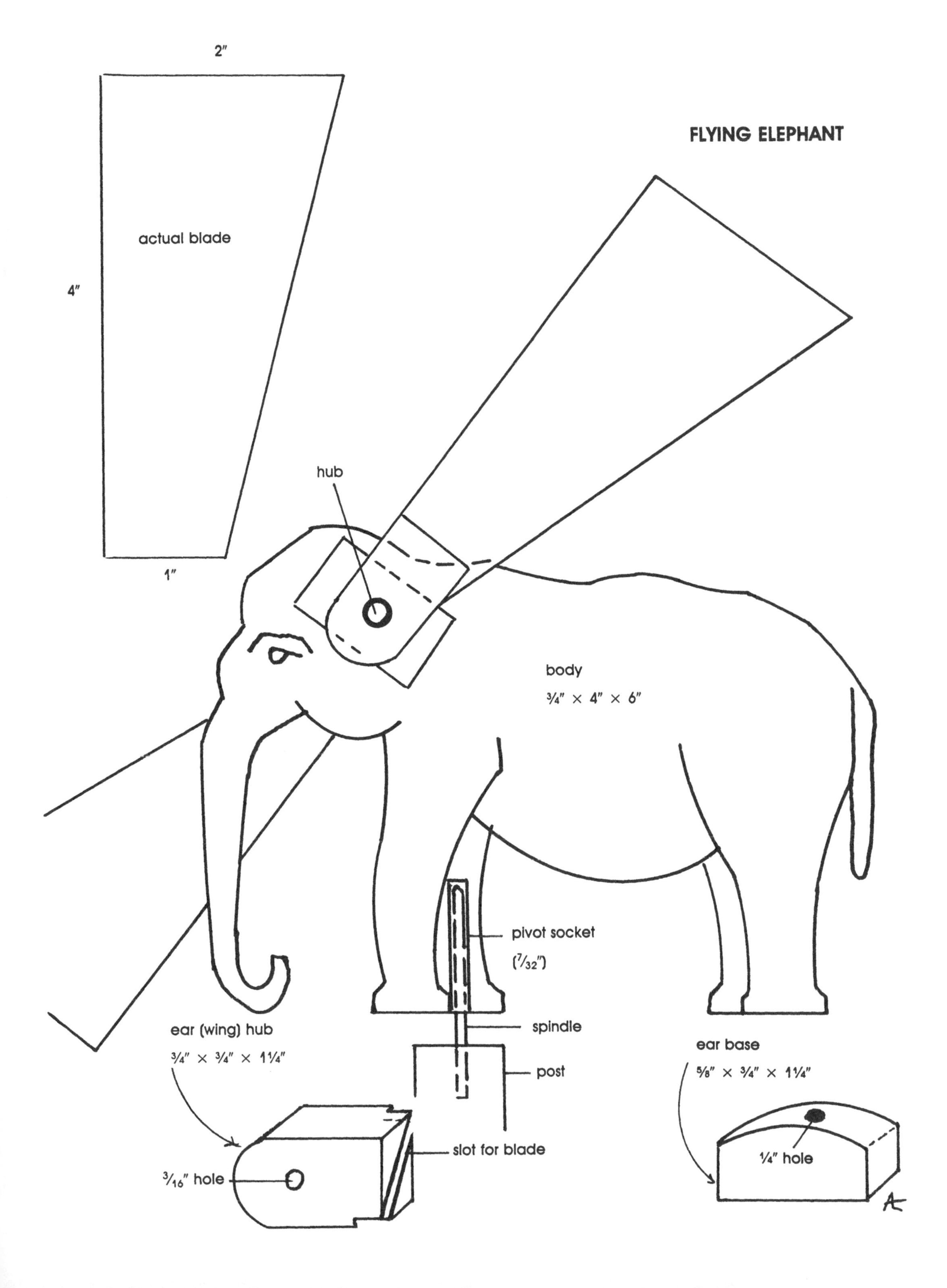
FLYING ELEPHANT
2"
actual blade
4"
1"
hub
body
3/4" × 4" × 6"
pivot socket
(7/32")
spindle
post
ear (wing) hub
3/4" × 3/4" × 1 1/4"
3/16" hole
slot for blade
ear base
5/8" × 3/4" × 1 1/4"
1/4" hole

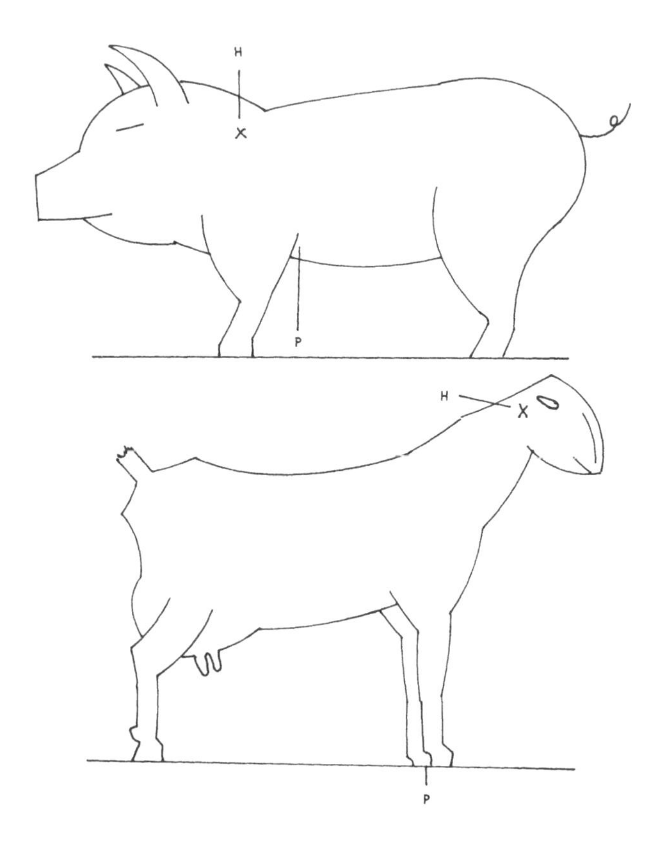

socket $1\frac{1}{4}$″ deep. Line it with brass tubing if you have it; in any case, place a cap (a 16d nail end or a BB) at the bottom of the socket. Drill a $\frac{5}{16}$″ hole at H for the ear hub.

2. Cut out the *ear bases* and drill a hole through the middle with a $\frac{1}{4}$″ bit. Glue the ear bases to the hub hole with brass tubing in place. A C-clamp will hold them until the glue dries.
3. Construct the *ear wings* as shown in the drawing. First, cut out the *hub pieces* and drill them with a $\frac{1}{4}$″ bit through H. Round off one of the ends. Draw diagonal lines at the other end for the wing slots. Check the pieces against the body, and think of the wind blowing across it to make sure your diagonals are correct. Cut out the *wing blades* as well as the hub slots.
4. Glue the wing blades in the hub slots.

Note: In this type of blade or wing, the straight side must be next to the body. Check this out before finally gluing the blades in the slots.

5. Glue the *axle* to one of the ear hubs and insert it through the body with a washer in place. Then, holding the other ear in a straight line, glue it onto the axle.

Suggested Colors

The Flying Elephant is now ready for painting. Because the ears are so large, perhaps you would prefer to paint the pieces separately. It is up to you. I suppose everything will be the same color anyway—elephant gray. But maybe you like your elephant pink? To make the elephant really funny, as a whirligig should be, use a bright color with polka dots.

Other Animals Using the Same Wings

Many people have written to me asking if I could make a whirligig of their favorite animals. One of my sons wanted a pig with large ears for wings. At one time my daughter had goats, and I made her a Nubian goat with ears for wings, too. (Nubians have bigger ears than most goats.) You can put wings on just about anything.

Chapter 5

Special and Weathervane Whirligigs

There are a number of whirligigs that do not fit into any special category. Many simply turn into the wind and move only a propeller. Some of these are called weathervane whirligigs because, for the most part, they look like weathervanes and they indicate wind direction. Others are a combination of several types and are very decorative.

Whirligigs of different designs can be quite small or very large. A folk artist in the Appalachian Mountains makes frames that hold several small propellers; the frames are pointed into the wind by a big rudder. Then there is Vollis Simpson, an ironworker who lives east of Raleigh, North Carolina, who builds whirligigs thirty to forty feet tall. One of his creations has nearly lifesize mules pulling a big wagon; he uses truck transmissions to keep the gigantic propellers from running away in a strong breeze. His whirligigs are very special and have been exhibited on the grounds of the North Carolina Museum of Art.

You can make all kinds and sizes of whirligigs. Almost any object can be made into a whirligig if it can be made to swing sideways and have a turning propeller or propellers on it somewhere.

The whirligigs on the following pages are special in some way. The Cruise Ship is a true weathervane whirligig because it faces into the wind at all times and has a propeller that turns. You can make many of this type, such as a simple airplane or other type of aircraft. Cut out the aircraft, put a large rudder on it and a propeller in front, and you have it! Unfortunately, you can't make a modern jet aircraft into a whirligig because it has no propeller. But you can make a whirligig of any animal—like an alligator or crocodile. Put the pivot point (P) less than a third of the way back on the body, put a propeller on its snout, and you will have an unusual whirligig.

The Gondola whirligig is special because it has a propeller placed sideways at the end of a long whirligig and works on the principle of lateral balance. The gondola always lies sideways to the wind and the propeller (the gondolier's arms and sweep) will always turn.

The Juggling Clown is also unique because it doesn't have the usual arm-waving configuration. It acts more like a weathervane—but it is not that, either. It is an offside whirligig because the pivot point (P) is off to one side. This causes the offside to swing with the wind and keeps the propeller arms spinning. You can make many objects with an offside pivot point and, if you can balance it properly and plan to put a propeller on it somewhere, you will have an unusual whirligig. The Balancing Clown is also an offside whirligig but has a different configuration and two independent propellers. The Dancing Sailor whirligig follows this pattern and has different propellers.

The Football Player whirligig shows what can be done with sports figures. He (or she) has a football in his/her hands. Other whirligigs hold baseballs, gloves, tennis rackets, and other objects related to their sport.

Remember, there is nothing to stop you from making any object into some kind of whirligig if you have a lively imagination!

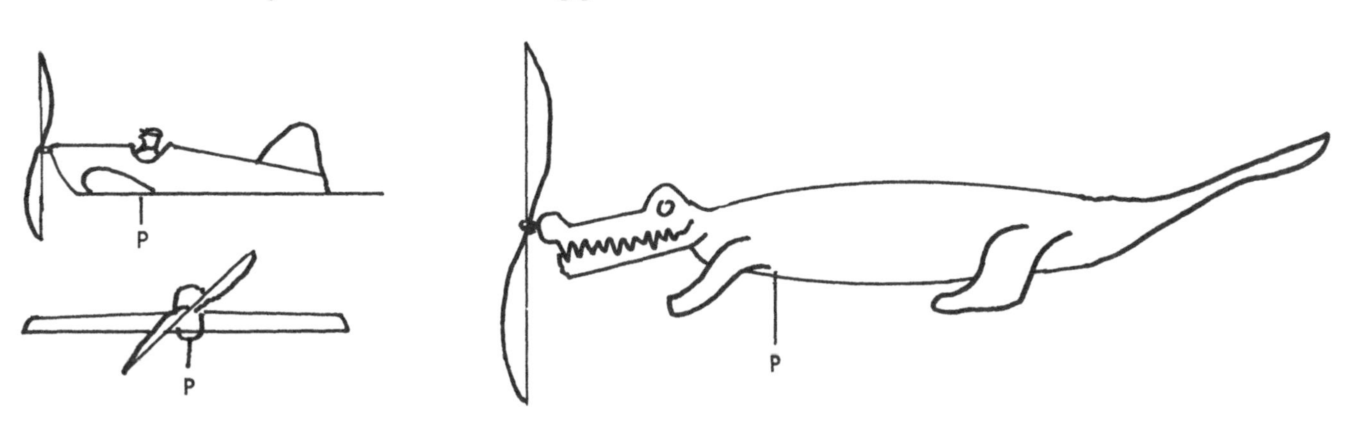

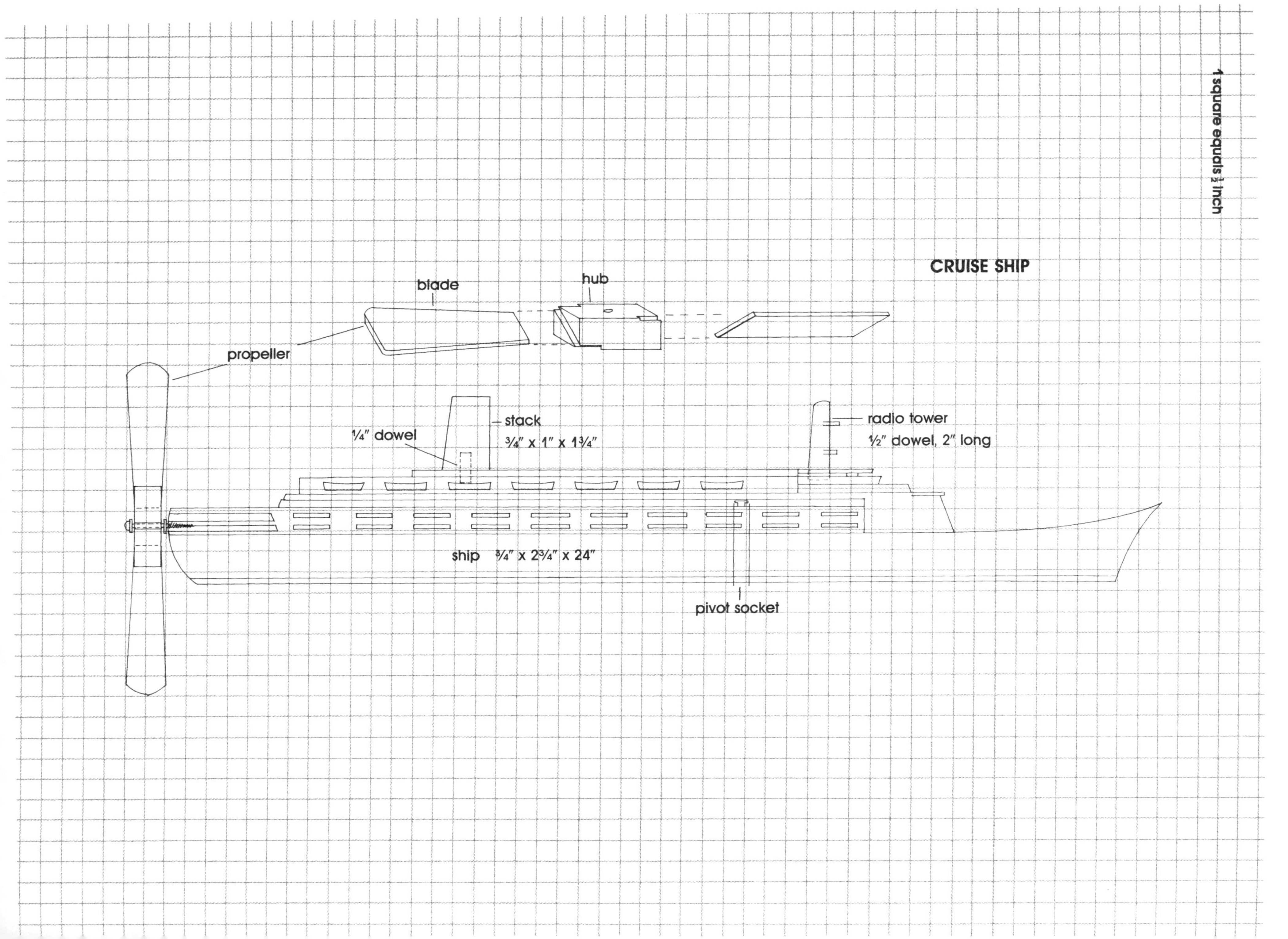
1 square equals ½ inch
CRUISE SHIP
blade
hub
propeller
stack
¼" dowel
¾" x 1" x 1¾"
radio tower
½" dowel, 2" long
ship ¾" x 2¾" x 24"
pivot socket

Cruise Ship

Making ship and boat whirligigs is an old tradition, and you can make sailboats, tugboats, submarines, battleships, and all kinds of boats into whirligigs by putting a propeller on them. Whirligig makers didn't use propellers on boats until John Ericsson invented the screw propeller in 1836, so this kind of boat whirligig is about 150 years old.

With this particular whirligig in your yard, people will think you've been on a world cruise. It is a weathervane whirligig similar in design to the Cunard Line's *Queen Elizabeth II*. The two-bladed propeller acts as a drag or rudder; it will spin in any breeze. If you would prefer another type of propeller, see the alternate Angel Whirligig or Mary in Her Garden; these have four-bladed propellers. You also can make this one bigger by lengthening the blades.

Materials

Ship	$\frac{3}{4}'' \times 2\frac{3}{4}'' \times 24''$
Stack	$\frac{3}{4}'' \times 1'' \times 1\frac{3}{4}''$
Radio tower	$\frac{1}{2}''$ dowel, 2″ long
Pivot socket liner	$\frac{3}{8}''$ tension pin, or $\frac{1}{4}''$ brass tubing, 2″ long
Propeller	
hub	$\frac{3}{4}'' \times \frac{3}{4}'' \times 2''$
blades (2)	$\frac{3}{8}'' \times 1'' \times 3\frac{1}{2}''$
axle	No. 6 round-headed brass screw, $1\frac{1}{2}''$
washers	No. 6 or No. 8 brass washers

Procedure

1. Before cutting out the *ship*, trace or draw it on the wood block and mark the location of the stack, tower, and pivot point. Cut out the ship. Drill the pivot socket hole 2″ deep; it is located 10″ from the bow. Put in the socket liner and cap. Drill a pilot hole in the stern for the propeller screw/axle. On the top deck drill a $\frac{1}{4}''$ hole for the stack-holding dowel and drill a $\frac{1}{2}''$ hole for the tower base. File and sand the ship smooth.
2. Cut out the *stack* and drill a $\frac{1}{4}''$ hole in the middle of the base about $\frac{1}{2}''$ deep. Glue a $\frac{3}{4}''$ piece of dowel in the hole and glue the stack with the dowel inserted in the top deck. File the *radio tower* into shape and glue that in the $\frac{1}{2}''$ hole about $\frac{1}{4}''$ deep.
3. Make the propeller. Cut out the *hub piece* and drill a $\frac{3}{16}''$ hole in the center. Line it with tubing. Mark the angles for the blade slots and cut out the slots $\frac{1}{2}''$ deep. Cut out the *blades* and trim them. Glue them in the slots.
4. The boat may now be painted. The hull is black; if you are clever, you can paint the bottom and a waterline red. The upper decks are white. When you have finished painting (perhaps two coats) decide how much detail you wish to add, such as deck lines, cabin windows or portholes, and lifeboats. Use a thin waterproof black ink marker in drawing lines or objects.
5. The propeller may now be painted silver or gold. When it is dry, mount it with a screw and washers and your whirligig is ready to sail the seven seas.

Gondola

A gondola is a boat that has been used on the canals of Venice, Italy, for hundreds of years. It is thirty-two feet long and can carry up to six passengers. Since 1562, all gondolas by law must be painted black. The boat is propelled by a gondolier, who stands at the stern and pushes with a long oar or sweep held in a wooden fork.

Notice the position of the pivot point (P) as related to the hub (H); this relationship permits a lateral balance to be maintained when wind blows against it and

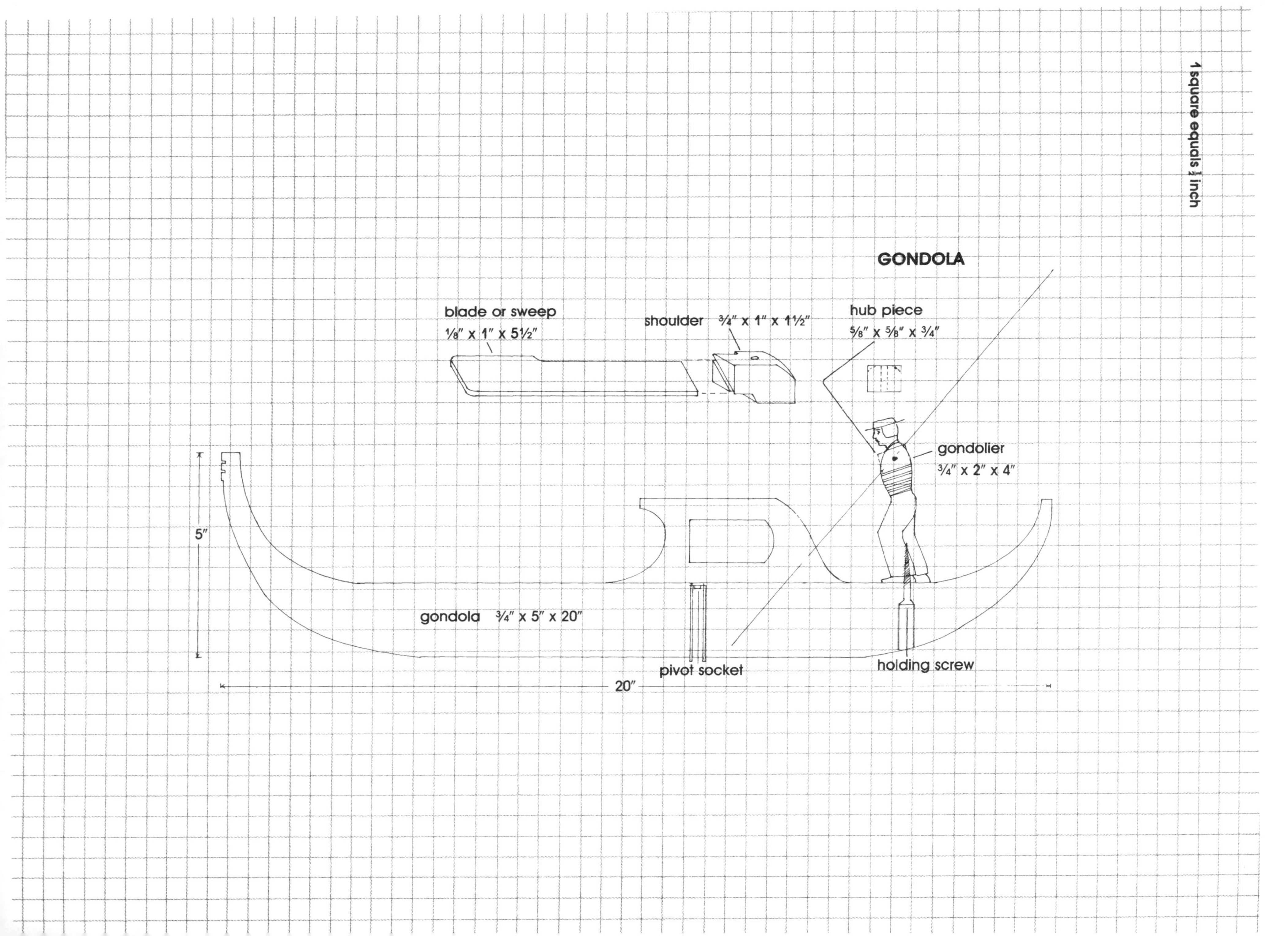

GONDOLA
blade or sweep
1/8" x 1" x 5½"
shoulder 3/4" x 1" x 1½"
hub piece
5/8" x 5/8" x 3/4"
gondolier
3/4" x 2" x 4"
5"
gondola 3/4" x 5" x 20"
pivot socket
holding screw
20"
1 square equals ½ inch

the propeller turns. If P were a couple of inches back, the boat would turn away from the wind and the propeller would probably stop. If P were some inches forward, the reverse would be true, and the propeller would also stop. Keep this in mind when making larger and longer whirligigs that have propeller blades at one end. When this pivot point is in the right position, the whirligig remains sideways to the wind and the propeller (gondolier's sweeps) keeps turning. The position of the pivot point will change as whirligigs become longer and bigger, and the proper position can only be determined by testing different locations. I drilled three pivot sockets before I found the best one for this whirligig.

Materials

Gondola	$\frac{3}{4}$" × 5" × 20"
Gondolier	
body	$\frac{3}{4}$" × 2" × 4"
hub pieces (2)	$\frac{5}{8}$" × $\frac{5}{8}$" × $\frac{3}{4}$"
shoulders (2)	$\frac{3}{4}$" × 1" × 1$\frac{1}{2}$"
sweeps (2)	$\frac{1}{8}$" × 1" × 5$\frac{1}{2}$"
Hub liner	$\frac{3}{16}$" brass tubing, 2" long
Axle	$\frac{1}{8}$" brass rod, 2" long threaded both ends
Pivot socket liner	$\frac{3}{8}$" tension pin, 2" long
Spindle	20d or 30d nail, head cut off
Washers	As needed

Alternate Materials

Hub liner	$\frac{5}{16}$" tubing, 2" long
Axle	$\frac{1}{4}$" wood dowel, 4$\frac{1}{4}$" long
Pivot socket liner	$\frac{1}{4}$" brass tubing, 2" long

Procedure

1. Prepare a piece of wood $\frac{3}{4}$" thick and slightly larger than 5" wide and 20" long. Square it off. Draw the gondola on it or trace a pattern, making sure the lines are correct. As indicated in the drawing, the main hull is 1$\frac{3}{4}$" high. The cabin is 2" high and stretches from about 9$\frac{1}{4}$" to 15" along the top of the hull from the front. The pivot point is at 8$\frac{1}{2}$" from the stern, and the gondolier's holding screw hole is 3$\frac{1}{2}$" from the stern.

   Cut out the *gondola with cabin*. File and sand it smooth. Mark the gondolier's screw hole centered on top and bottom of the boat and drill it with a $\frac{1}{8}$" bit halfway from the top and bottom. Then, from the bottom, with a $\frac{3}{8}$" bit, drill a hole up 1$\frac{1}{4}$" for the screw. Redrill the hole from the top with a $\frac{7}{64}$" bit for the holding screw. Drill the hole for the pivot socket with either a $\frac{3}{8}$" bit for a tension pin or a $\frac{1}{4}$" bit for the socket liner tubing. Put a metal cap in the socket.

Fitting the sweeps on the Gondola.

   The head of a 16d nail will fit into the tension pin, and a small screw can be used with the other tubing. It is a good idea to make a stand for this whirligig as soon as you can.

2. Cut out the *gondolier*. Sand him smooth. Drill a $\frac{3}{16}$" hub hole in his shoulder. Cut out the *hub pieces* and drill a $\frac{3}{16}$" hole through them. Glue them to the body at the hub with the tubing, and hold them in place with a C-clamp. If you are using a wooden dowel axle, drill a $\frac{1}{4}$" hole through the body and the hub pieces, and use $\frac{1}{4}$" tubing for a liner. When the glue is dry, mount the gondolier in place on the deck with glue and the holding screw. It is advisable to drill a small pilot hole in the gondolier to avoid splitting the wood.

3. Make the propeller and the shoulder/sweeps. Cut out the *shoulders*. Drill $\frac{7}{64}$" holes $\frac{1}{2}$" from the top if your axle is a $\frac{1}{8}$" rod. Drill $\frac{1}{4}$" holes if you are using a wooden dowel. Then cut out the diagonal slots for the sweeps. If the shoulders are put side by side in

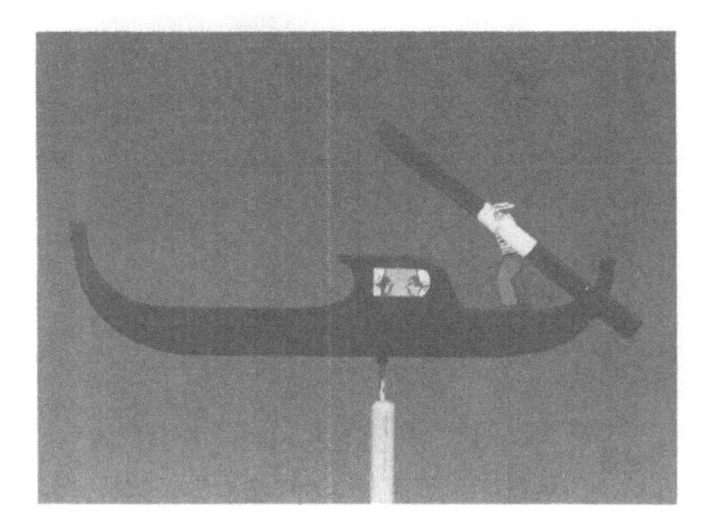

the same position, the diagonals will be the same. Cut out the *sweeps* and glue them in the slots, making sure that the extra wide part juts out away from the body. When the glue is dry, cut the sweeps back so they look more like paddles (see the illustration). Try them on the axle to make sure they balance. Then place them on the gondolier's body to see if they work properly. Paint the pieces separately before final mounting.

Suggested Colors

Gondola (by law): black. The cabin window usually has curtains in it, and if you are good at it, you can paint people looking out. The gondolier has blue pants, white shirt with horizontal red stripes, and a white hat with a red ribbon. The sweeps are red.

Juggling Clown

The Juggling Clown whirligig is fun to make and everyone enjoys watching him juggle. He is full of tricks—and the best one is a whirligig maker's secret. Look at the illustration and you will see that the pivot point (P) is well off to one side. This means that the rest of his body acts as a *vane*. He will automatically turn sideways to the wind, and this will insure that his arms will spin. There are two very different kinds of arms used in the Juggling Clown and the Balancing Clown (which follows).

Materials

Figure	$\frac{3}{4}'' \times 2\frac{1}{2}'' \times 9\frac{1}{2}''$
Arms	
shoulders (2)	$\frac{3}{4}'' \times 1'' \times 1\frac{1}{2}''$
blades (2)	$\frac{1}{8}'' \times \frac{3}{4}'' \times 3\frac{1}{4}''$
balls (2)	$\frac{1}{8}'' \times 1\frac{1}{4}''$ in diameter
Axle	$\frac{3}{16}''$ dowel, $4\frac{1}{2}''$ long
Metal	
pivot socket	$\frac{7}{32}''$ brass tubing, 2″ long
hub liner	$\frac{1}{4}''$ brass tubing, $2\frac{1}{2}''$ long
Washers (2)	$\frac{1}{4}''$ brass washers

Procedure

1. For this clown, trace the *figure* on the woodblock and cut it out. Smooth it with a file and sandpaper. Mark on it the location of the pivot point (P) and the hub (H). Drill a $\frac{1}{4}''$ hub hole through H. To make sure it is straight across, drill halfway in from each side. Line it with brass tubing if you have it. Drill the pivot socket to one side, as shown, with a $\frac{7}{32}''$ bit and line it with tubing. Put a metal cap in the bottom.
2. Make the *arm pieces*. Cut out the *shoulders* and drill a $\frac{3}{16}''$ hole through them for the axle. Shape the shoulders and draw angles on the bottom for the blade slots. Check the angle of these slots to make sure they will work as a propeller.
3. Cut out the *blades*. Then cut out the shoulder slots, checking with the width of the blades. Glue the blades in the slots.
4. For the *balls*, cut out two round pieces of $\frac{1}{8}''$ or $\frac{1}{4}''$ thick wood and glue them to the bottom of the arms. They should extend a little below the level of the blades. Be sure they extend out from the figure; otherwise they will strike the figure. When the glue is dry, take your file and thin down the balls from the inside to the edges to make them lighter. Put the arms in a temporary axle and balance them.

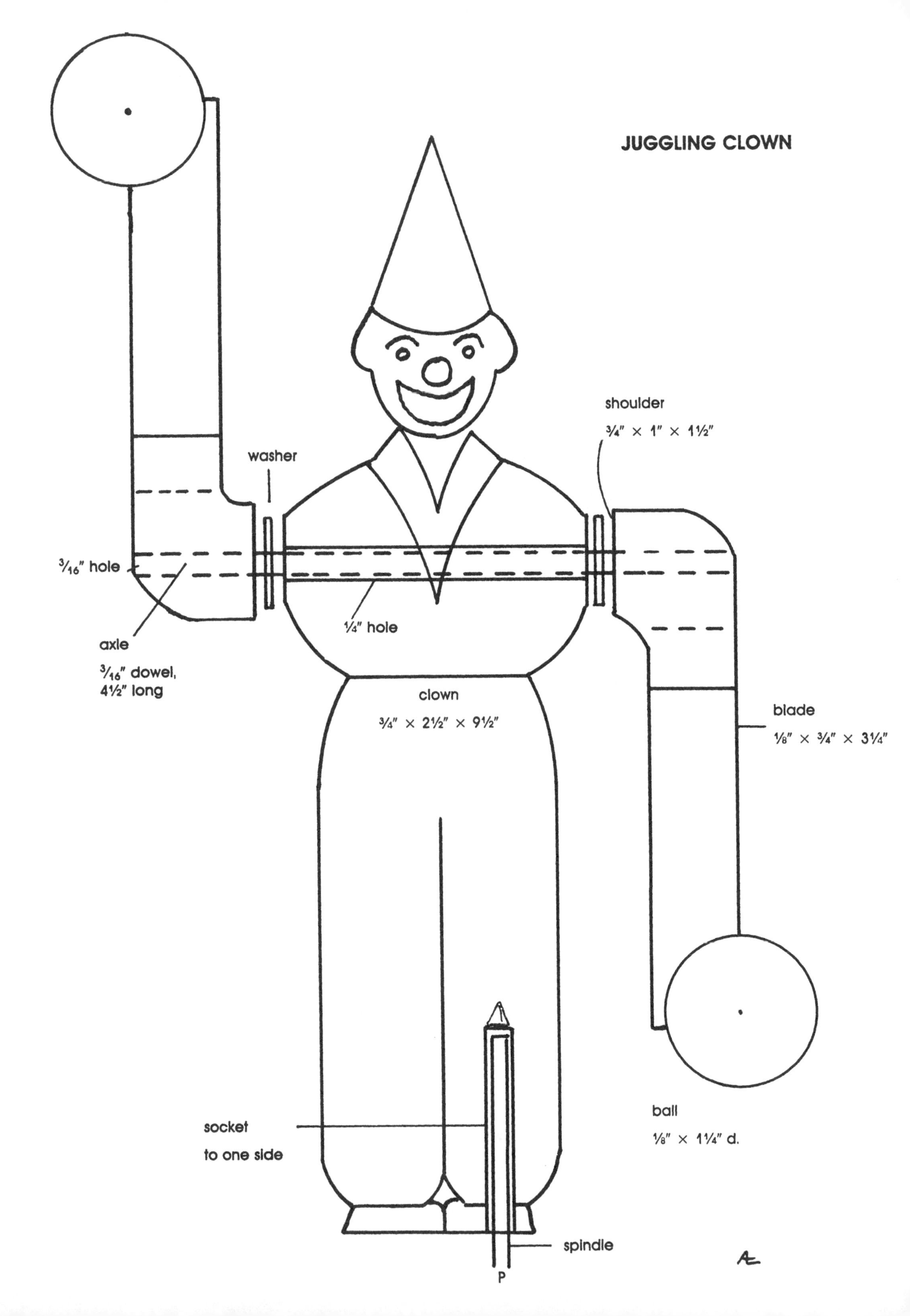
JUGGLING CLOWN
shoulder
¾″ × 1″ × 1½″
washer
³⁄₁₆″ hole
¼″ hole
axle
³⁄₁₆″ dowel,
4½″ long
clown
¾″ × 2½″ × 9½″
blade
⅛″ × ¾″ × 3¼″
ball
⅛″ × 1¼″ d.
socket
to one side
spindle
P

5. Attach one end of the *axle* to a shoulder with glue. Then put it through the hub with a washer and, after making sure the other arm is in line with it, glue the other end to the shoulder. The arms must be in line and balanced or they won't work correctly. Leave enough space between the shoulders and the body so the arms may move freely.

Suggested Colors

Clown: white with red and blue polka dots, face: natural, hair: brown, balls: red and blue.

Balancing Clown

This whirligig also has an off-center or offside pivot point that makes it turn sideways to the wind. This enables the propellers to get the wind's power constantly. There are two independent propellers, one larger than the other, so this whirligig is not an arm-waver like the Juggling Clown. To add to the rudder effect, a ball has been inserted in the right foot (although the whirligig will work without it). The design of the propellers is similar to those for the Vane and the Cruise Ship.

Materials

Clown	
figure	$\frac{3}{4}'' \times 9'' \times 11''$
ball	$\frac{1}{8}'' \times 3''$ diameter circle
Propellers	
hubs (2)	$\frac{5}{8}'' \times \frac{5}{8}'' \times 1\frac{1}{4}''$
blades (2 no. 1)	$\frac{1}{8}'' \times 1'' \times 2''$
blades (2 no. 2)	$\frac{1}{8}'' \times 1'' \times 3''$
hub liners (2)	$\frac{3}{16}''$ brass tubing

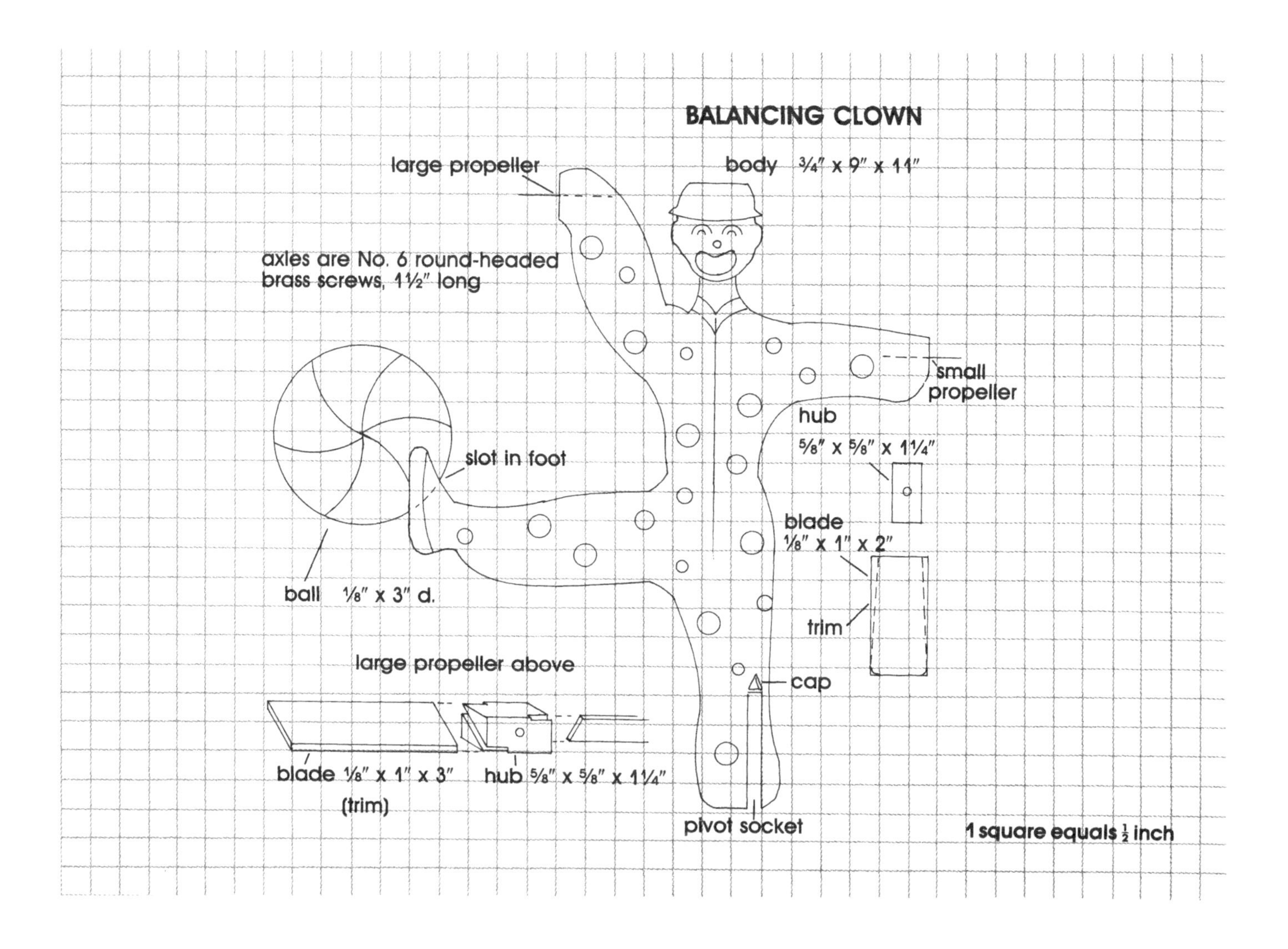

axles (2)	No. 6 round-headed brass screws, 1½" long
washers (2)	No. 6 or No. 8 brass washers
Pivot socket liner	$\frac{7}{32}$" brass tubing, 2" long

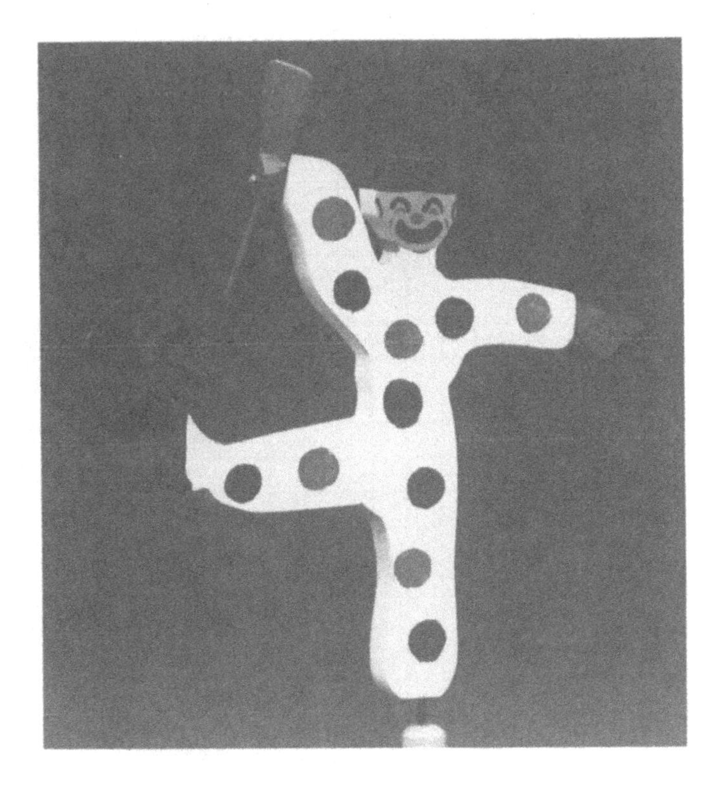

Procedure

1. Cut out the *clown figure*. Drill a $\frac{7}{32}$" hole in the upright leg 2" deep and line it with tubing if you have it. Put a metal cap in the base. Drill small pilot holes in the ends of the arms for the propeller screws or axles. Cut out a ⅛" slot in the right leg about ½" deep.
2. Make the propellers. Cut out the *hubs* and drill $\frac{3}{16}$" holes through the centers. Then mark the angles for the blade slots. There are two things to watch for. Each propeller must have blades at opposite angles in order to work. Also, each propeller should turn in a different direction. The hubs should be marked with these two points in mind. Cut out the slots after you have cut out the blades, so you can fit them properly.
3. Cut out the *blades* and make sure they will fit into the slots. Then glue them.
4. Cut out the *ball* and glue it into the foot slot. Secure it with a small nail.
5. Paint the figure and the propellers separately. When dry, attach the propellers with the screws and washers in place. The washers should be on the lee side of the propellers (away from the wind). Also, the smaller propeller should be in front so that the wind will catch it first. The larger propeller, in back, will add to the rudder effect.

Suggested Colors

Clown suit: white or yellow (or any color) with large polka dots (red, blue, or contrasting to the suit color); propellers: one blue and one red; ball: multicolored; face: any style of clown face.

Dancing Sailor

In olden days sailors danced the hornpipe. The name of this dance was taken from an ancient wind instrument made of bone and a cowhorn bell, and it became the name of old Irish, Scottish, and English solo dances. The hornpipe dance was fast and similar to a jig. So you can imagine our sailor dancing the hornpipe with two propellers in his hands. This may look complicated, but it is easy to make. It has an offside pivot point and the propellers should always be turning in the wind.

Materials

Body	¾" × 7" × 10¾"
Large propeller	
hub square	¾" × 1" × 1" or circle of 1" diameter
blades	⅛" × ¾" × 2¼"
Small propeller	
hub square	¾" × ¾" × ¾" or circle of ¾" diameter
blades	⅛" × ¾" × 1⅞"
Axles (2)	No. 6 round-headed brass screws, 1" or 1½" long
Washers (4)	No. 6 or No. 8 brass washers
Metal	
pivot socket	$\frac{7}{32}$" brass tubing, 2" long
hub liner	$\frac{3}{16}$" brass tubing, small lengths
cap for socket	End of 16d nail, or small screw

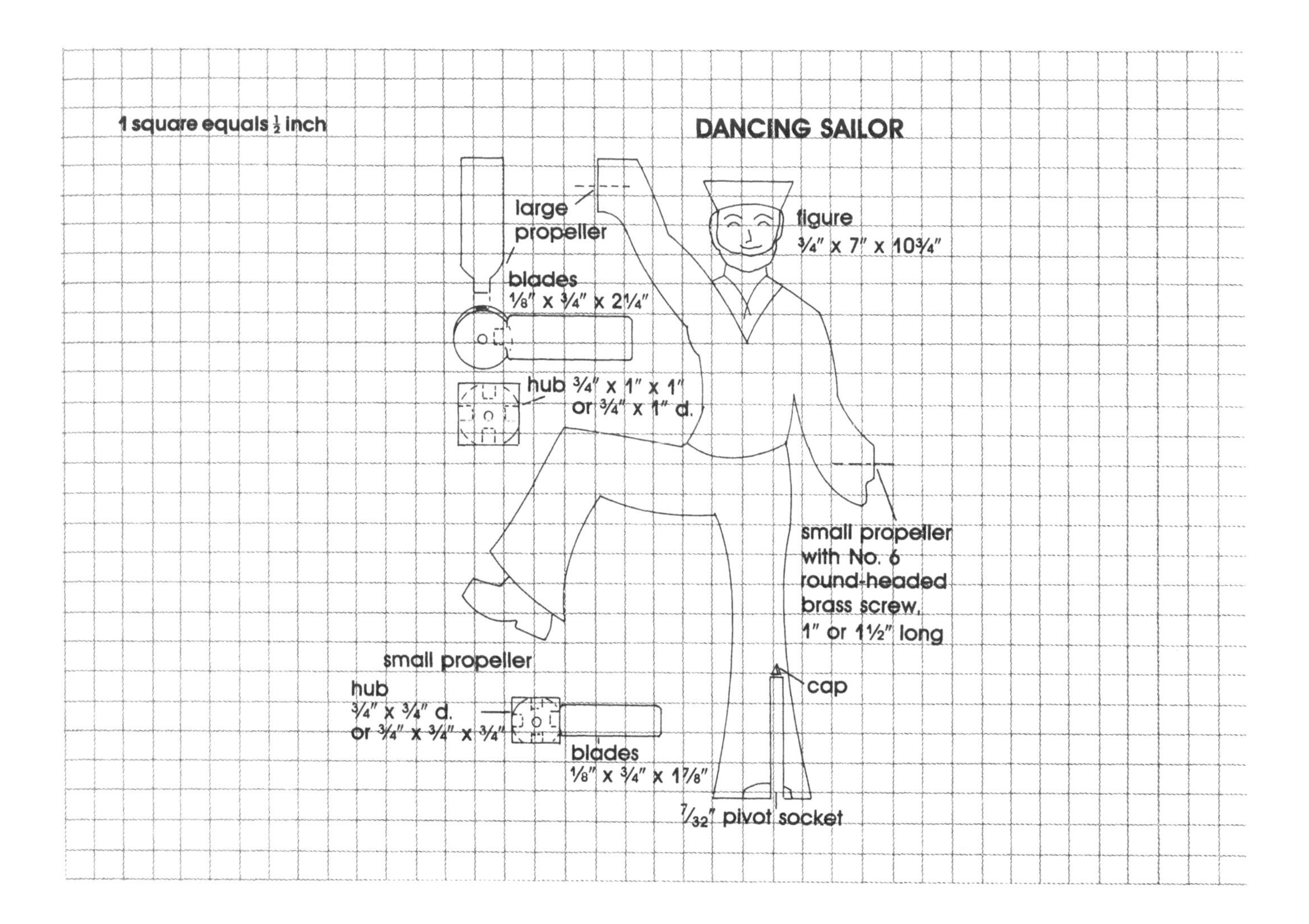

Procedure

1. Trace the sailor on a piece of wood and mark the pivot point (P) and the pivot socket carefully. Cut out the *figure* and file and sand it smooth. Drill the pivot socket (P) 2" deep with a $\frac{7}{32}$" bit, line it with tubing (if you have it), and place a cap at the bottom of the socket.

2. Mark the *axle holes* at the ends of the arms. Drill a small pilot hole (a $\frac{7}{64}$" hole will do for a No. 6 screw) into the arms, straight across but not all the way through.

3. Make the *large four-bladed propeller*. Cut out a 1" square block. With a pencil mark the center of the square, which will be the hub hole. Then mark the midpoints of the four sides. First drill a $\frac{3}{16}$" hole through the center. Line it with $\frac{3}{16}$" brass tubing if you have it. Then drill $\frac{1}{4}$" holes at the midpoints of the four sides, going in $\frac{1}{4}$" (don't go into the center hub hole!) You can now round off the edges of the hub piece with a file. If you have the ability, you may wish to begin with a round hub, 1" in diameter but it is not necessary to do this (and it is more difficult to make and to get the blade holes just right).

4. Cut out the *blades*. With a pencil mark the end of each blade so it will taper down to $\frac{1}{4}$". Then trim down the ends to fit into the $\frac{1}{4}$" holes in the hub. When you have all the blades ready, glue them into the four holes at a 45-degree angle so the propeller will go counterclockwise when the wind blows against it. When the glue is dry, mount the propeller in the sailor's right hand with a No. 6 screw and washers.

5. Put the sailor on a spindle, propeller in place, and put him in the wind (or in front of a fan). The body should go edgewise to the wind and the propeller should spin quickly counterclockwise. (If it spins

clockwise, don't worry; make the small one go the other way.) The reason for making it go clockwise is that the screw is right-handed; if the propeller goes counterclockwise in the sailor's right hand, it would tend to loosen the screw. Think about it. Perhaps it will make no difference with this small whirligig, but it certainly makes a difference with large ones! Always think of the effect of the wind and rotation on whirligig activity.

6. Make the small four-bladed propeller in the same way. First cut out a $\frac{3}{4}''$ block, mark it off, and drill the center hub hole with a $\frac{3}{16}''$ bit. Line the hole if you have brass tubing. Then drill the four side holes with a $\frac{1}{4}''$ bit, but do not drill as deep as on the large propeller (and don't go into the hub center hole!) Cut out the four *blades*, trim them, and glue them in position at an angle that will turn the propeller in a clockwise direction. Mount the propeller in the sailor's left hand.
7. Put the sailor on a spindle and see how he operates in the wind. Both propellers should turn fast and in opposite directions.

Suggested Colors

Sailor: blue with white trim, hat: white, shoes: black, propeller blades: different colors, skin: your choice.

Football Player

The Football Player is an example of the sports figure whirligig that waves an arm handling a ball or racket. It is similar to arm-wavers like the Smiling Lady and the Cheerleader except that the figure has an offside or off-center pivot point. When you become familiar with the many ways in which figure whirligigs can be made to operate (the pivot point/hub relationship, with tail or rudder extension, and offside pivot point), you will be able to design all kinds of whirligigs and make them work.

Materials

Figure	$\frac{3}{4}'' \times 2'' \times 8\frac{1}{4}''$
Propeller	
shoulder	$\frac{3}{4}'' \times 1'' \times 1\frac{1}{2}''$
arms	$\frac{1}{8}'' \times 1'' \times 3\frac{1}{2}''$
Axle	$\frac{3}{16}''$ dowel, $4\frac{1}{2}''$ long
Hub liner	$\frac{1}{4}''$ tubing, 2″ long
Footballs (2)	$\frac{1}{8}'' \times 1\frac{1}{2}'' \times 2\frac{1}{2}''$
Washers (2)	$\frac{1}{4}''$ brass washers
Pivot socket liner	$\frac{7}{32}''$ brass tubing, $1\frac{1}{2}''$ long
Socket cap	Point of 16d nail, BB, or screw

Procedure

1. Before cutting out the figure, cut the woodblock to exact size ($2'' \times 8\frac{1}{4}''$) and draw or trace the pattern on the block. Make sure the lines of the hub/axle are square across the body and the line of the pivot socket is straight up. Then, with a $\frac{1}{4}''$ bit, drill the axle hole halfway through the body from both sides. Drill the $\frac{7}{32}''$ pivot socket hole $1\frac{1}{2}''$ deep. Then cut out the figure and file and sand it smooth. Line the hub and the socket with tubing.

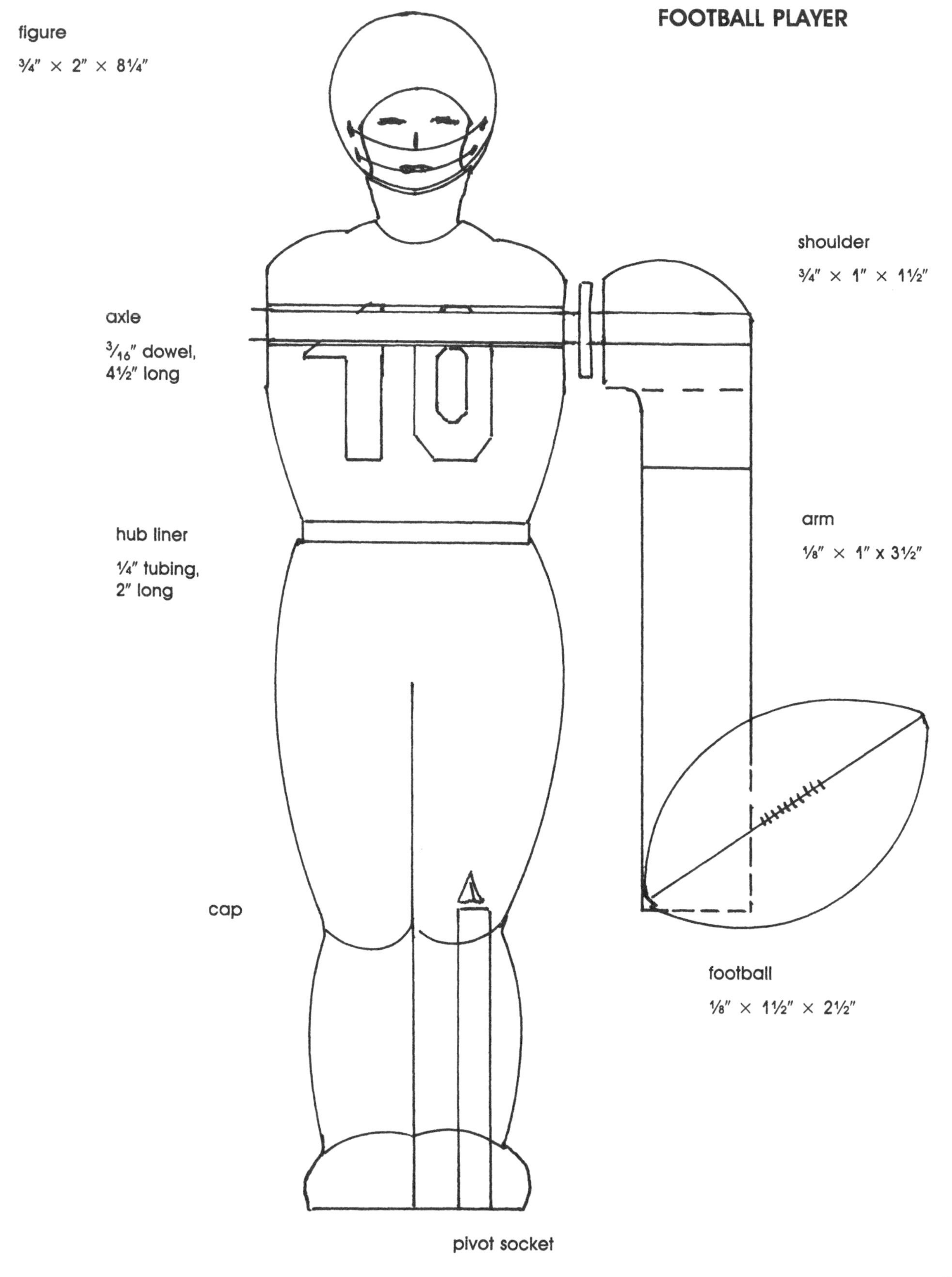
FOOTBALL PLAYER
figure
¾″ × 2″ × 8¼″
shoulder
¾″ × 1″ × 1½″
axle
3⁄16″ dowel,
4½″ long
arm
⅛″ × 1″ x 3½″
hub liner
¼″ tubing,
2″ long
cap
football
⅛″ × 1½″ × 2½″
pivot socket
'91

2. Make the propeller/arms. Cut out the shoulder pieces. Drill a $\frac{3}{16}''$ hole through the shoulders at $\frac{1}{2}''$ from the top, and shape the pieces. Mark where the slots for the arms will be and cut them out. Cut out the arms/blades and glue them in the slots. Cut out the footballs and glue them to the ends of the arms, holding them with spring clamps. When the pieces are dry, test the arms to make sure they are balanced. The pieces may be painted separately at this point.
3. Cut out the axle. Glue one end into a shoulder hub hole, then insert it in the body with a washer. Glue the other end, washer in place, to the other shoulder, making sure that the arms are in a straight line.

Suggested Colors

Your favorite team colors will do nicely.

Chapter 6
Mechanical Whirligigs

A mechanical whirligig has a wind propeller on it that turns a driveshaft; as the driveshaft turns it makes things connected with it move. In this case the driveshaft is called a camshaft because it has a rotating pin on it that is connected to another moving part. The principal parts of a mechanical whirligig are the propeller, camshaft, connecting rod, and the object it moves. There is also a tail or rudder to steer the whirligig into the wind. Of course, the whirligig also has a base or platform and supports for the camshaft. Then there is the pivot socket by which the whirligig is supported. It really is not as complicated as it sounds.

This chapter of the book discusses simple mechanical whirligigs for beginners. Chapters 7 and 8 provide instructions for the construction of more complicated mechanical whirligigs and discuss advanced techniques of whirligig making. (See specifically Other Camshafts for Mechanical Whirligigs, Other Cams, and Use of Propellers in Chapter 7 and the whirligigs in Chapter 8).

The Mechanism for Mechanical Whirligigs

The next three whirligigs are simple mechanical whirligigs with the same mechanism and the same parts. This section tells how to make the parts and put them together. The next three sections tell how to complete the different whirligigs: Danny the Dinosaur, David the Wood Chopper, and Mary in Her Garden.

Materials

Platform or base	3/4" × 3/4" × 12"
Pivot socket block	3/4" × 1" × 1"
Support blocks (2)	3/4" × 3/4" × 1 1/4"
Camshaft	1/4" dowel, 6" long
Cam block	3/4" × 1 1/4" × 1 1/4"
Spacer	3/4" × 3/4" × 3/4"
Propeller hub	3/4" × 3/4" × 1 1/4"
Propeller blades (2)	1/8" × 2" × 4"
Socket	7/32" brass tubing
Screws (2)	No. 6 flat-headed, 1 1/2"
(1)	No. 4 round-headed, 3/4"
Washers (3)	Brass, to go over 1/4" dowel
Wire	Stiff, for connecting rod

Procedure

1. Cut out the *platform* and measure off very carefully where the parts will be connected on it. This will include the slot for the rudder (in 2" from the rear of the platform for Danny the Dinosaur and Mary in Her Garden, and 1" for David the Wood Chopper); the holes for screws to hold the support pieces (3/8" and 2 5/8" from the front); and the position of the socket block (3" from the front). Then cut the rudder slot (3/16" wide or 1/4" wide, depending on the size of your wood). Drill the holes for the support screws using a 1/8" bit, and your platform is ready for the parts.
2. Cut out the camshaft *support pieces* and drill a 5/16" hole through them about 1/4" from the top, as shown. Line the holes with 5/16" tubing (if you have it). Cut out the *camshaft* now. Attach the support pieces to the platform with glue and screws, but before tightening the screws, put the drive shaft through the holes to make sure it will turn easily.
3. When everything is set correctly, tighten the screws. Then cut out the *pivot socket block* and drill two small pilot holes through it to nail it onto the underside of the platform. Attach it with glue and 1" nails or brads. You may have to use a C-clamp to hold it while it dries. When it is dry, drill a 7/32" hole in it about 1" deep and put a cap in the bottom. The cap can be the end of a 16d nail, a small screw, or a BB. Be careful about the cap; you may drive it through the platform. If you use a BB, put some glue on it to hold it.

The Mechanism for Mechanical Whirligigs

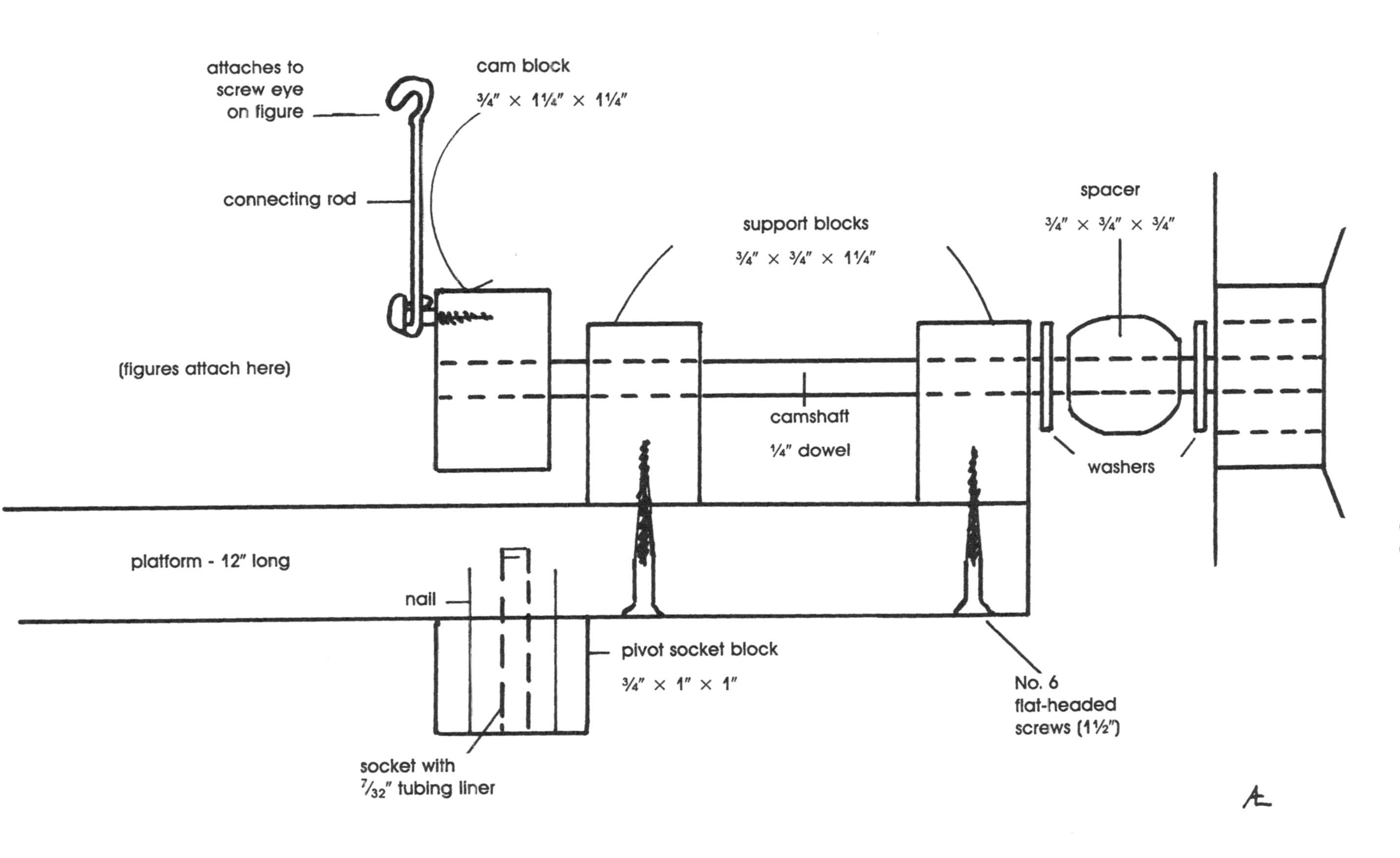

4. Cut out the *rudder* or *tail* of your choice (see the next sections) and glue/brad it into the slot. Two $\frac{1}{2}$" or $\frac{3}{4}$" brads will do the trick.
5. Cut out the *cam block* and drill a $\frac{1}{4}$" hole through the middle. On one corner drill a small pilot hole ($\frac{1}{16}$") and turn in the $\frac{3}{4}$" round-headed screw, leaving about $\frac{1}{4}$" of the shaft exposed. Then glue the drive shaft into the cam block.
6. Make the *propeller*. Cut out the hub and drill a $\frac{1}{4}$" hole through the center. Mark the angles on the edges for the blade slots and make sure the angles are opposite. Cut out the blades and, checking their width, cut out the angled hub slots. Glue the blades in the slots. Keep the straight edges of the blades on one side of the hub.
7. Cut out the *spacer* and drill a $\frac{5}{16}$" hole through it.
8. You can put the platform and pieces aside now and work on the dinosaur, chopper, or girl figures while the glue dries on the mechanism. You might also want to make a *stand* for the whirligig.

Materials for a Simple Stand

Base	$\frac{3}{4}$" × $4\frac{1}{2}$" × $4\frac{1}{2}$"
Post	$\frac{5}{8}$" or $\frac{3}{4}$" wood dowel, 2" long
Spindle	16d nail, head cut off and filed smooth

Procedure

Cut out the base. Drill a $\frac{5}{8}$" or $\frac{3}{4}$" hole in the center. Glue the post in the hole. When the glue is dry, drill a $\frac{5}{32}$" hole into the top of the post about 1" deep. Tack the 16d nail in the hole.

When you are ready to return to the platform, follow the instructions in the following sections.

Danny the Dinosaur

You are about to make the king (rex) of the tyrant lizards: Tyrannosaurus Rex, the biggest allosaurus. You are going to cut him down to eight inches. But he will be a happy dinosaur, chewing on his trees.

Materials

Body	$\frac{3}{4}$" × $3\frac{1}{2}$" × 8"
Legs (2)	$\frac{1}{4}$" × $2\frac{3}{4}$" × 4"
Rudder	$\frac{1}{4}$" × $3\frac{1}{2}$" × $4\frac{1}{2}$"
Body liner	$\frac{5}{32}$" brass tubing
Axle	$\frac{1}{16}$" brass rod, about 3" long
Connecting rod	$\frac{1}{16}$" brass rod, about 4" long
Screw eye	About $\frac{3}{8}$" in width

Procedure

1. Complete the platform and mechanism shown in The Mechanism for Mechanical Whirligigs, including the *rudder*, which is cut out of a piece of thin wood or $\frac{1}{4}$" plywood measuring $3\frac{1}{2}$" × $4\frac{1}{2}$".
2. If you haven't made a *stand* for your whirligig, now is the time to do it.
3. Cut out the *legs* and sand them smooth. In one of the legs (*not* both) drill a $\frac{1}{8}$" hole at H. Mount the drilled leg with the heel $7\frac{1}{2}$" from the front of the platform. Tack two brads in place first and then secure the leg on the platform with glue. It is a good idea to drill the same pilot holes in the legs to make sure the wood does not split. Then nail and glue the other leg in place opposite the first. When it is in position, take your drill and put the bit through the hole. Check that it is straight across and level and then drill a hole in the other leg. Do this because it is hard to get two predrilled holes even. To make sure the legs will hold, use a C-clamp on them until the glue dries.
4. Cut out the *body* and file and sand it smooth. Drill a $\frac{5}{32}$" hole in the body at H and line it with tubing if you have it. Drill a pilot hole in the tail and turn in the screw eye. When the glue is dry on the legs, cut out a *spacer* from a small piece of wood or a dowel about $\frac{13}{16}$" long (which is $\frac{1}{16}$" longer than $\frac{3}{4}$"). Glue it between the legs beneath where the body will be. This will keep the legs apart and the body free to move.
5. Make the *leg axle*. Put a $\frac{1}{16}$" brass rod or other metal rod through the legs and body with one end bent over about $\frac{1}{4}$" (so you can move the body if you wish). Test the body movement. It should move freely.
6. Make a *connecting rod* of stiff wire or $\frac{1}{16}$" brass rod. Put a loop at one end to go around the cam screw. Put another loop around the screw eye on the tail. The dinosaur's mouth should be at the trees when the cam is in the up position. Make sure it does not

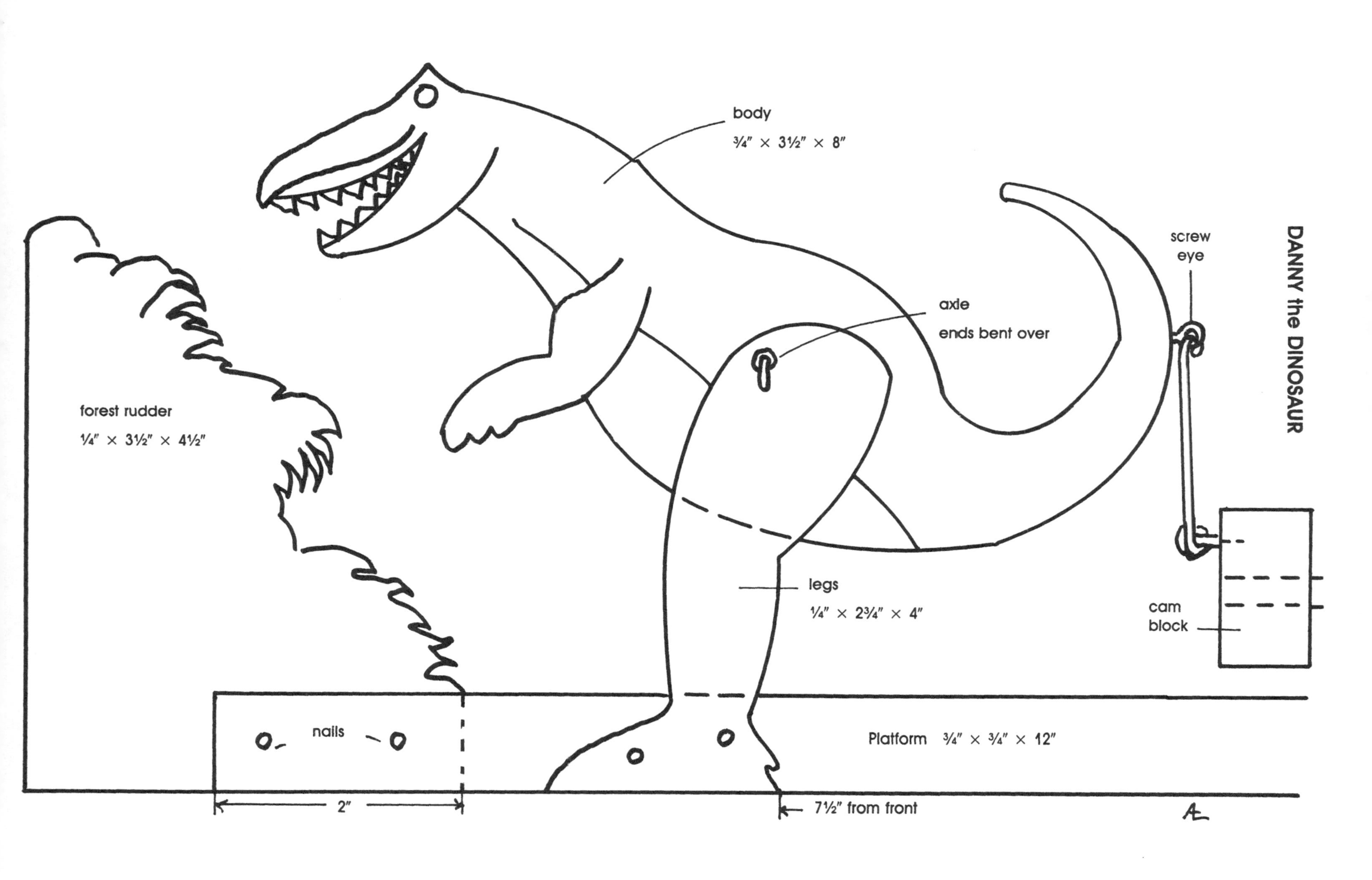
DANNY the DINOSAUR
body
3/4" × 3 1/2" × 8"
screw
eye
axle
ends bent over
forest rudder
1/4" × 3 1/2" × 4 1/2"
legs
1/4" × 2 3/4" × 4"
cam
block
nails
Platform 3/4" × 3/4" × 12"
2"
7 1/2" from front

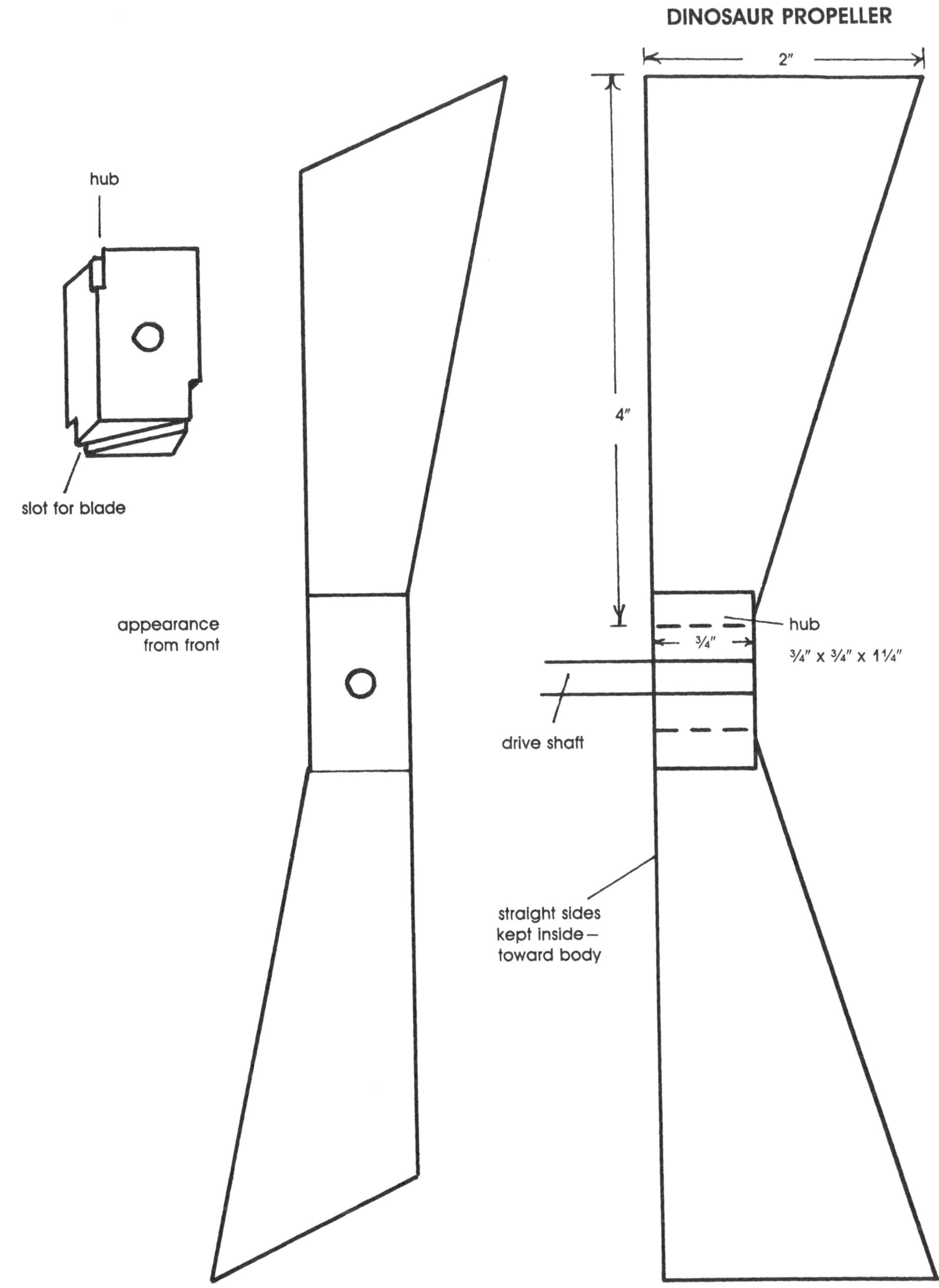
DINOSAUR PROPELLER
2″
4″
hub
slot for blade
appearance
from front
hub
3/4″
3/4″ x 3/4″ x 1 1/4″
drive shaft
straight sides
kept inside—
toward body

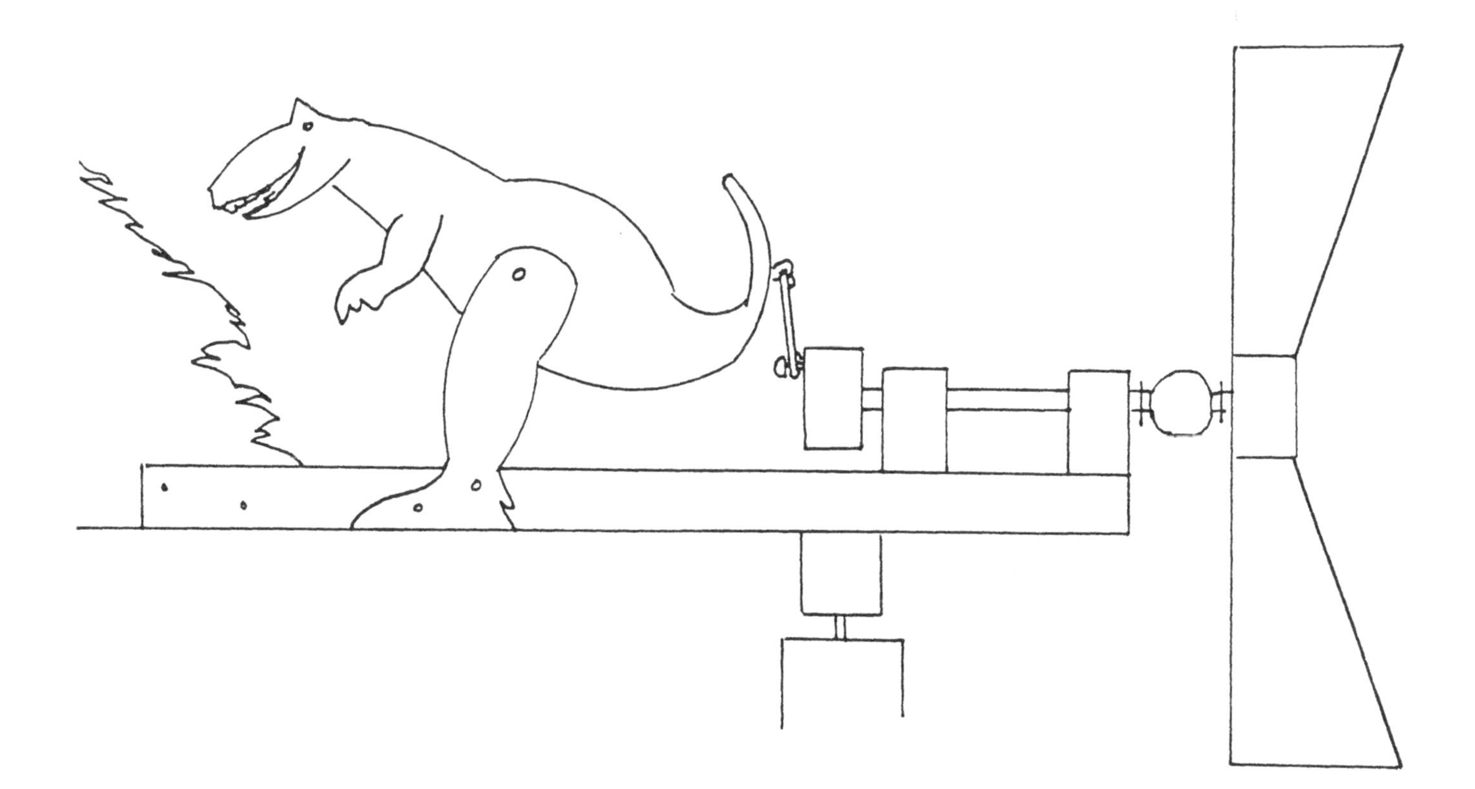

hit the trees. The distance between the cam screw and the screw eye in my model was about 2″ when the loops were finished.

7. When the dinosaur works perfectly, make the final bend in the axle, secure the connecting rod, and put the propeller in place. With the spacer and washers in position, the end of the cam should be between 4″ and $4\frac{1}{4}$″ from the front, and the connecting rod should move from being vertical to leaning slightly forward. Glue the propeller in final position and the whirligig is complete.

Suggested Colors

Dinosaur and legs: green with dark lines and spots, wood: junglelike plants and giant trees, platform: light green with strokes of paints for grasses of various colors.

David the Wood Chopper

This is one of the oldest American whirligig patterns, about as old as the Man Sawing Wood. As with the Danny the Dinosaur, you should follow these steps.

Materials

Chopping block	$\frac{3}{4}$″ × 1″ × $1\frac{1}{2}$″
Logs	Small pieces of wood or dowel about 1″ long

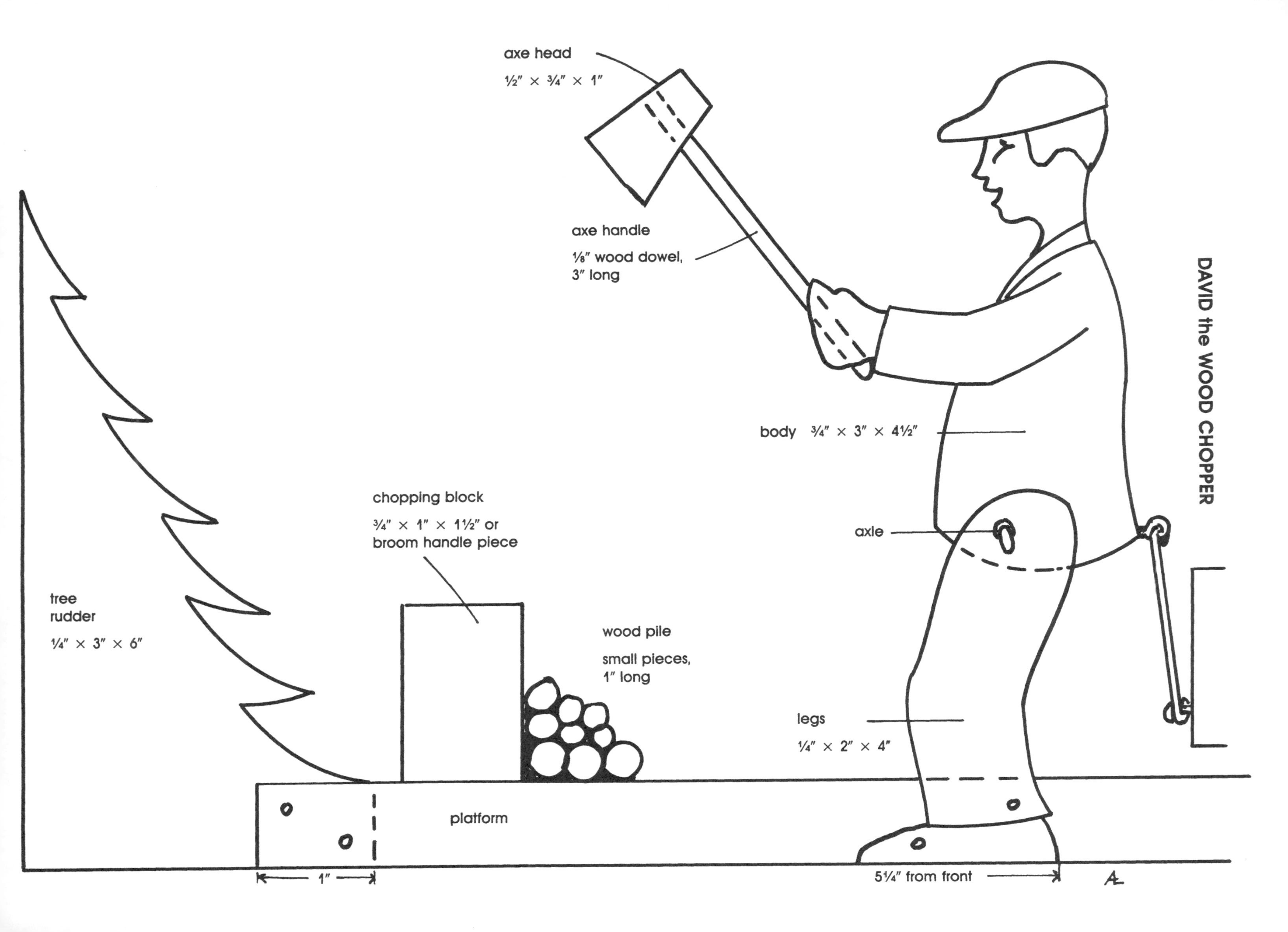
DAVID the WOOD CHOPPER
axe head
½″ × ¾″ × 1″
axe handle
⅛″ wood dowel,
3″ long
body ¾″ × 3″ × 4½″
axle
chopping block
¾″ × 1″ × 1½″ or
broom handle piece
tree
rudder
¼″ × 3″ × 6″
wood pile
small pieces,
1″ long
legs
¼″ × 2″ × 4″
platform
1″
5¼″ from front
AL

Wood chopper	
legs (2)	$\frac{1}{4}$" × 2" × 4"
body	$\frac{3}{4}$" × 3" × $4\frac{1}{2}$"
axe head	$\frac{1}{2}$" × $\frac{3}{4}$" × 1"
axe handle	$\frac{1}{8}$" dowel, 3" long
body liner	$\frac{5}{32}$" brass tubing
Axle	$\frac{1}{16}$" brass rod, about 3" to 4" long
Connecting rod	$\frac{1}{16}$" brass rod, about 4" to 5" long
Screw eye	About $\frac{3}{8}$"

Procedure

1. Complete the platform and mechanism in The Mechanism for Mechanical Whirligigs and add the fir tree *rudder* shown here with glue and brads.
2. Make a stand for the whirligig.
3. Cut out the *chopping block*. Drill a screw hole in the platform at $10\frac{1}{4}$" from the front and glue/screw the block in position. Cut out five or six logs and fasten them with glue and brads in front of the chopping block. If you use brads, drill a small pilot hole in the wood first to prevent splitting.
4. Cut out the *legs*. Drill a $\frac{1}{8}$" hole in one (*not* both) of them. Mount this so the heel is $5\frac{1}{4}$" from the front with glue and brads. Then fasten the other leg and hold them both with a C-clamp until the glue is dry. Put the drill bit through the first leg hole and, while holding it straight and level, drill through the other leg.
5. Cut out the *body*. Drill a $\frac{5}{32}$" hole through H and another hole ($\frac{1}{8}$") through the hands for the axe handle. Drill a pilot hole in the back for a *screw eye* and attach it. Make the *axe*. Drill a $\frac{1}{8}$" hole through the axehead and glue it to the handle. Don't glue the axe in the hands yet; put it in the hands temporarily.
6. Cut out a *spacer* $\frac{13}{16}$" long (this is just $\frac{1}{16}$" longer than the platform is wide). Glue and brad it in place between the legs below the body line. This will keep the body moving freely.
7. Make an *axle* of a metal rod (like a $\frac{1}{16}$" brass rod) about 4" long, and put it through the hub holes with the body in place. Check to see that the body moves easily and correctly.
8. With a pair of pliers make a loop in one end of the *connecting rod* so that it goes around the cog screw. Test the movement; the axe should come down just over the chopping block but not strike it. Glue the handle at the proper length. Make a loop for the other end of the connecting rod around the screw

Propeller for Chopper and Mary

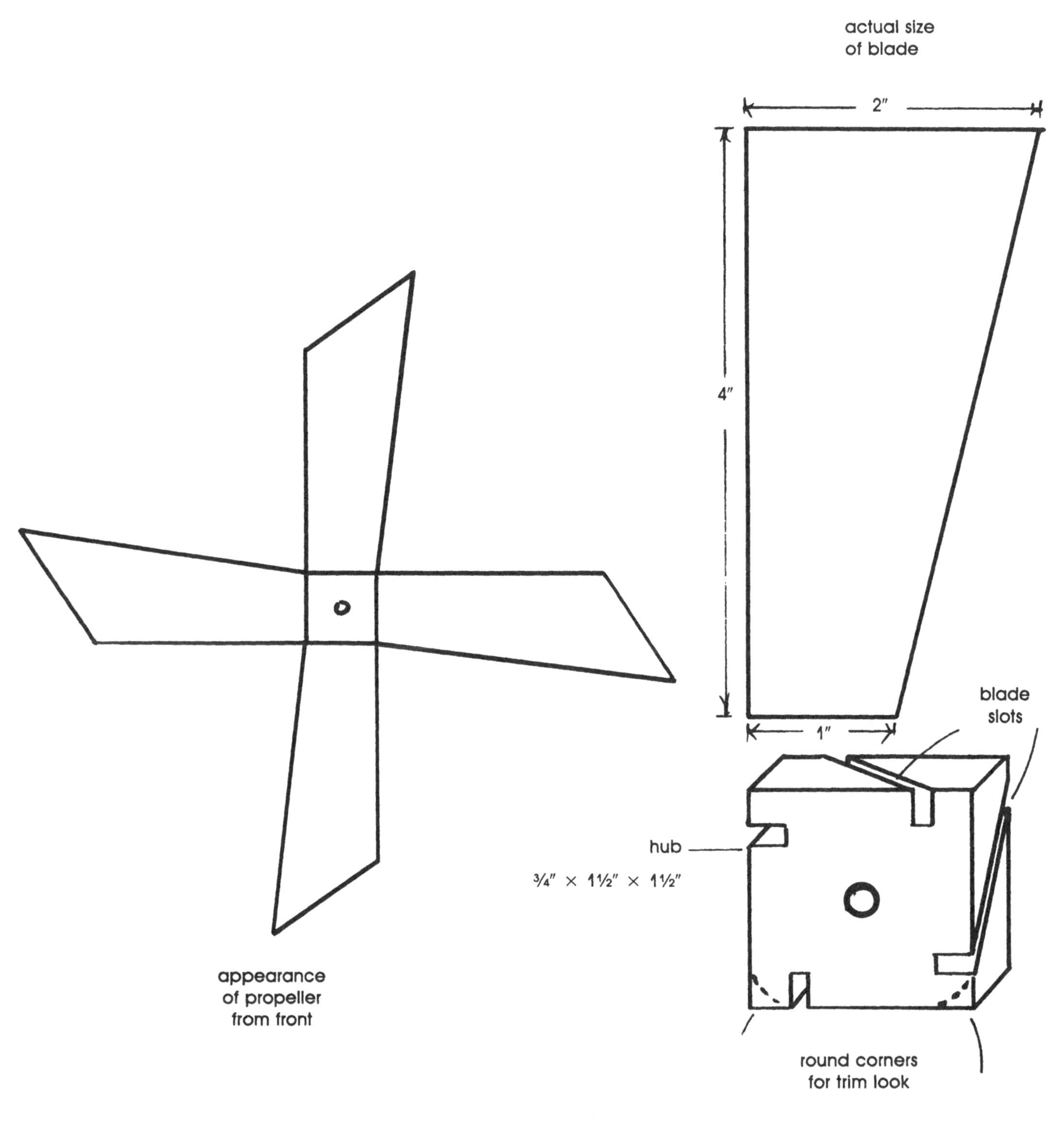

eye. (On my model the distance between the cam screw and the screw eye was $1\frac{3}{4}''$.) When you have decided the proper length, loop it permanently around the screw eye.

9. When the chopper works to your satisfaction, secure the axle with a final bend, tighten the loops in the connecting rod, check the washers at either end of the drive shaft spacer, and put the propeller in position. Remember that the cam should be located between 4″ and $4\frac{1}{2}''$ from the front of the platform, and the connecting rod should be vertical or slightly leaning toward the rear. Then glue the propeller in place, and your whirligig is finished.

Suggested Colors

Platform: white, jacket and hat: red, pants: blue, tree: green with white snow, axe: yellow handle and gray blade.

Mary in Her Garden

Mary in Her Garden is an old design. If she is not watering flowers, she is moving an old pump handle up and down pumping water into a pail. Follow the same steps as with the other whirligigs.

Materials

Body	$\frac{3}{4}'' \times 4'' \times 5''$
Legs (2)	$\frac{1}{4}'' \times 1\frac{3}{4}'' \times 3''$

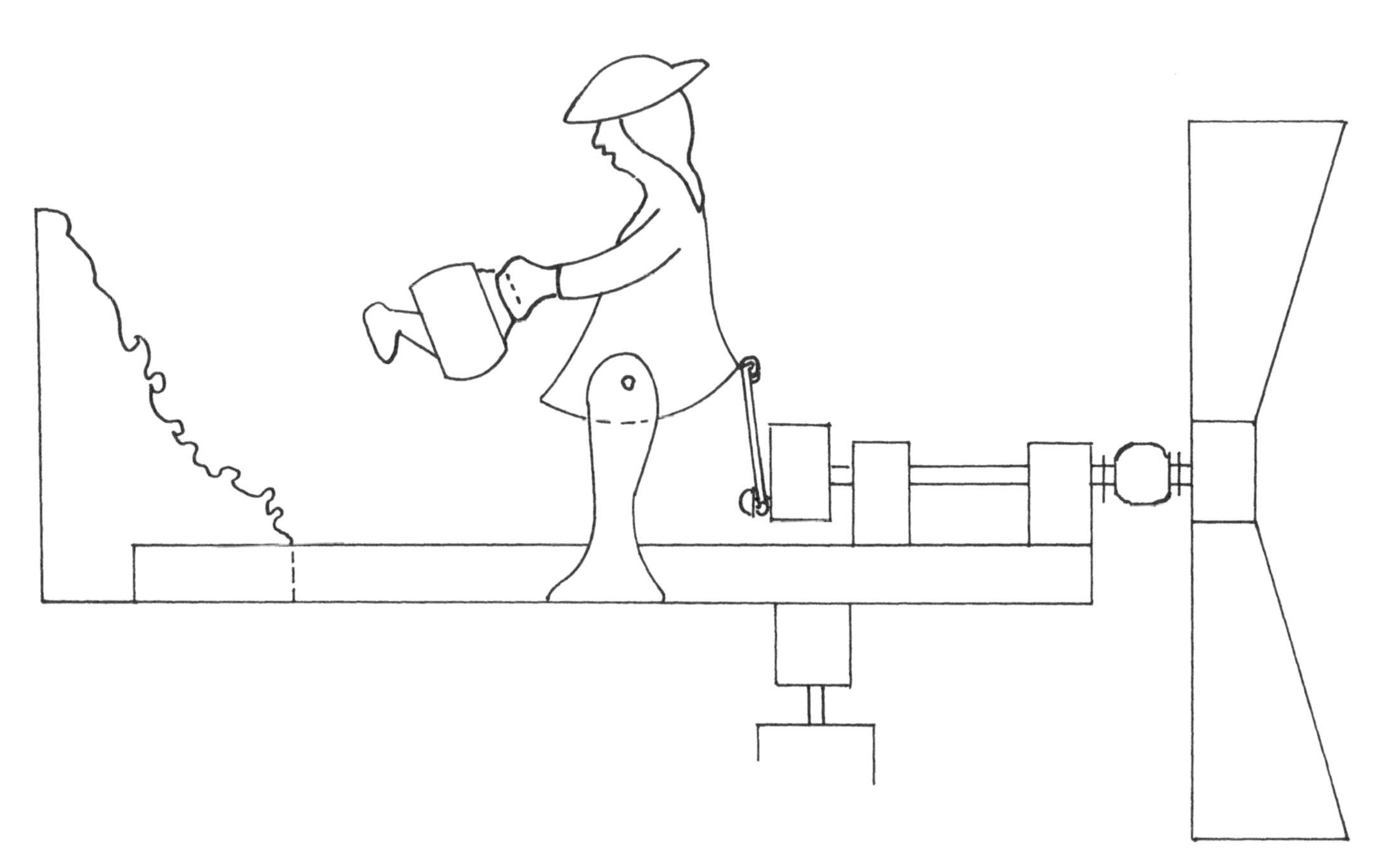

MARY IN HER GARDEN

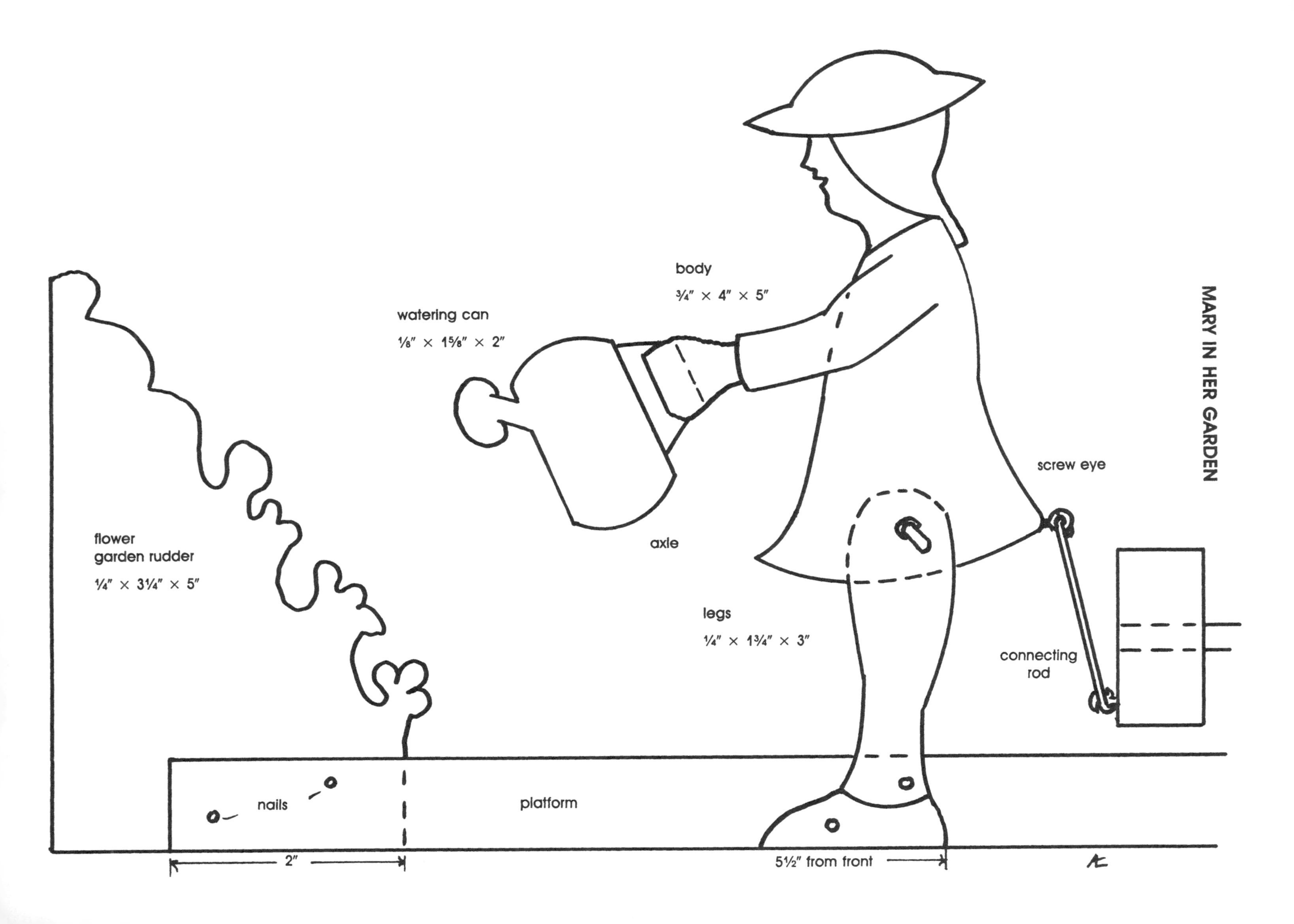

Watering can	$\frac{1}{8}$" × $1\frac{5}{8}$" × 2"
Flower garden rudder	$\frac{1}{4}$" × $3\frac{1}{4}$" × 5"
Body liner	$\frac{5}{32}$" brass tubing
Axle	$\frac{1}{16}$" brass rod, about 4" long
Connecting rod	$\frac{1}{16}$" brass rod or other stiff wire
Screw eye	About $\frac{3}{8}$"

Procedure

1. Complete the platform and mechanism as in The Mechanism for Mechanical Whirligigs and add the flower garden *rudder* shown here.
2. Make a *stand* for the whirligig.
3. Cut out the *legs* and drill a $\frac{1}{8}$" hole at H in one of them (*not* both). Glue and brad this one in place with the heel $5\frac{1}{2}$" from the front. Then nail and glue the other leg in place opposite the first. When it is in position, take your drill and put the bit through the hole. Check that it is straight across and drill a hole in the other leg. To make sure the legs will hold, use a C-clamp on them until the glue dries. Make a *spacer* just a little larger than the width of the platform and glue/brad it between the legs.
4. Cut out the *body*. Drill a $\frac{5}{32}$" hole at H and line it with tubing if you have it. Drill a pilot hole for the screw eye and attach it. Cut out the *watering can* from thin wood ($\frac{1}{8}$" or $\frac{1}{4}$" thick) and then cut a slot in the hands for it. Glue the can in place, and perhaps drill a tiny hole through the hands for a $\frac{1}{2}$" brad to hold the can firmly.
5. Put the body between the legs and put the *axle* through at H. Make sure the body moves easily.
6. Make the *connecting rod* by bending a loop around the cam screw first with a pair of pliers. See how far you want the girl to bend over. The can should go near the flowers but not hit them. (On my model the distance between the cam screw and the screw eye was $1\frac{1}{2}$" when the connecting rod was completed.)
7. When everything is complete, secure the axle with a final bend, check the loops on the connecting rod, make sure the drive shaft spacer and washers are in place, and add the propeller. The connecting rod should be vertical or lean slightly toward the rear when moving, and the end of the cam should be between 4" and $4\frac{1}{4}$" from the front. When the whole mechanism is correct, mark the location of the propeller and glue it in place.

Suggested Colors

Rudder: green and whatever other colors you wish (for flowers); watering can: gray; Mary—dress: yellow, hair: brown, hat: blue, shoes: brown, stockings: red.

Part II

Complex Whirligigs

Chapter 7

Advanced Methods in Whirligig Construction

This section is for those who have made some of the whirligigs in the previous chapters and wish to make larger or more complicated ones. It also contains further instructions on other ways of making propellers, camshafts, connecting rods, and so on, which will be useful for those designing new whirligigs.

Making Designs Larger

First, we will begin by learning to enlarge the whirligig patterns in the book. In this way we can immediately start making larger whirligigs. In some cases the model may be so simple that you can make a larger pattern by simply measuring it and drawing it freehand or with a ruler of any size. But where you wish to have an accurate reproduction of one that may be more complex, there are two ways to make patterns larger: by using a grid and by using a pantograph.

The Grid Method

This is a simple, homemade way to enlarge a drawing. Place or draw a grid (horizontal and vertical lines ½″ inch apart) over the drawing. On a larger, separate sheet of paper, draw another grid with lines 1″ apart. Then draw freehand lines corresponding to those on the ½″ grid on the 1″ grid. Sometimes it is easier to find corresponding points where the drawn line crosses a grid line by then drawing a line between the points. You will be surprised at how accurate your drawing will be, and you can eliminate errors through checking measurements. In this illustration the drawing on the 1″ grid will be twice as large as that on the ½″ grid. You can make different sizes by changing the sizes of the grids.

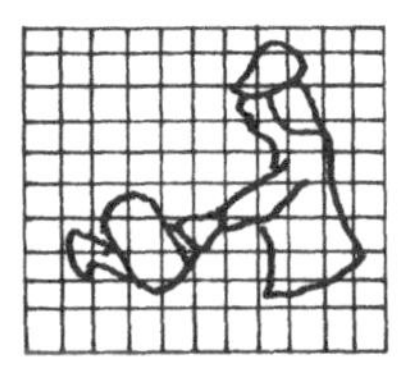

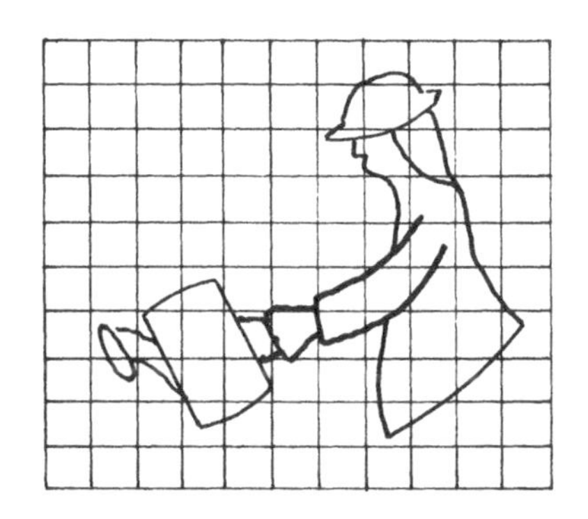

To give you an example of how enlargements are done, I have included another whirligig, the Baseball Player. Over the drawing showing his figure, which is 10″ high, I have placed a ½″ grid. If you make a ¾″ grid on a separate, large sheet of paper, you can draw a 14½″ Baseball Player whirligig. Trace this on a (at least 15″ long) piece of 2″ × 4″ (measures 1½″ × 3½″) wood. Use the same hub (H) construction, and a ⅛″ metal rod axle. Enlarge the shoulder and arms, make the baseball and glove correspondingly larger, and you will have the larger model.

The Pantograph Method

This is a marvelous instrument used by engineers and artists to copy a figure exactly and make enlargements in a number of sizes. Adjustments are made for the size of the desired enlargement, then one end of the pantograph is secured on a table. The original drawing or picture is taped down with the larger blank sheet beside it. The pantograph has two moving points. One is a pin that moves over the original drawing; the other is a pencil that moves over the blank page. As the pin traces the lines of the original picture, the pencil draws an enlargement. Inexpensive pantographs are available in art stores and hobby shops. They are fun to use for other things besides whirligigs.

Most of the nonmechanical whirligigs in this book may be made larger without any problems, except that arms (propellers) have to be made larger, and sometimes the pivot socket has to be made longer and stronger.

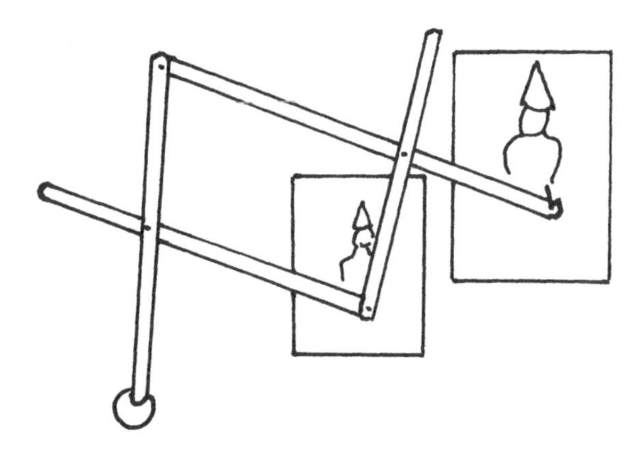

Enlargement of the mechanical whirligigs will probably necessitate changes in the design. The first thing to decide is how large you want the whirligig to be and draw the whole pattern on a large sheet of paper, measuring every line with a ruler. While the platform will be longer and the tail larger and higher, the camshaft itself will not have to be changed except in terms of length. The connecting rod will be longer. A larger propeller may be necessary. Danny the Dinosaur, David the Wood Chopper, and Mary in Her Garden can easily be enlarged with the use of a grid or the pantograph.

Remember that you can enlarge any picture, photograph, or drawing by these two methods. It will help you to make accurate enlargements when you wish your models to be representative or natural. But remember, too, that whirligig makers never thought of themselves as great artists, and did the best they could. It really makes no difference if your whirligig figure doesn't look perfect. It's the idea that counts!

Other Axles for Winged and Arm-Waving Whirligigs

The axles for the arms and hubs of whirligigs from the Toy Soldier to the Football Player were made of wood ($\frac{3}{16}$″ and $\frac{1}{4}$″ hardwood dowels). The same axles may be made of steel or brass rods, obtainable in a hardware store or hobby shop.

Simple Metal Rod Axles

A number of early whirligig models used thin metal axles. A small hole was drilled through the body for the axle and a hole smaller than the axle hole was drilled in the arm or hub. The rod was then pressed into the arm with some adhesive. You also can use this method. The only problem is that in time the axle will work loose and you will have to reglue the piece or otherwise wedge it firm. The metal rod should be stiff and ordinarily will not exceed $\frac{1}{8}$″ in diameter for the small whirligigs in this book.

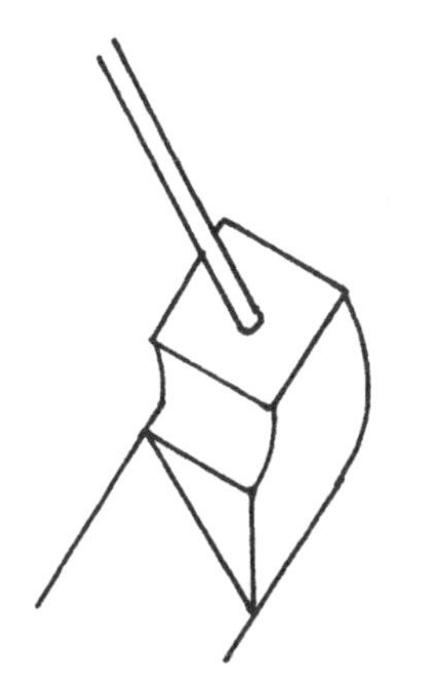

The Threaded Axle

A much better axle can be made from $\frac{1}{8}$″ brass rod threaded $\frac{3}{4}$″ on both ends. This makes it possible for the arms or wings to be turned on the axle; with a little glue they will hold firm. To make such an axle you will need a vise, $\frac{6}{32}$ die, hacksaw, die holder, and a file.

4″ long, threaded ¾″ at each end

The *die,* which cuts threads, and the *die holder* will be new to you; they can be purchased in any hardware store. The "6" refers to the wire or metal thickness, and the "32" means that thirty-two turns of the die will produce 1″ of thread.

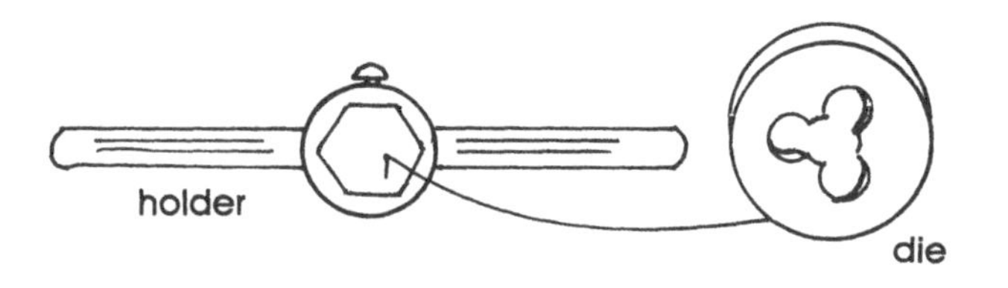

To make the axle, cut the rod to the correct size (the length through the body, into the arms or hubs, leaving enough room for the washers and movement).

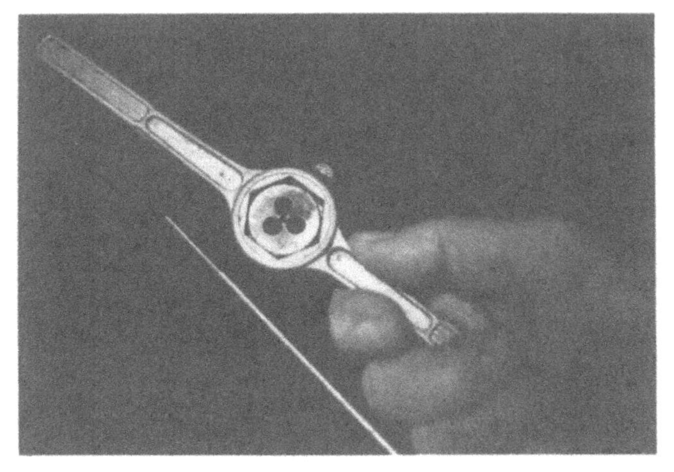

A $\frac{6}{32}$ die in a die holder and threaded rod.

The thread-cutting process.

File down any rough edges. Then place the rod in a vise and place the marked open end of the die against it. Turn it clockwise (to the right). When the die begins to cut, turn the die holder twenty full turns. This should cut a thread $\frac{3}{4}$" long, enough to go into the arms or hubs. As regards the hub hole through the body, a $\frac{3}{16}$" hole will do. This can be lined with $\frac{3}{16}$" brass tubing, but a lining is not absolutely necessary. To illustrate the use of this axle, I have included instructions for a winged whirligig, the Carolina Wren, and two arm-wavers, the Cheerleader and the Signaling Scout.

For larger whirligigs with heavy arms or wings, it may be necessary to use stronger metal axles. For example, the axle for the 16" baseball player, instead of being a $\frac{1}{4}$" wood dowel, could be a $\frac{3}{16}$" rod. Most large rods are only available in iron or steel and not in brass. Do not use stainless steel; it is too difficult to cut with small dies. A $\frac{16}{32}$ die in the same die handle will easily cut threads in a $\frac{3}{16}$" rod. Drill a $\frac{5}{32}$" hole in an arm or wing hub and these easily can be turned onto the rod and held securely.

Other Camshafts for Mechanical Whirligigs

The drive shafts or camshafts of the mechanical whirligigs in Part II of this book are made of $\frac{1}{4}$" hardwood dowels. Most old whirligigs were made completely of wood, but camshafts also may be made of metal. Two examples follow.

The Carriage Bolt Camshaft

This method uses a $\frac{1}{4}$" carriage bolt 6" long. Make a cam piece of $\frac{3}{4}$" thick wood about $1\frac{1}{2}$" square or round by drilling a $\frac{1}{4}$" hole through the center. Trim the wood to hold the head firm so it doesn't slip around. At the hub of the propeller, drill a $\frac{1}{4}$" hole and secure the propeller with $\frac{1}{4}$" nuts. The connecting rod can be attached to a $\frac{1}{2}$" or $\frac{5}{8}$" screw placed near the edge of the cam. The support pieces of the bolt will usually be $1\frac{1}{2}$" corner irons, as shown in the illustration.

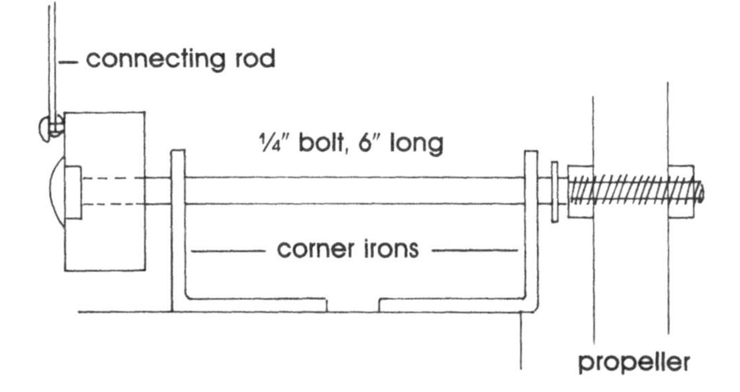

Metal Rod Shaft

A preferred method is the use of a $\frac{1}{8}$" rod with threaded ends and a bent cam secured with machine nuts. Cut a $\frac{1}{8}$" steel or brass rod to the required length, in this case $7\frac{1}{2}$". Thread one end 1" (about thirty complete turns of the die holder), and thread the other end $\frac{3}{4}$". The 1" end is for the propeller, and the other is for the cam end. Using the vise, a pair of pliers, and a hammer, put a bend in the cam end at $1\frac{3}{4}$". Then make a second bend to make a cam $\frac{1}{2}$" or $\frac{3}{4}$" deep, depending on the length of the motion required for your whirligig.

The connecting rod is attached between two $\frac{6}{32}$ machine nuts on the threaded end. On the other end, the propeller (with a $\frac{7}{32}$" hole through a $\frac{3}{4}$" hub) can be

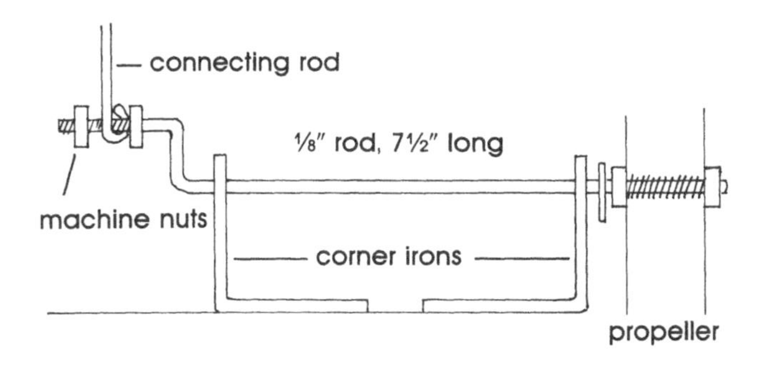

turned on the rod and secured between two $\frac{6}{32}$ machine screws. The shaft may be supported between two 1½" angle irons or a more solid support. This camshaft is used in the Fisher in the Boat whirligig. Note that the construction is simple enough so that you could use a ¼" wooden camshaft to make this model if you wish to do so.

Other Cams

We already have discussed the use of the wooden cam with a screw in it for the connecting rod as well as the metal rod cam with machine screws. There are other commonly used cam connections. The first is the cam with a collar, and the other is the double cam.

The Cam with a Collar

This is used when a connecting rod might slip off a shaft while it is turning. It is used most often when a cam is made along a shaft and not at the ends. If the drive shaft is ⅛" in diameter and the length of the space is 1", cut out a piece of wood about ½" × ½" × ¾" or somewhat thicker. Drill a $\frac{5}{32}$" hole through it. Then cut the piece in half lengthwise. Glue the wood over the shaft and hold it with a clamp. When dry, cut a notch in the middle for the connecting rod. The collar will turn easily around the shaft, and the connecting rod will not slip to one side. This is illustrated in the Clashing Knights whirligig.

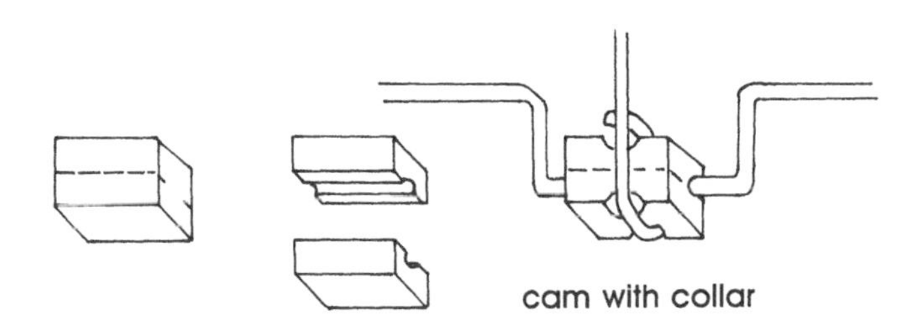
cam with collar

Note that the square cam does not always need a collar. In whirligigs where arms are connected with the cam, for example, they usually will hold their position without moving sideways, as in the first example that follows.

The Double Cam

This has two forms. In the first, the two interlinked cams are square. They are used when, as in the case just mentioned, two sets of arms are positioned in the cam (usually from figures stationed opposite each other). This is illustrated in the instructions for the Machine Lab whirligig.

square double cam

In the second, the camshaft is bent at an angle and notches are filed in the shaft itself to hold a connecting rod (usually of a thin diameter). This type of cam is used in whirligigs that require rhythmical up and down movements, such as in the Farmer Milking the Cow whirligig (which is not shown in this book). At the end of Chapter 8, two different uses are made of this type of camshaft in the Patriotic Drummer and the Daniel Boone and the Bear.

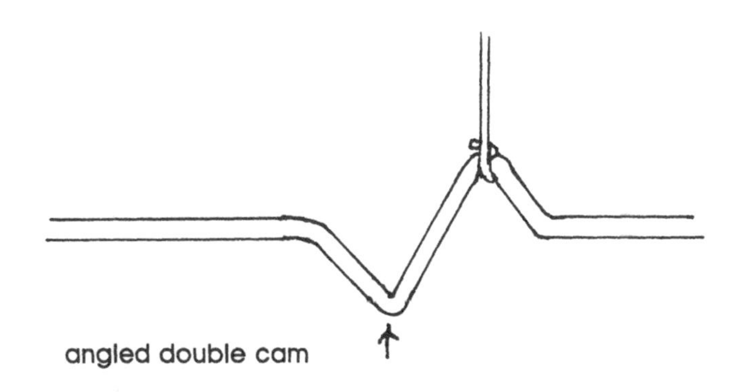
angled double cam

Use of Propellers

In making propellers for a particular whirligig, one of the first requirements is to know the typical wind conditions in the area in which the whirligig will operate. A consistently high wind will require a smaller propeller or one designed to limit its power. An area where only a light breeze predominates requires a larger propeller or one that moves more efficiently. This has to be balanced against the size of the whirligig and the force required to move its parts. Larger whirligigs generally require larger propellers for force and power. A basic rule, however, is not to provide more power than is necessary to operate the whirligig. The reason is that a powerful propeller spinning in a high wind can wreck the mechanism and tear apart the whirligig. That is why many people take their whirligigs indoors when a storm is on the horizon.

Where does all this leave us? High winds, small propeller, light breezes, large propeller? At this stage of whirligig making, do not worry. The solution is to make an average-size propeller, similar to those shown in this book, for most whirligigs. If the conditions require a different propeller, then make one later. You will learn some basic principles as you go along. A small propeller will spin faster than a large one and will go faster with more blades (like a turbine). However, it may not have as much power as a larger propeller. A large propeller will provide more power *only* if it has large blades and more blades. On the other hand, it will move more slowly—and there are whirligigs where more power is needed but fast spinning is unnecessary.

The tradition of trial and error in whirligig making still lives on in propeller design. There are literally thousands of types and sizes of propellers. All you need are the basic parts and principles: a center hub and balanced blades with freedom to move into or away from the wind. Any number of blades may be fitted around the hub. Blades add power and speed. But one can never be sure that he or she has the correct propeller for the whirligig until it is tested in the wind. I keep propellers of several types and sizes on hand to use as test propellers for my whirligigs. Even if I think I have the right one I warn my customers that they should consider using another propeller if the wind conditions are different from those in my area.

The Basic Propeller

This is the two-blade version made from a single piece of wood and shaped by hand. It is most readily made with a sharp knife, so it should not be attempted by anyone who cannot handle a knife. At the same time, making a simple propeller can be a good knife-training project under proper supervision.

The knife may be a good, solid pocketknife or a knife with a built-in handle. It should fit comfortably in your fist and should have a firm blade that cannot double back on your fingers. The blade should be sharp; dull knives are sometimes more dangerous than sharp knives. Woodcarvers always keep their knives clean and sharp. Part of any knife-training project should involve learning how to sharpen knives.

A good propeller for various uses can be made from a piece of wood with dimensions of $\frac{3}{4}'' \times \frac{3}{4}'' \times 8''$. With a pencil mark the center of the wood, mark the ends with opposite diagonals, and mark a $\frac{1}{2}''$ area on each side of the center. This will determine the center hub and the limit of the blade cuts.

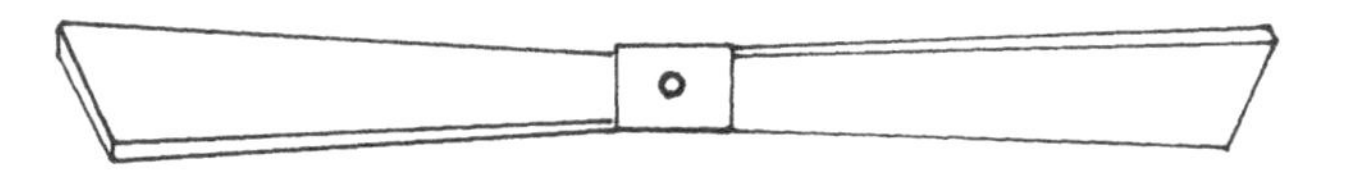

Holding one end firmly in the hand, shave off pieces of the other end of the wood down toward the diagonal mark. Then turn the piece over and cut down on the other side. Think of making a $\frac{1}{8}''$ thick blade so you don't cut too close to the diagonal line. Always cut away from yourself. Then turn the wood around and cut off the edges of the opposite side while holding the cut end.

When you have the blades cut down, put the propeller on a table or workbench, hold it steady, and cut notches by the penciled hub marks. Then cut the propeller blade back by the notches. This is difficult; watch out for your hands. When you have finished all you can do with the knife, file the blades smooth. Balance the propeller with a nail in the hub. If one end is too heavy, file it down until it balances. You then will have a square-ended working propeller, and it should spin easily in any breeze.

To make the propeller look more interesting—like a bird's wing or anything else—shape it accordingly. Curve the wing tips and trim down toward the hub. You can make larger or smaller propellers with this method. Very large propellers may require other tools,

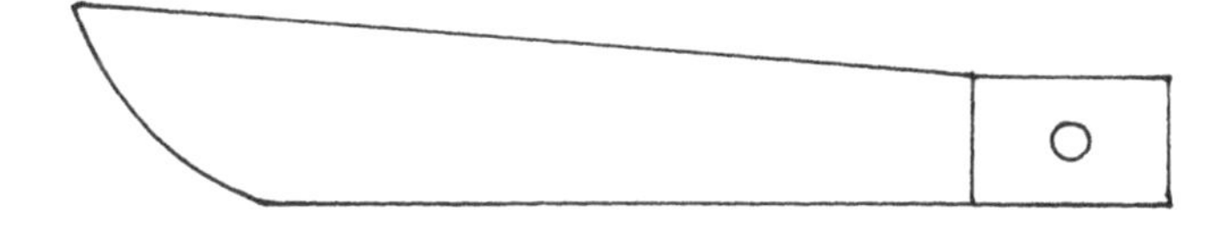

like a spokeshave or a chisel. But all two-bladed propellers are made according to the same principles: two balanced blades and a central hub.

Propellers with Separate Hubs and Blades

Propellers for other purposes require a separate hub and blades.

Hubs

One usually begins with the hub. The following illustration shows a square-cut hub for multibladed propellers. When making such a hub, mark off the center first. Mark off opposite sides for a two-bladed propeller or a four-bladed propeller. Edges can be rounded for effect. Such hubs are illustrated for the Vane, the Guardian Angel, and mechanical whirligigs such as Danny the Dinosaur, David the Wood Chopper, and Mary in Her Garden.

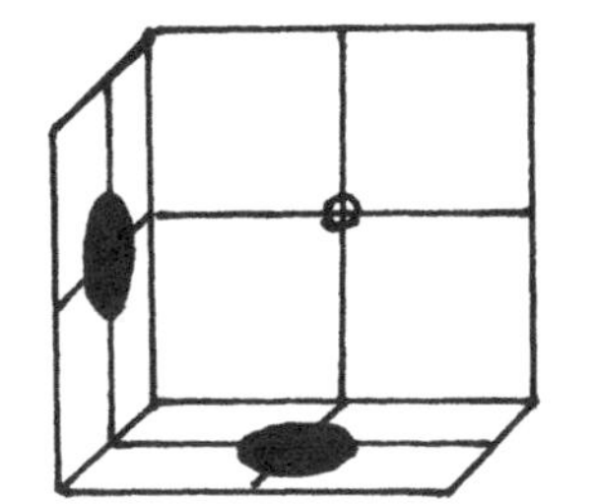

A circular hub, made with a compass, makes it possible to locate any number of blades. A circle has 360 degrees, so if you wish to have a three-bladed propeller, measure off three points 120 degrees apart. Four blades are 90 degrees apart, five blades are 72 degrees apart, six blades are 60 degrees apart, and eight blades are 45 degrees apart.

Working with a small compass can lead to errors, and drilling holes in a circle hub does not always make for a balanced propeller. There are faster ways to make multibladed propeller hubs. For a five-bladed propeller, draw a circle the size of the hub and draw a line for the radius. Mark off a 72-degree angle; you can check this because it should make five equidistant points around the circumference of the circle. By joining these points you will form a pentagon. Find the middle of these points and draw a line from the center of the circle through them. Then cut out the pentagon. Extend the lines over the edge to the center and you will have a good point from which to make the blade slot or the armhole. A pentagon hub is suggested for the propeller of the Clashing Knights.

For a six-bladed propeller, draw a circle the size of the hub. Using the radius of the compass, mark off six points on the circumference. Join those points, find the middle, and draw a line from the center of the circle through these points. Cut out the hexagon and continue the line over the edge to the center of the side. You will find it easier to work with a square edge than a round one. A hexagon hub is recommended for the propeller of Johnny Appleseed.

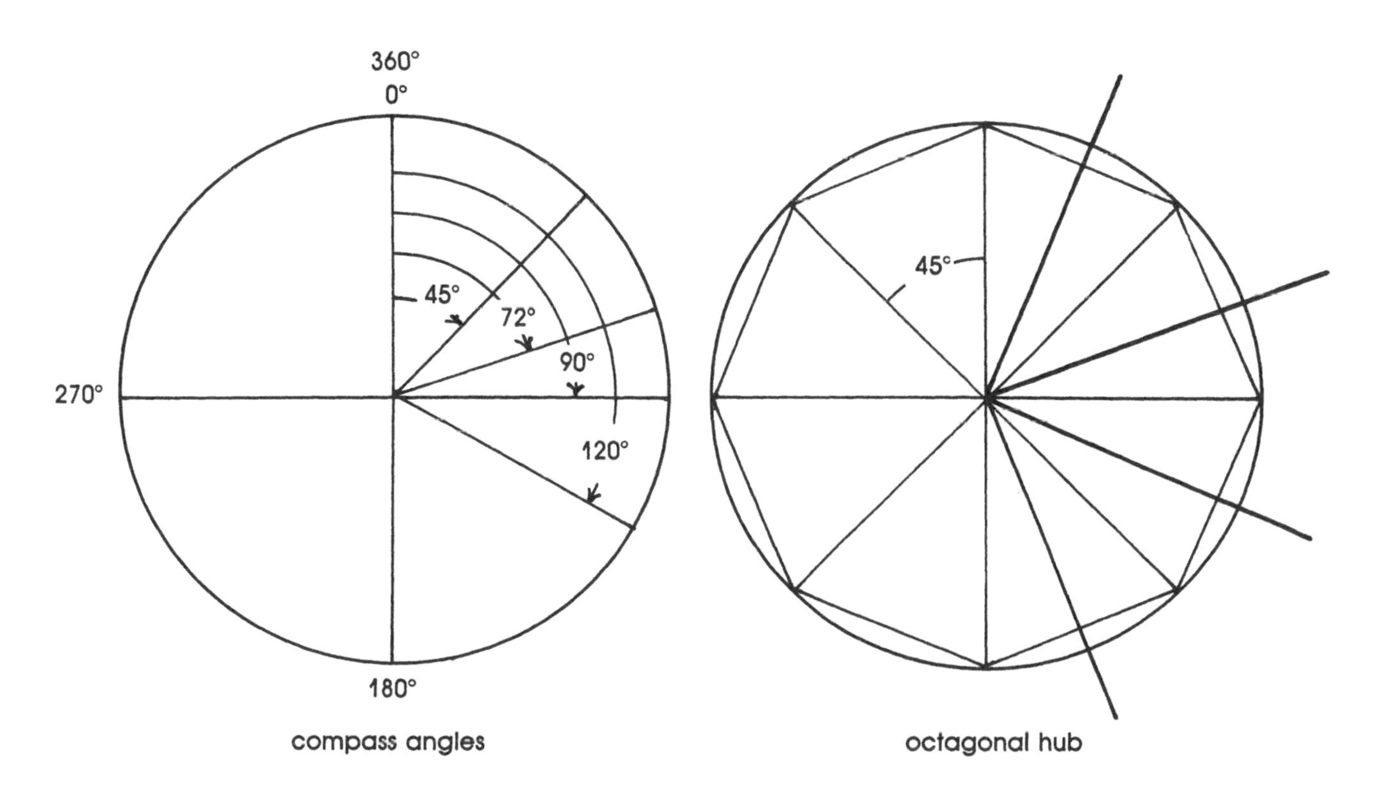

compass angles

octagonal hub

For an eight-bladed propeller, divide the circle into four parts (90 degrees) and then eight (45 degrees). Join the points where the lines (radii) meet at the circle. Find their middle point and draw a line from the center of the circle to those midpoints. Cut out the octagon and carry the lines over the edge to make the center of the slot or the arm blade hole. You can go on from there to make hubs for any multibladed propeller.

Blades

The blades may be attached directly to the hub or may be extended on arms.

Blades attached directly. There are two ways of attaching blades to hubs. One way is to cut slots in the hubs and glue the blades in the hub slots. (See the propellers for David the Wood Chopper and Mary in Her Garden.) The other method is to drill holes in the sides of the hubs and shape the ends of the blades to fit in the holes. (See the propellers for the Dancing Sailor.)

Blades attached on extended arms. This method also involves drilling holes in hubs. The propellers for the Fisher in the Boat and other mechanical whirligigs in Chapter 8 are made this way. The points for the hub holes are located at the sides of the hubs (four-sided, five-sided, and so forth, or circular), as shown in the previous section on hubs. Then they are drilled with the bit (corresponding to the size of the dowel or arm) as deep as required. In most of our propellers that depth is $\frac{1}{2}''$. For example, if a $\frac{3}{8}''$ diameter dowel is used, a decision is made regarding the *length* of dowel to use. A short length is required if a fast rotating propeller is desired and long arms are needed if a more stately, slow revolution is wanted. The end of the arm is usually cut out for wooden blades or slit for thin metal blades 2″ or more in length, depending on the size of the blades. The blades are attached to the arms before being glued into the hub holes at as close to a 45-degree angle as possible. It is said that a 50-degree angle will provide more power, but few whirligig makers would worry about that; no two arms are ever inserted at precisely the same angle anyway!

The construction of propellers for the advanced whirligigs is shown on pages 86 and 91.

Using More Advanced Tools

This section is near the end of the book because I started out, like an old whirligig maker, to show you how to make whirligigs using only or almost only wood. I was not interested in having very young persons use sharp knives or power tools. But as you progress in whirligig making, you will learn about electric power tools used in woodworking. As you grow older, you may be taught to use them in manual training classes in school. Or, some or all of them may be in your home or a friend's home, and may be used by a parent or other relative or friend. These tools save time and energy and increase productivity. They should never be used by anyone without instruction. They can be very dangerous. When you use them you have to concentrate on what you are doing. Even experienced people get injured. A power saw can take off a finger in the wink of an eye; it can happen so fast you won't even feel it until you notice that it is not there! Be extremely careful around power tools.

Cutting out complex shapes, such as the contours of the gondola, is made easier with a scroll saw. Always wear goggles when working with power tools.

The power tools most commonly used by hobbyists and craftspersons include the following.

Bench or table saw. This saw is used to cut large boards into useable sizes. It makes straight (rip) cuts and square crosscuts (across the grain). It takes only a minute, for example, to cut out a whirligig base or platform measuring $\frac{3}{4}'' \times 2\frac{1}{4}'' \times 24''$ from a board $\frac{3}{4}'' \times 8'' \times 72''$.

Band saw. This saw has a long, "endless" blade about $\frac{1}{2}''$ deep that turns on wheels and makes curved cuts in thick wood. There are small band saws on the market designed for hobbyists that do not take up much room. While the band saw cuts fast, cuts out curves that dress up whirligig platforms, and makes circular hubs, it cannot make tight curve cuts. These are made by a scroll saw.

Scroll saw. This has a thin blade that goes up and down like a coping saw and is used to cut curves in wood. It can cut out a figure like Danny the Dinosaur in just a few minutes. It does not cut as quickly as a band saw, but it makes sharp turns. A smaller version, made for young hobbyists, is available; this has a vibrating blade and is safer to use. It is slow and does not cut thick wood, but it is excellent for whirligig work.

Electric drill. The electric hand drill makes holes in wood very quickly, but young people may find it heavy to handle. This drill operates best for our purposes when it is used in a holder, making a *drill press*. Drill presses as such are one-piece machines.

Electric sander. This machine usually is equipped with a 5″ disc sander and an endless belt sander. With the coarse grit disc, it can do some fast shaping, as in finishing bird's wings. The medium or fine sanding belt is excellent for finishing work.

Use protective gear, like goggles for the eyes and dust filters for your nose, with all of these power tools. And watch those fingers!

Chapter 8
More Intricate Whirligigs

As it is said that the proof of the pudding is in the eating, the proof of the whirligig is in its operation. A number of whirligig construction ideas have been introduced in this book, and you may have tried some of the models. At this point it is time to consider a few whirligigs that are more complicated to make although not beyond the capacity of persons who have patience and persistence. There is nothing new about them; the essentials of their construction already have been discussed in this book. If you follow the instructions you should have no unusual problems. Let's see if you can make them and then make them work. That will be proof enough of your ability as a whirligig maker.

The Baseball Player demonstrates one way of enlarging the smaller models from the first part of the book. The Carolina Wren shows how the metal axle works in a split-wing model. The Cheerleader and the Signaling Scout do the same for arm-wavers; the Cheerleader has an extended tail, and the Signaling Scout has two pivot sockets to show how the position of each makes a difference in activity. The Kayak shows how to make a fascinating boat model in which the position of the hub and pivot point are different from those of the Gondola. The Fisher in the Boat has related action parts. The Clashing Knights shows how the double-arm mechanism works, and the Machine Lab demonstrates square double cams; both have long camshafts. The Patriotic Drummer shows how double-angled cams operate. The Winning Race Car and Daniel Boone and the Bear combine several of the advanced techniques and were designed just for fun of young and old.

It is hoped that, as you become more acquainted with whirligig making, you will think about creating your own designs and whirligigs!

Baseball Player

Baseball is the old American sport and was, according to tradition, invented by Abner Doubleday at Cooperstown, New York, in 1839. It is said to be derived from the old English game of Rounders and an American childrens' game called Old Cat. The Baseball Hall of Fame is in Cooperstown, New York, which is also famous as the home of James Fenimore Cooper, who wrote *The Last of the Mohicans* and other books of adventure.

Our baseball player has a ball in one hand and a glove in the other. Like the clowns, he has an offset pivot point so he should be tossing the ball whenever there's a breeze. He also can be made with a rudder (see the Smiling Lady) to insure he works correctly. He also can be enlarged if you want him bigger.

Materials

Figure	$\frac{3}{4}$" × 2" × 10"
Shoulders (2)	$\frac{3}{4}$" × 1" × $1\frac{1}{2}$"
Blades (2)	$\frac{1}{8}$" × 1" × $3\frac{1}{2}$"
Ball	$\frac{1}{8}$" × $1\frac{1}{4}$" diameter
Glove	$\frac{1}{8}$" × $1\frac{1}{4}$" diameter
Axle	$\frac{3}{16}$" dowel, $4\frac{1}{2}$" long
Metal	
pivot socket	$\frac{7}{32}$" brass tubing, 2" long
socket cap	End of 16d nail or small screw
hub liner	$\frac{1}{4}$" brass tubing, 2" long
washers	$\frac{1}{4}$" brass

Procedure

1. Trace the pattern of the *figure* on the wood. With a pencil mark the positions of the hub points (H), making sure that when you drill the hub hole it will be straight across the body. Drill a $\frac{1}{4}$" hole through the body, going in halfway from both sides. Find the pivot point (P) and then drill the $\frac{7}{32}$" pivot socket hole $1\frac{1}{2}$" to 2" deep. Cut out the figure. File or sand it

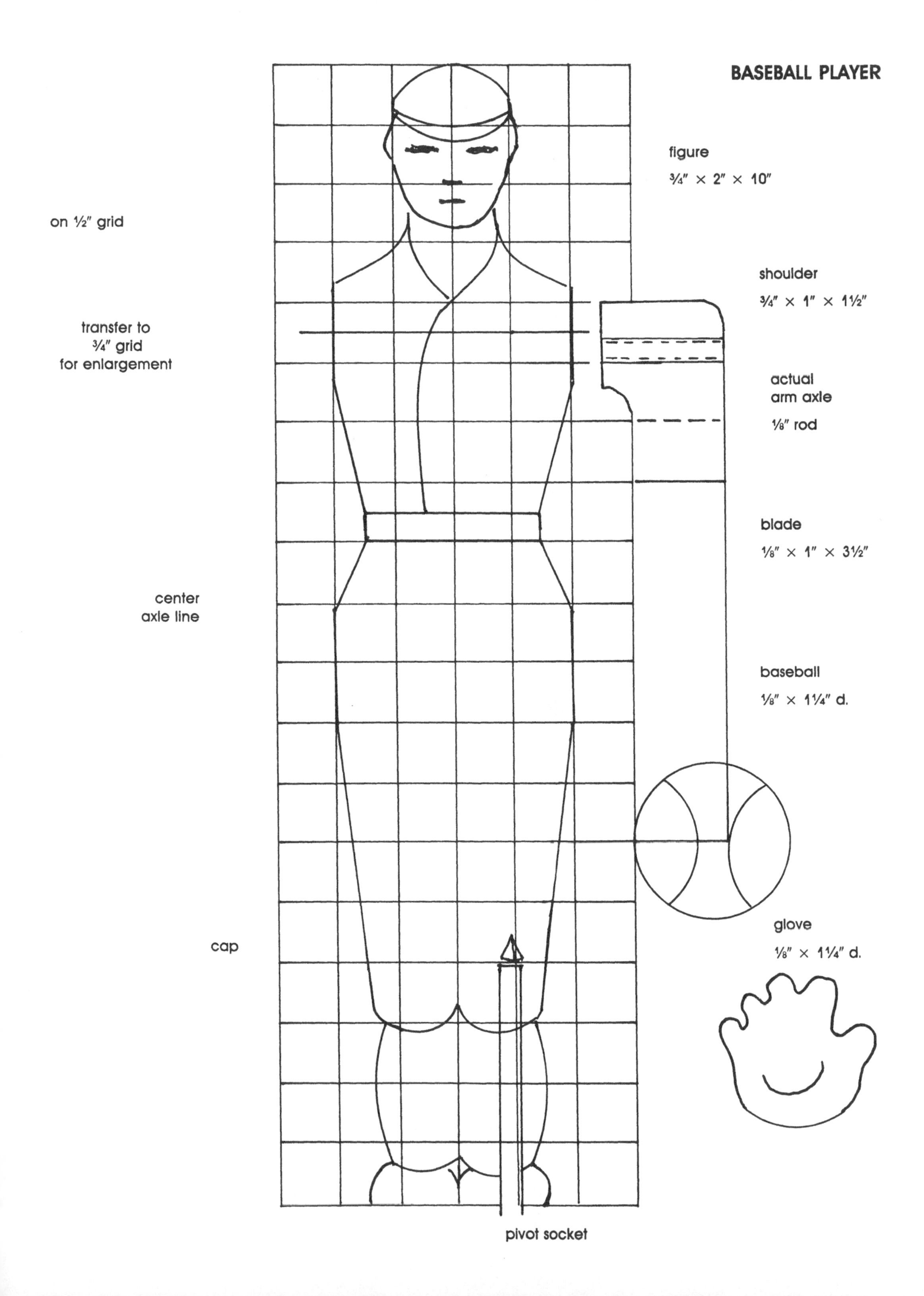
BASEBALL PLAYER
figure
¾″ × 2″ × 10″
on ½″ grid
shoulder
¾″ × 1″ × 1½″
transfer to
¾″ grid
for enlargement
actual
arm axle
⅛″ rod
blade
⅛″ × 1″ × 3½″
center
axle line
baseball
⅛″ × 1¼″ d.
glove
⅛″ × 1¼″ d.
cap
pivot socket

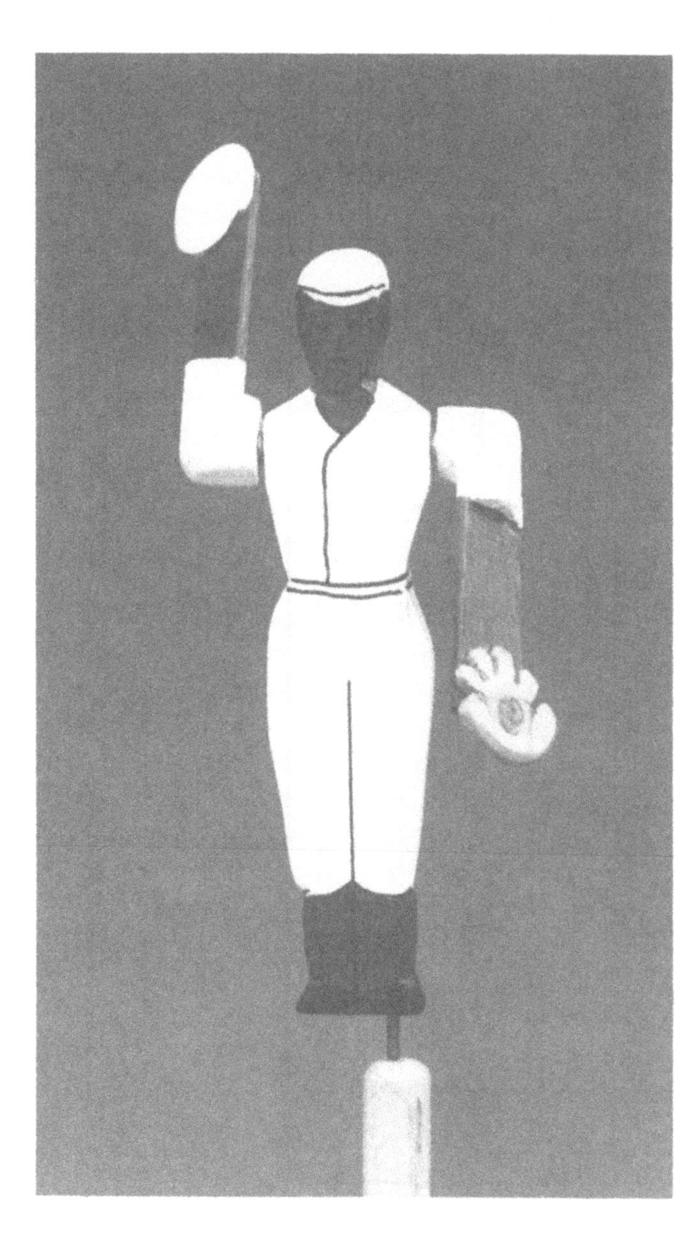

smooth. Line the hub hole with $\frac{1}{4}''$ brass tubing and the pivot socket with $\frac{7}{32}''$ brass tubing. Put a metal cap in the socket.

2. Follow the directions on page 15 for making whirligig *arms.* Cut out the *shoulder pieces* and shape them. Drill $\frac{3}{16}''$ holes in the upper part. On the bottom mark the angles for the blade slots. Remember that they must slant in different directions when on the body.

3. Cut out the *blades.* Then cut out the slots in the shoulder pieces $\frac{1}{2}''$ deep to fit the blade ends. Glue the blades in the slots. After the glue dries, shape the shoulders with a file. Put a temporary axle in the hub and test the balance of the arms. If they are out of balance, file down the heavier side until they balance.

4. Cut out the *ball* and the *glove;* they should be cut from similar pieces of wood so they weigh about the same. Glue them to the ends of the arms. Put them in a temporary axle and test the balance once more.

5. Glue the *axle* into one arm first, then insert the axle into the hub with a washer in place. Glue the other arm (with a washer in place) into the axle on the other side of the figure. The glue will hold fast, so make sure that the arms are directly opposite each other.

Suggested Colors:

Uniform, including arm sleeves and cap: white or blue-gray; socks: red or blue; shoes: black; skin color: your choice. You can put the logo or name of your team on the shirt and the name of your favorite player on the back.

For those interested in an enlarged version of the ballplayer, the following are materials used in a $1\frac{1}{2}''$ enlargement (from a $\frac{1}{2}''$ grid to a $\frac{3}{4}''$ grid).

Materials

Body	$1\frac{1}{4}'' \times 3'' \times 14\frac{1}{2}''$
Shoulders (2)	$1\frac{1}{4}'' \times 1\frac{1}{2}'' \times 2\frac{1}{4}''$
Arms (2)	$\frac{1}{8}'' \times 1\frac{1}{4}'' \times 5\frac{1}{2}''$
Glove and ball	$\frac{1}{8}'' \times 2''$ diameter
Pivot socket	$\frac{1}{4}''$, lined with tubing
Hub hole	
(A)	$\frac{3}{16}''$, lined with tubing for $\frac{1}{8}''$ metal axle
(B)	$\frac{5}{16}''$, lined with tubing for $\frac{1}{4}''$ dowel axle
Spindle	20d nail with the head cut off

Approximately the same materials can be used in enlarging the other arm-wavers shown in the book.

Carolina Wren

The Carolina Wren, *Thyrothorus ludivicianus,* is our largest wren and is only 6″ long. You can tell it by the white stripe over its eyes. It does not migrate, but it is a great singer; its beautiful songs are heard all year long. This model is 6″ long, too, or 7″ with its tail down, and has a split-wing propeller. Unfortunately, it does not sing.

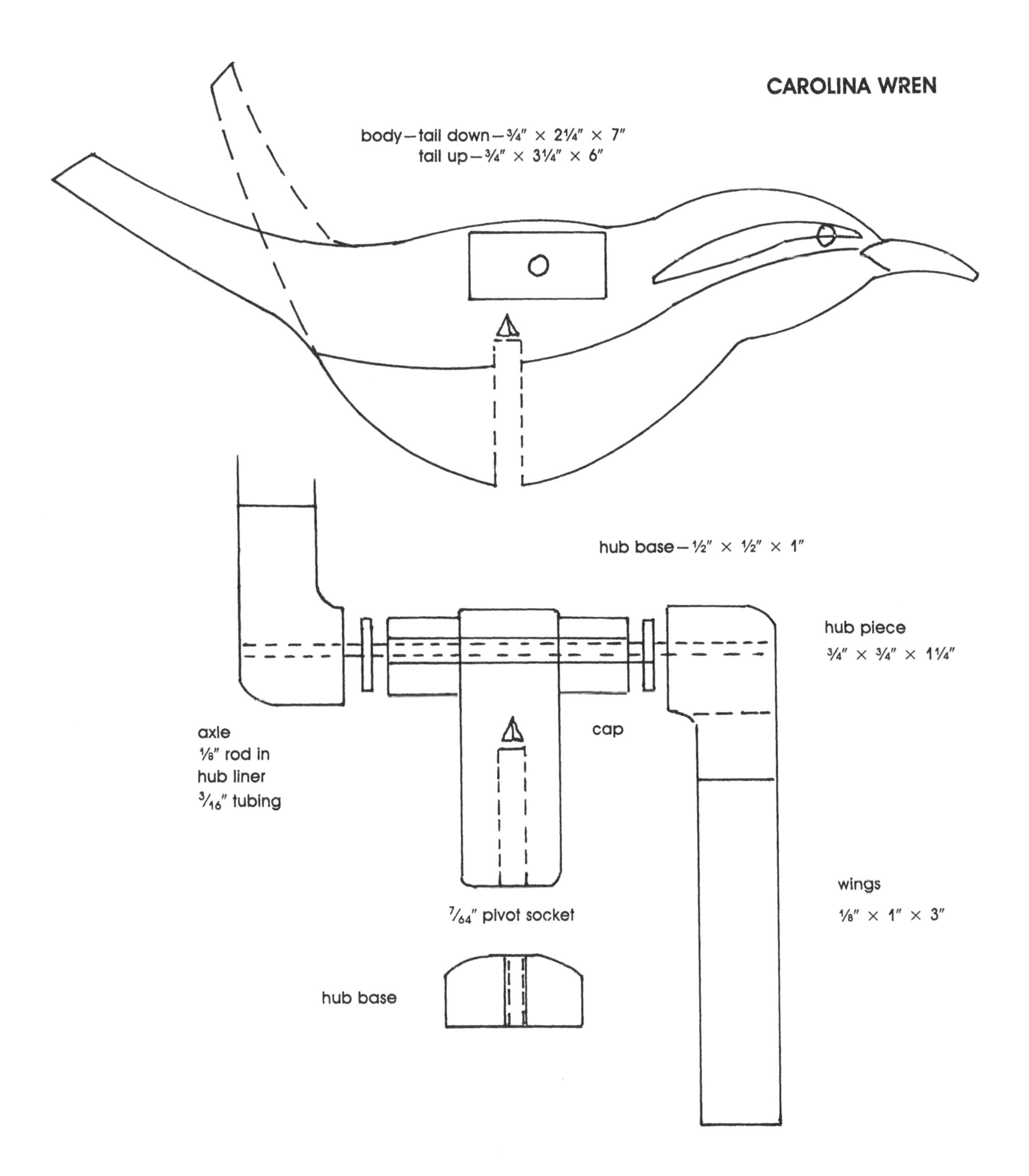
CAROLINA WREN
body—tail down—¾″ × 2¼″ × 7″
tail up—¾″ × 3¼″ × 6″
hub base—½″ × ½″ × 1″
hub piece
¾″ × ¾″ × 1¼″
axle
⅛″ rod in
hub liner
3/16″ tubing
cap
wings
⅛″ × 1″ × 3″
7/64″ pivot socket
hub base

Materials

Body	
tail down	$\frac{3}{4}'' \times 2\frac{1}{4}'' \times 7''$
tail up	$\frac{3}{4}'' \times 3\frac{1}{4}'' \times 6''$
Hub bases (2)	$\frac{1}{2}'' \times \frac{1}{2}'' \times 1''$
Wings	
hubs (2)	$\frac{3}{4}'' \times \frac{3}{4}'' \times 1\frac{1}{2}''$
blades (2)	$\frac{1}{8}'' \times 1'' \times 3''$
Metal	
axle	$\frac{1}{8}''$ rod, threaded both ends, $4\frac{1}{4}''$ long
socket liner	$\frac{7}{32}''$ brass tubing, 1″ long
hub liner	$\frac{3}{16}''$ brass tubing, 2″ long
washers (2)	No. 6 or No. 8 brass washers

Procedure

1. Trace the *body* on the wood, marking the pivot point (P) and the hub (H). Drill the $\frac{7}{32}''$ pivot socket hole 1″ deep and line it with brass tubing if you have it. Put a metal cap in the base of the socket; this can be the point of a 16d nail or a small screw or BB. Drill a $\frac{3}{16}''$ hole through the body at H.

2. Cut out the two *hub bases*. Drill a $\frac{3}{16}''$ hole through the centers. Round them off and glue them on the body at the hub with a 2″ piece of $\frac{3}{16}''$ brass tubing for a liner. A C-clamp will hold the pieces until the glue dries.

3. Make the *wing* parts. Cut out the *hub pieces* and shape them. At the upper end drill a $\frac{7}{64}''$ hole for the axle. Mark the ends with angles for the wing blade slots. Remember that the wings must turn in opposite directions, like a propeller, when they are on the body.

4. Cut out the *blades* and, using them as reference, cut out the blade slots $\frac{1}{2}''$ deep. Glue the blades in the slots. When dry, shape them so they look like wings.

5. Prepare the *axle*. Each end is threaded $\frac{3}{4}''$ with a $\frac{6}{32}$ die. Turn one wing onto the axle and insert it into the hub hole in the body with a washer in place. Then secure the other wing with a washer. The wings should balance. Trim the heavier wing until balance is achieved. Then attach the wings permanently with a drop of glue on the thread to hold the piece firmly.

Suggested Colors

Back: reddish brown; breast and belly: buff or yellow; chin: white, with a slash of white across the eyes; bill: yellow. The tail is barred with dark brown or black lines.

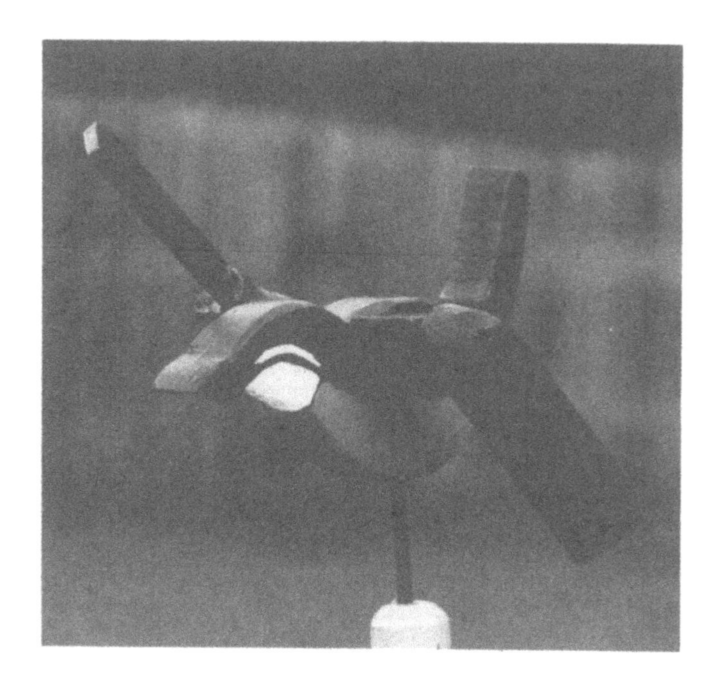

Cheerleader

Probably every school that has team sports also has hardworking male and female cheerleaders. Some put on dazzling shows, perform acrobatics, and build human pyramids. The girls and young women often wave pom-poms as they dance and kick. Pom-poms make marvelous wind-catchers, and if you make this whirligig, you may wish to make another one even larger. A former student of mine made a wonderful cheerleader sculpture, with the body carved in the round.

This whirligig is designed to have a rudder extension. To see how this is made, see the Smiling Lady.

Materials

Body	$\frac{3}{4}'' \times 2'' \times 10''$
Arms	
shoulders (2)	$\frac{3}{4}'' \times 1'' \times 1\frac{1}{2}''$
arms (2)	$\frac{1}{8}'' \times \frac{3}{4}'' \times 3\frac{1}{2}''$
pom-poms (2)	$\frac{1}{8}''$ thick, 1″ radius
Metal	
axle	$\frac{1}{8}''$ brass rod, $3\frac{3}{4}''$ long
hub liner	$\frac{3}{16}''$ brass tubing, $1\frac{3}{4}''$ long
socket liner	$\frac{7}{32}''$ brass tubing 2″ long
washers (2)	No. 6 or No. 8 brass washers

CHEERLEADER

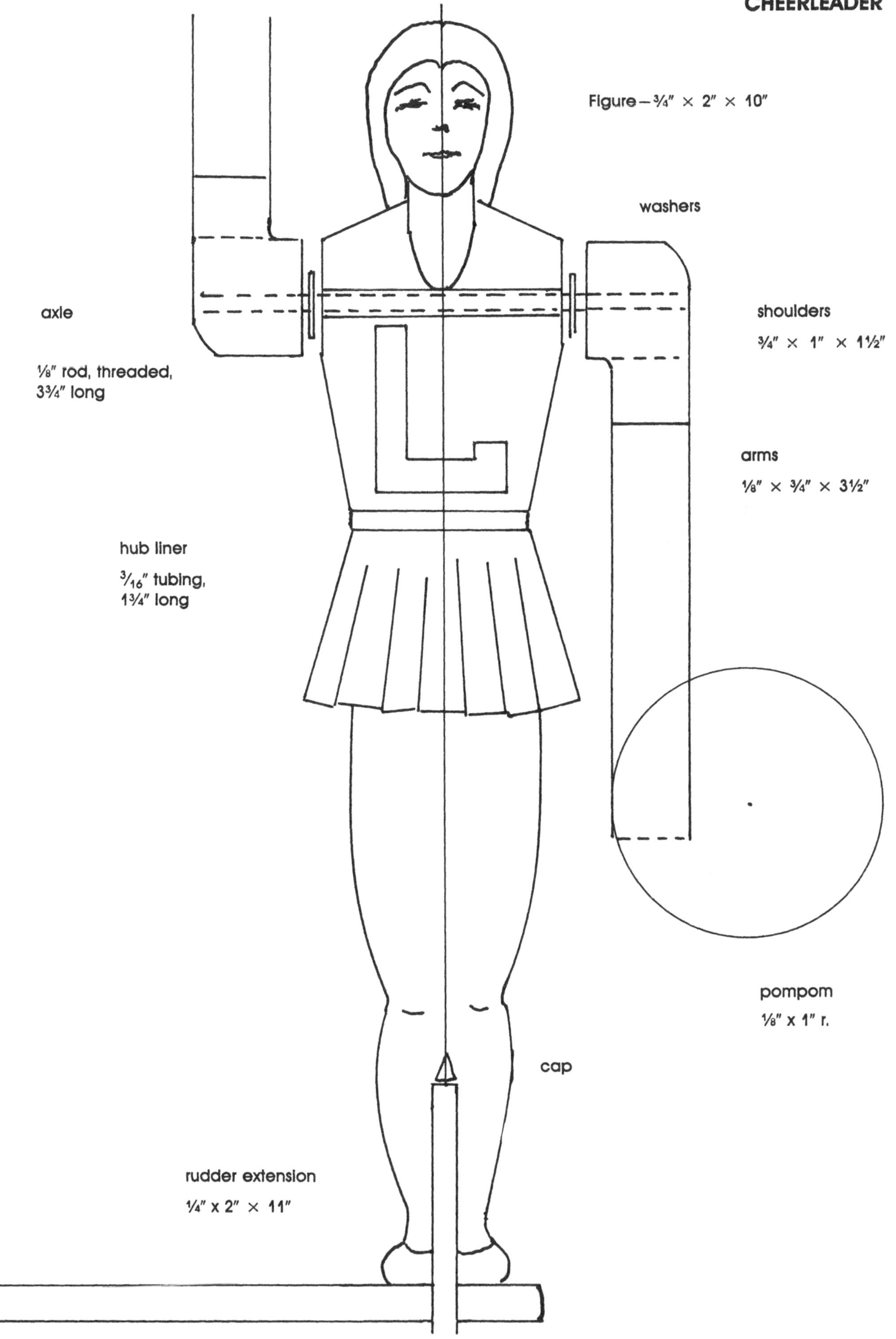

socket cap	Point of 16d nail, or screw
spindle	16d nail with the head off
Rudder extension	$\frac{1}{4}$" × 2" × 11"
Rudder	$\frac{1}{8}$" or $\frac{1}{4}$" × 3" × 4"

Three Cheerleaders in various stages (from left): a finished but unpainted weathervane version with a rudder, a pattern, and a finished enlarged arm-waver. Using patterns is essential when enlarging whirligig designs.

Procedure

1. Trace the *body* on the wood, marking the location of the pivot socket (P) and the hub (H). Draw a straight line across the body where the axle will pass and mark the sides. When the body is cut out, drill the pivot socket about $1\frac{3}{4}$" deep (this will allow the 2" tubing to stick out and go through the tail extension. Put in the tubing liner and the cap.
2. Make the $\frac{3}{16}$" *hub hole* through the body, drilling in halfway from each side. Put the tubing liner in the hole if you have it.
3. Cut out the *shoulder pieces* as shown in the drawing. Drill a $\frac{7}{64}$" hole through the shoulder at the top. On the bottom mark the angle for the blade slots, remembering that the arms must be slanted in opposite directions when mounted on the body. Cut out the shoulder slots $\frac{1}{2}$" deep.
4. Cut out the *arms* and glue them in the slots. Round off the shoulders. Temporarily balance the arms on the axle. Then cut out the pom-poms; try to keep them equal in size and weight. Glue them on the arms so they will extend outward from the body.
5. Cut out the tail extension, locate the position of the pivot socket, and then drill a $\frac{3}{16}$" hole for the socket.

Proper placement and balance of the arms is important for any whirligig—and especially important for the Cheerleader, who must help cheer her team to victory.

At the other end of the extension, cut out the $\frac{1}{8}''$ or $\frac{1}{4}''$ slot for the tail. Cut out the tail. The tail shape should have some connection with the school or university; perhaps the school mascot could be used. Glue the tail in the slot. When it is firm, glue and nail the extension to the bottom of the figure. This whirligig will really take off!

Suggested Colors

School colors, perhaps. If not, dress: white, with a colored letter, shoes: any color, skin color and hair: your choice, pompoms: light blue (for University of North Carolina) or other colors for your favorite school.

Signaling Scout

The first time we learned about signaling, it was probably when we were in the Girl Scouts or the Boy Scouts. We learned the International Morse Code and its system of dots and dashes. We also learned the Semaphore Signaling Code as used by the U.S. Coast Guard and the U.S. Navy. This scout is using the regulation white and red signal code flags. Incidentally, this is a Boy Scout, but anyone can make a Girl Scout out of the figure by adding long hair and making a skirt out of the shorts. The hat would be different, too. This whirligig uses a metal axle instead of a wooden one. The ends of the axle can be forced into the $\frac{7}{64}''$ holes in the arms (or even glued into $\frac{1}{8}''$ arm holes), but it is much easier to thread the axle ends and turn the arms onto the axle.

Materials

Figure	$\frac{3}{4}'' \times 2'' \times 10''$
Arms	
shoulders (2)	$\frac{3}{4}'' \times 1'' \times 1\frac{1}{2}''$
blades (2)	$\frac{1}{8}'' \times 1'' \times 4''$
flags (2)	$\frac{1}{8}'' \times 1\frac{1}{2}'' \times 1\frac{1}{2}''$
Hub pieces (2)	$\frac{5}{8}'' \times \frac{5}{8}'' \times 1''$
Axle	$\frac{1}{8}''$ brass rod, $4\frac{1}{2}''$ long
Hub liner	$\frac{3}{16}''$ brass tubing, 2″ long
Pivot socket liner	$\frac{7}{32}''$ brass tubing, 2″ long
Washers (2)	$\frac{3}{16}''$ brass

Procedure

1. Trace the pattern of the *figure* on the wood and cut it out. File or sand it smooth and, with a pencil, mark where the pivot point (P1 or P2, your choice) and the hub (H) are located. Drill a pivot socket hole 2″ deep with a $\frac{7}{32}''$ bit and a hub hole through H with a $\frac{3}{16}''$ bit. If you have $\frac{7}{32}''$ tubing, cut a piece for the socket liner and insert it. Put a cap in the socket base; this can be the point of a 16d nail or a small screw.

2. Cut out the *hub pieces* and drill $\frac{3}{16}''$ holes through the center. If you have brass tubing for a liner, cut a piece to go through the body and the hub pieces. Glue them together with the liner in place. Use a C-clamp to hold everything tight.

3. Cut out the two *shoulder pieces* and shape them as shown. First drill $\frac{7}{64}''$ holes through the top part. Then, at the bottom, mark the angles for the blade slots, remembering that the blades must slant in opposite directions when they are mounted on the figure. The arms are, after all, a propeller.

SIGNALING SCOUT

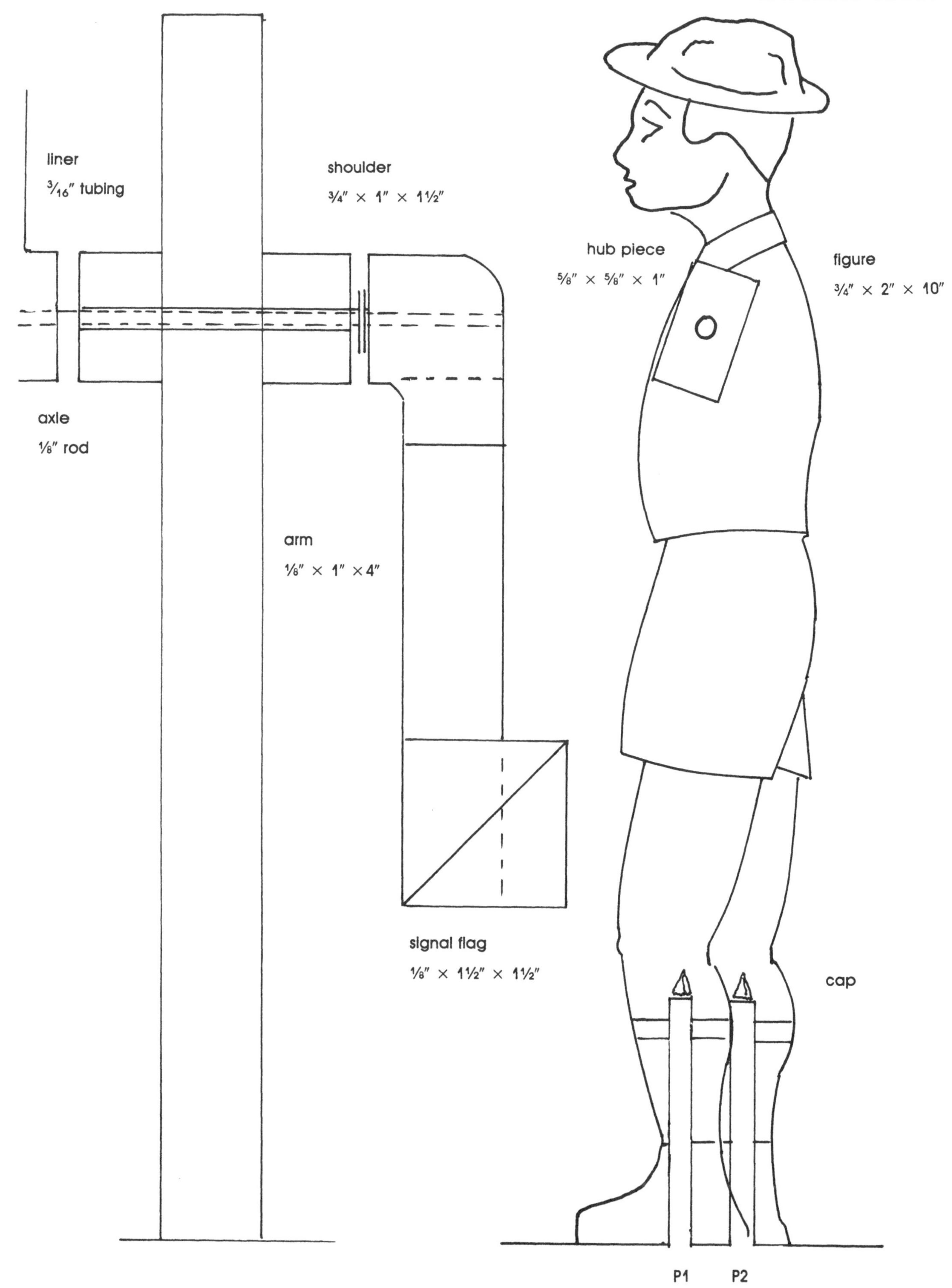

4. Cut out the arm *blades;* then cut out the arm slots in the shoulder pieces to fit the blade ends. The slots are $\frac{1}{2}$" deep. Glue the blades in the slots. After the glue dries, finish shaping and smoothing the shoulders.
5. Make the *axle* of a $\frac{1}{8}$" brass rod $4\frac{1}{2}$" long. Thread each end $\frac{3}{4}$" with a $\frac{6}{32}$ die. Put the axle in the shoulder hub holes and test the balance of the arms. Trim them until they balance.
6. Cut out the *signal flags;* they should be of the same size and weight. Glue them to the ends of the arms, making sure that they will face out from the body. Otherwise, they may strike the body when they rotate. Once again, check the balance of the arms.
7. Attach the arms permanently. Turn the axle into one arm first; then insert it through the hub (with a washer). Then turn on the other arm (with a washer). The arms should be directly opposite each other and in a straight line.

Suggested Colors

Uniform: tan, green, or blue, neckerchief: a bright color, signal flags: red and white diagonally, skin color: any color.

Kayak

This Eskimo boat also uses a split-propeller design and a $\frac{1}{8}$" metal axle. It may be made with a $\frac{1}{4}$" wood dowel axle. The overall design is similar to that of the Gondola and presents the same problem for model makers: Where do you put the pivot point (P) in relation to the hub (H) so the whirligig remains broadside to the wind? In this case, with the hub near the center of balance (B) and near the center of the boat, the pivot point is quite close to the hub.

Note that in the Gondola there is quite a bit of distance between H and P. There are many different models you can draw that will have the same construction and similar H and P locations. Think about making an Indian paddling a canoe or a man rowing a boat. Remember, when you move the propeller (and its hub) to a different location, you will have to change the location of the pivot point as well.

Materials

Kayak and Eskimo	$\frac{3}{4}$" × $5\frac{3}{4}$" × 24"
Hub pieces	$\frac{5}{8}$" × $\frac{5}{8}$" × 1"
Paddle/prop	
shoulders	$\frac{3}{4}$" × 1" × $1\frac{1}{2}$"
paddles (2 ea.)	$\frac{1}{8}$" × 1" × $6\frac{1}{2}$"
Hub liner	$\frac{3}{16}$" tubing, 2" long
Pivot socket liner	$\frac{3}{8}$" tension pin or $\frac{1}{4}$" brass tubing, 2" long
Axle	$\frac{1}{8}$" brass rod, $4\frac{1}{2}$" long, threaded both ends $\frac{3}{4}$"
Washers (2)	No. 8 brass washers
Wood axle	
hub liner	$\frac{5}{16}$" tubing, 2" long
axle	$\frac{1}{4}$" dowel, $4\frac{1}{2}$" long
washers (2)	$\frac{1}{4}$" brass washers

Procedure

1. On a block of wood trace the *kayak,* marking the location of the hub hole and the pivot socket. Drill the $\frac{3}{16}$" hole through the Eskimo's shoulder and a $\frac{1}{4}$" or a $\frac{3}{8}$" hole for the socket depending upon the size of the liner you use. If using a wooden dowel axle, drill a $\frac{5}{16}$" hole in the shoulder. File and sand the kayak. Put a liner in the socket with a metal cap.
2. Make the *hub pieces.* Drill a $\frac{3}{16}$" hole through the centers. Round off the outside edges. Glue the pieces to the body at the hub hole with a $\frac{3}{16}$" piece of brass tubing in place. Hold this firmly with a C-clamp until the glue is dry.
3. Make the paddle/propeller. Cut out the *shoulder pieces* and mark their shape for cutting. Drill a $\frac{7}{64}$" hole $\frac{1}{2}$" from the top for the axle ($\frac{1}{4}$" if using a wooden dowel). Then cut out the final shape. Mark the angles for the blades; they have to slant in opposite directions when on the axle. Cut the slots out $\frac{5}{8}$" deep.
4. Cut out the *paddles.* You can shape them to show an arm and a hand as in the illustration. Glue them in the slots so the larger part of the paddle extends outward from the body.
5. Make the *axle* of an $\frac{1}{8}$" metal rod threaded $\frac{3}{4}$" from each end. Temporarily attach the paddles and make sure they are balanced. (Make the wooden axle out of a $4\frac{1}{2}$" long piece of $\frac{1}{4}$" dowel.)
6. Permanently attach one of the paddle/arms to the axle by turning it like a screw and inserting it into the hub with a washer in place. Then carefully attach the other shoulder/paddle to the axle, making sure both are in a straight line. (Glue the axle to the

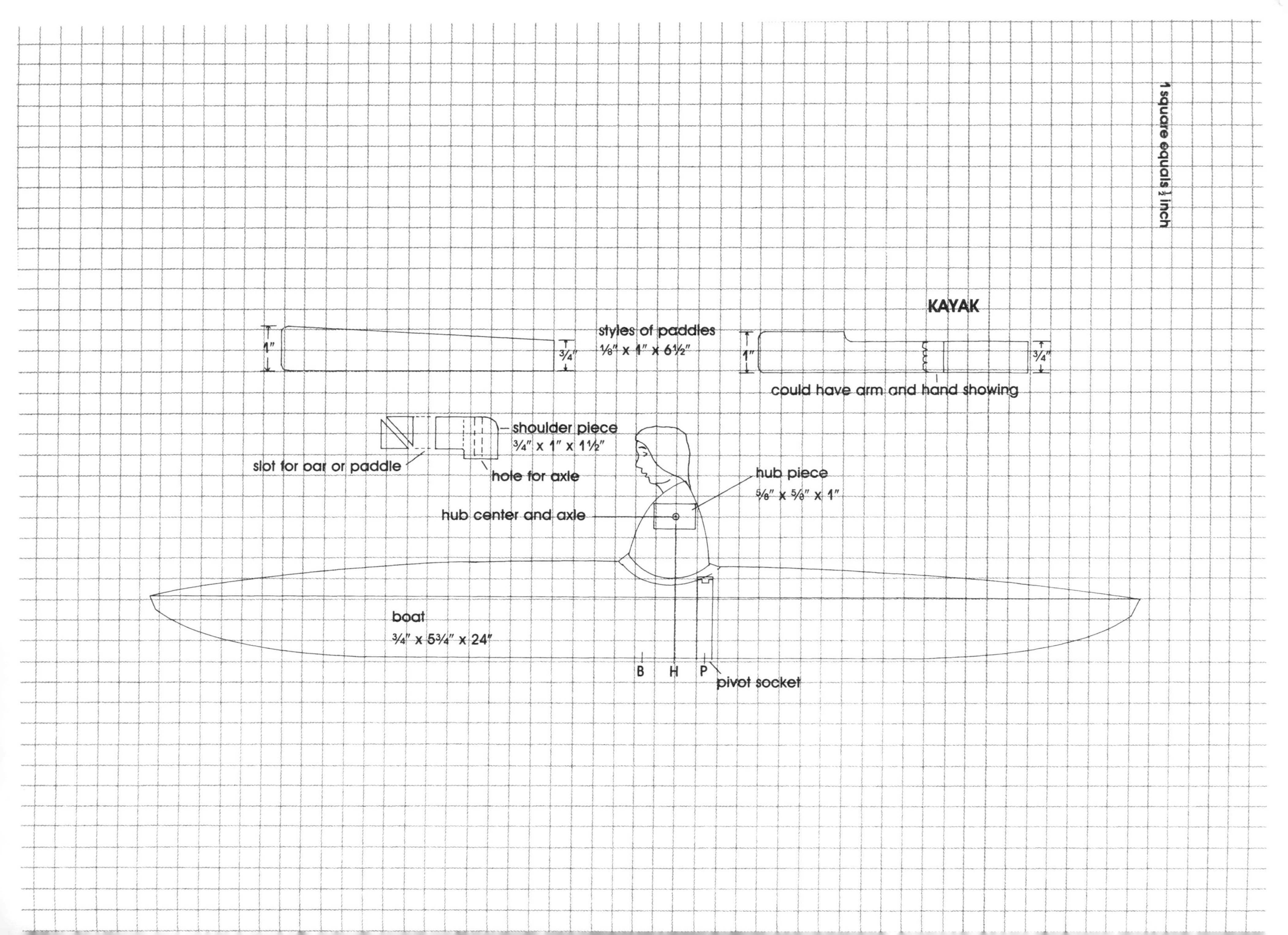
1 square equals ½ inch
KAYAK
1″
¾″
styles of paddles
⅛″ x 1″ x 6½″
1″
¾″
could have arm and hand showing
shoulder piece
¾″ x 1″ x 1½″
slot for oar or paddle
hole for axle
hub piece
⅝″ x ⅝″ x 1″
hub center and axle
boat
¾″ x 5¾″ x 24″
B
H
P
pivot socket

paddle/arm when using a wooden dowel.) You can paint the parts before assembly.

Suggested Colors

The Eskimo kayak is made of animal hide, so brown, yellow, and white may be used to indicate sections sewn together. The Eskimo also wears furs. The paddles are dark wood but can be painted any color.

Fisher in the Boat

There are many fishing whirligigs and many designs from which to choose. The essential parts include a man or woman fishing, an aquatic setting, and a fish. Sometimes a boat is added, as in this case. It is a large whirligig—about 25" in length—but its mechanism is simple. The camshaft idea is the same as in previously described mechanical whirligigs, except that it is made with a brass instead of a wooden rod. Instructions are included for those who want to make the whirligig with a wooden camshaft. In some ways this larger whirligig is easier to make than the smaller ones because the pieces are larger and there is more space in which to work. If you follow the directions carefully, you will have little difficulty in making the Fisher in the Boat whirligig.

Some ripsawing is needed with the platform, which is 24" long and $2\frac{1}{4}''$ wide. To make it more interesting, it is suggested that a bottom section be cut out. Before you begin this project, study it carefully and decide how best to cut out the platform. The rest is not so complicated. Use $\frac{1}{4}''$ plywood for the waves and fish pieces.

Materials

Platform	$\frac{3}{4}'' \times 2\frac{1}{4}'' \times 24''$
Platform extension	$\frac{3}{4}'' \times 1\frac{1}{2}'' \times 4''$
Boat, with fisher	$\frac{3}{4}'' \times 4\frac{1}{2}'' \times 14''$
Boat waves (2)	$\frac{1}{4}'' \times 2\frac{3}{4}'' \times 11''$
Wave backing (2)	$\frac{1}{16}'' \times 1'' \times 11''$
Fish	$\frac{1}{4}'' \times 5'' \times 9''$
Fish sides (2)	$\frac{1}{4}'' \times 1\frac{1}{4}'' \times 2''$
Fish waves (2)	$\frac{1}{4}'' \times 4'' \times 4\frac{1}{4}''$
Fish pole	$\frac{3}{16}''$ wood dowel, 12" long
Metal	
camshaft	$\frac{1}{8}''$ rod, 7" long, threaded ends
extension liner	$\frac{3}{16}''$ brass tubing, 4" long
pivot socket liner	Either $\frac{5}{16}''$ brass tubing, 2" long, or $\frac{3}{8}''$ tension pin
boat and fish liners	$\frac{1}{8}''$ tubing, $\frac{3}{4}''$ long
boat and fish axles	$\frac{3}{32}''$ brass rod, $2\frac{1}{2}''$ long
screw eye	$\frac{3}{8}''$ or $\frac{1}{2}''$ size
cap	See instructions
spindle	20d nail, head cut off
washers	As indicated
screw and nails	As indicated
Wood camshaft	See Notes on Metal and Wooden Camshafts (later in this chapter).

Procedure

1. Construct the *platform* according to the details in the illustration. Cut out the whole piece first without trimming it. Then mark the various points where the different parts will be attached, measuring from the front. For example, the extension will reach to 3" from the front (with a 1" overhang); the extension screw hole will be at 2"; the pivot socket at 6"; the boat wave's end will be a $6\frac{1}{2}''$ and will extend 11" to $17\frac{1}{2}''$. The fish wave starts at $3\frac{1}{4}''$ from the rear of the platform. If you wish to do so, plan to cut off $1\frac{1}{4}''$ from the bottom of the platform to a point 15" from the rear. For guidance when drilling, locate the top and bottom points on the extension screw and the pivot socket by drawing connecting lines across the top, bottom, and sides of the platform. A square or ruler should be used to make these lines accurate.

2. When all the locations are marked off, drill the extension hole and the pivot socket hole. It is easiest to drill small holes first. With a $\frac{1}{8}''$ bit drill a hole from the center of the top of the platform halfway

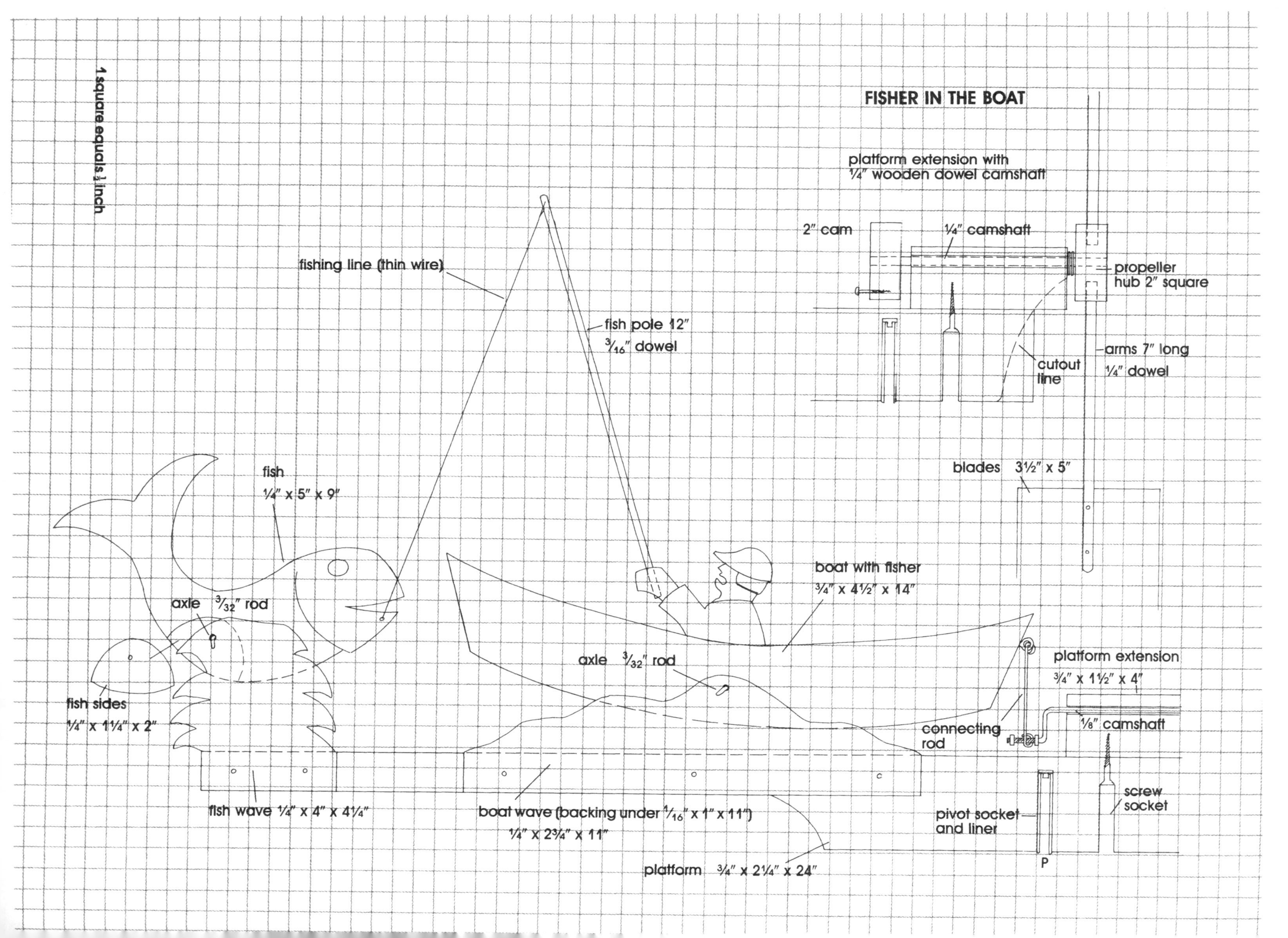
FISHER IN THE BOAT
platform extension with
1/4" wooden dowel camshaft
2" cam
1/4" camshaft
propeller
hub 2" square
arms 7" long
1/4" dowel
cutout
line
blades 3 1/2" x 5"
fishing line (thin wire)
fish pole 12"
3/16" dowel
fish
1/4" x 5" x 9"
axle 3/32" rod
boat with fisher
3/4" x 4 1/2" x 14"
axle 3/32" rod
platform extension
3/4" x 1 1/2" x 4"
1/8" camshaft
connecting
rod
fish sides
1/4" x 1 1/4" x 2"
fish wave 1/4" x 4" x 4 1/4"
boat wave (backing under 1/16" x 1" x 11")
1/4" x 2 3/4" x 11"
pivot socket
and liner
screw
socket
P
platform 3/4" x 2 1/4" x 24"
1 square equals 1/2 inch

down, and then drill from the center of the bottom halfway up. This will make a straight track for larger bits. With a $\frac{3}{8}''$ bit enlarge the extension hole to within $\frac{3}{4}''$ of the top of the platform. This will make it possible for a $1\frac{1}{4}''$ long No. 6 screw to hold the extension in place. Enlarge the pivot socket to within $\frac{1}{4}''$ of the top of the platform for the socket liner. The socket liner now can be put in place. If it is a 2″ tension pin, place the point of a 16d in one end to be used as a cap.

3. Cut out the *platform extension*. Drill a $\frac{3}{16}''$ hole lengthwise $\frac{3}{8}''$ from the top through the extension. It is easiest to drill halfway through from each end. Line this hole with $\frac{3}{16}''$ tubing. Glue it in place on the platform and secure it with a $1\frac{1}{4}''$ long No. 6 screw turned from the bottom. First, locate where the screw will go into the extension and drill a small pilot hole there so the extension will not split.
4. Cut out the *boat waves* of $\frac{1}{4}''$ plywood. Drill a $\frac{3}{32}''$ hole through the top of one of the waves. Prepare the *wave backing* pieces, which will keep the boat from being stuck between the waves. You can do without the backing pieces if you want to take the time to shave down or file down the sides of the boat so that it moves freely between the waves. Glue the backing pieces to the platform and glue/nail the waves over them. Use $\frac{3}{4}''$ small-headed nails. Brads without heads will do, but the headed wire nails hold better. To make sure the waves will remain firm, put a C-clamp on them with small pieces of wood between the clamp and the waves so they won't be damaged. Place the $\frac{3}{32}''$ bit through the hole and drill a hole through the other wave, making sure the bit is straight and level.
5. Cut out the *fish waves*. Drill a $\frac{3}{32}''$ hole near the top of one of them. Glue/nail them to the end of the platform. Drill through the other wave as noted earlier.
6. Cut out the *boat* and the *fisher* piece. File it and sand it smooth. Drill a $\frac{1}{8}''$ hole in the boat where indicated; line it with $\frac{1}{8}''$ brass tubing. Turn a $\frac{3}{8}''$ or $\frac{1}{2}''$ screw eye into the stern of the boat $\frac{3}{4}''$ down from the top side. Put the boat between the waves and put the $\frac{3}{32}''$ axle in place. Make sure that the boat rocks easily. Put No. 6 brass washers between the boat and the waves.
7. Cut out the *fish* and sand it smooth. Drill a $\frac{1}{16}''$ hole in the mouth for the fish line. Cut out the *fish sides* and glue them on the fish. Clamp them on with spring clamps until they are dry. Drill a $\frac{1}{8}''$ hole through the fish and line it with brass tubing. Put the fish between the waves with a $\frac{3}{32}''$ axle in place and No. 6 washers to see if the fish moves easily.

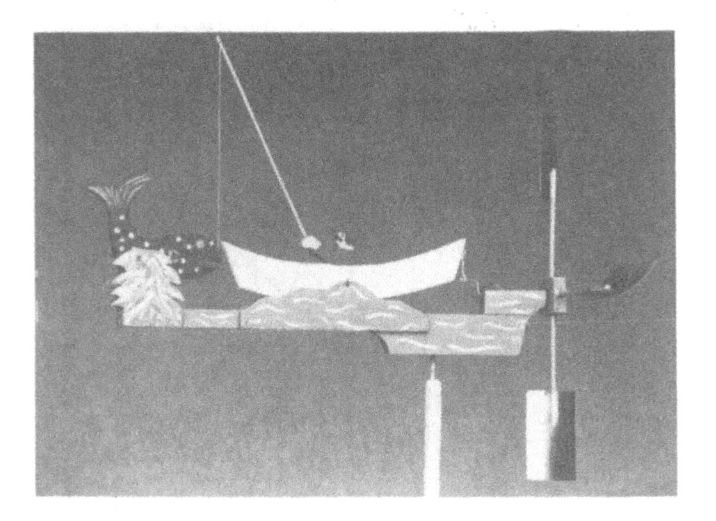

8. Drill a $\frac{3}{16}''$ hole for the *fishing rod* through the fisher's hands. Cut off a 12″ piece of $\frac{3}{16}''$ dowel and drill a $\frac{1}{16}''$ hole near the top of one end for the fish line. Put a temporary line in place about 11″ between the fish and pole and see if it all works. The weight of the fish should be so balanced that the head will drop as the line goes down. Make sure the fish does not hit the boat or lean over backward. If the fish and boat continue to collide, cut $\frac{1}{4}''$ off the stern of the boat and $\frac{1}{4}''$ off the tip of the fish's nose.

A Propeller for This Whirligig

This is a four-bladed armed propeller and is easy to make. (See Use of Propellers in Chapter 7 plus the illustration on basic propeller design.) You will need to use a brace with the $\frac{3}{8}''$ bit to make the hub holes for the propeller arms.

Materials

Hub	$\frac{3}{4}''$ × 2″ × 2″
Arms (4)	$\frac{3}{8}''$ dowel, 7″ long
Blades (4)	Thin metal (like aluminum flashing) Cut to $3\frac{1}{2}''$ to 5″

Procedure

1. Cut out the *hub* and mark the center. Then locate the centers of the four sides. Drill a $\frac{7}{64}''$ hole in the center if you have a $\frac{1}{8}''$ threaded camshaft. Drill a $\frac{1}{4}''$ hole if you have a wooden camshaft. Drill $\frac{3}{8}''$ holes $\frac{1}{2}''$ deep in the sides of the hub for the arms.
2. Cut out the *arms*. Measure down 2″ from one end of each arm. With a coping saw cut a slot down the middle of the dowels to the 2″ mark. Drill two small

Basic Propeller Design for Mechanical Whirligigs

For the Fisher in the Boat, Machine Lab, Patriotic Drummer, Winning Race Car, and Daniel Boone and the Bear whirligigs.

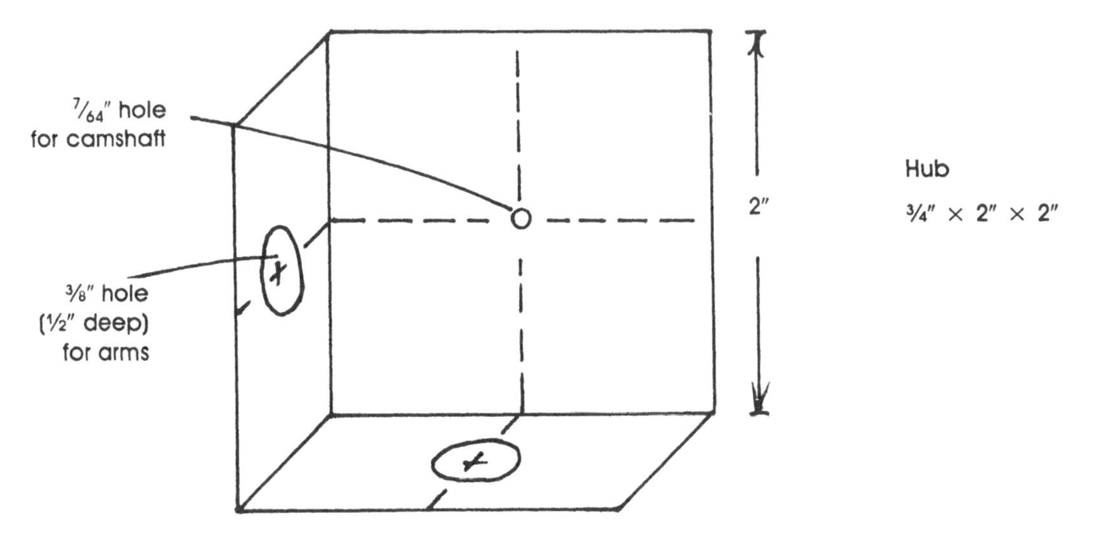

Arms (4) 3/8" wood dowel, various lengths (see directions)

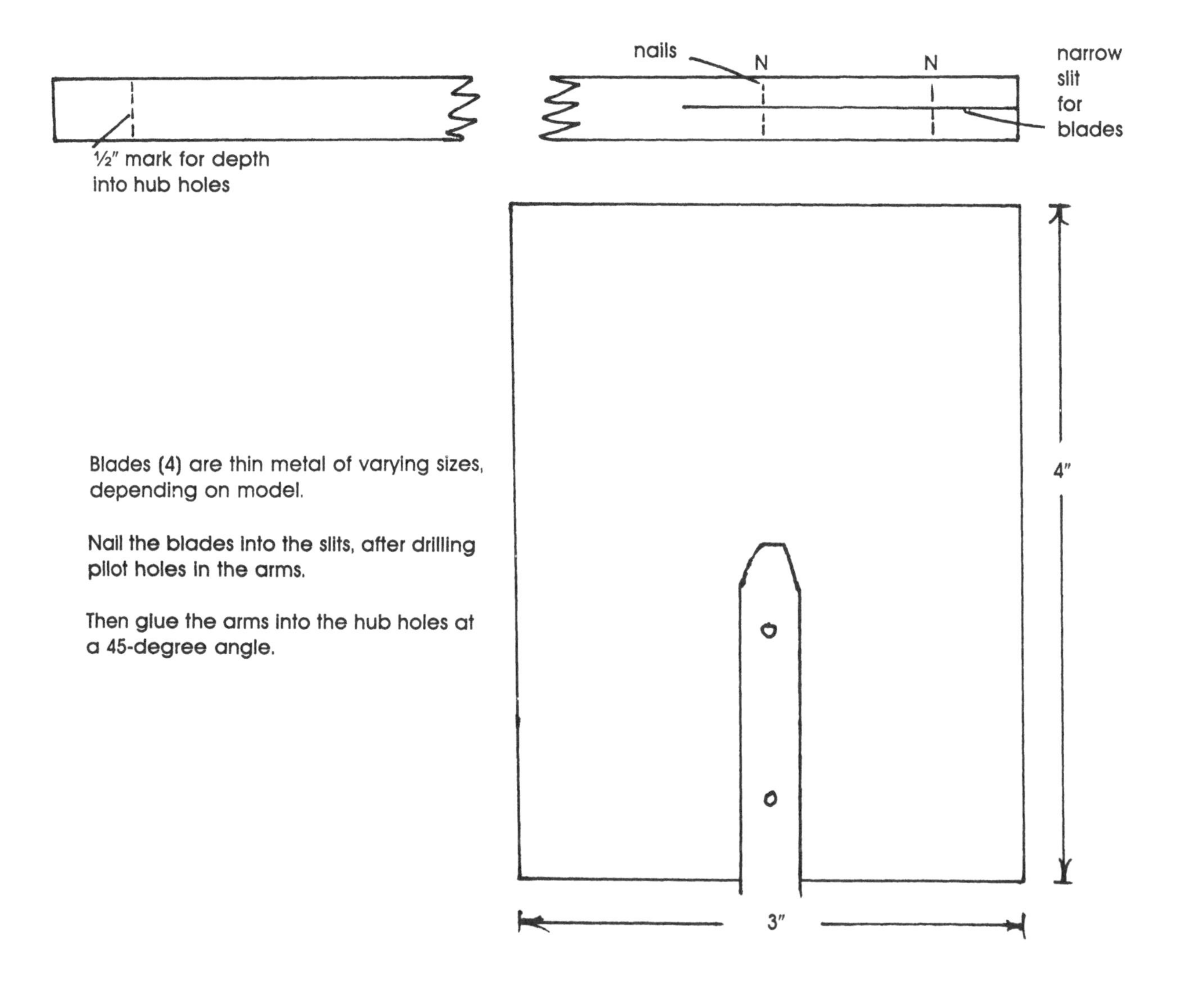

Blades (4) are thin metal of varying sizes, depending on model.

Nail the blades into the slits, after drilling pilot holes in the arms.

Then glue the arms into the hub holes at a 45-degree angle.

Cut out the metal blades with tin snips.

Fasten the blades to the dowels.

Attach the bladed dowels to the hub.

Place the finished propeller on the whirligig.

holes for nails through the ends of the arms as shown.

3. Cut out the *blades* with a pair of tin snips. Be careful. The edges of the aluminum may be very sharp. With a file smooth down the edges of the metal blades, and then sand them. Lightly sand the surface of the blades so the paint will stick better.

4. Glue the arms into the hub holes at a 45-degree angle. If they are loose, cut small wooden wedges to hold them firm. When they are dry, the propeller is ready to work. Turn the propeller onto the $\frac{1}{8}$" metal camshaft (or put the propeller onto the end of the 6" wooden camshaft). Test it to see that it works properly.

Notes on Metal and Wooden Camshafts

For a Metal Camshaft

Turn the propeller onto the ⅛″ metal camshaft, with a washer in place, to see that it works properly. Attach the connecting rod between the two machine nuts on the camshaft and the screw eye on the boat. (On my model the length of the rod between the screw eye and the cam was only 1½″.) Observe the motion of the boat and the fish. Make whatever adjustments are necessary.

For a Wooden Camshaft

The hole through the platform extension will be $\frac{5}{16}$″ and lined with tubing. Cut a 6″ long piece of ¼″ dowel. Cut a cam piece 2″ × 2″ square. Screw a 1″ round-headed No. 6 screw partway into one end of the cam piece. Glue the 2″ cam piece on the drive shaft. Place the camshaft in the platform extension. Force the propeller on the front end of the shaft with two washers in between the propeller and the extension. Attach the connecting rod. Test the action and the spacing. When you have the spacing correct, glue the propeller to the camshaft.

For Both Camshafts

Find the best operating location for the cam and the connecting rod. Place the propeller hub, with two washers in place, as close to the front of the extension as possible. This will eliminate the need for a spacer between the hub and propeller. If a spacer is necessary, make one from a piece of tubing.

Suggested Colors

Platform, extension, and all waves: sea green, with white caps here and there; boat: white; fisher's hat: blue; fisher's jacket: red; fisher's skin color: your choice; fishing pole: yellow; fish: dark green and red with yellowish belly.

Clashing Knights

"When knighthood was in flower" could be the subtitle of this whirligig. It shows two knights in battle, but they will never shed blood because they can't get near each other. They will fight forever. We don't know why they are fighting, whether they are in a war or fighting for a fair lady in distress. That's an idea! Put a weeping princess on the platform and you will have even more of a story. That's how imaginative whirligigs are created.

General construction is similar to that of Daniel

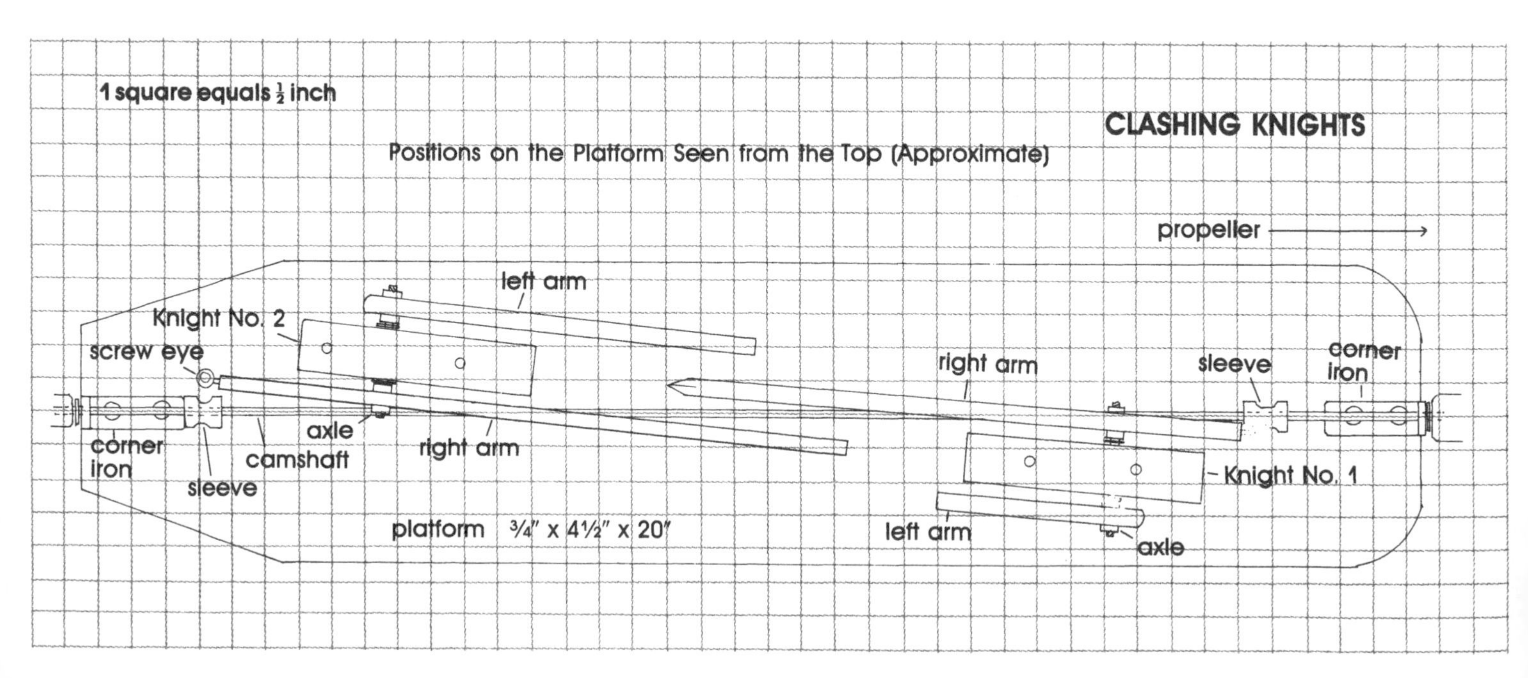

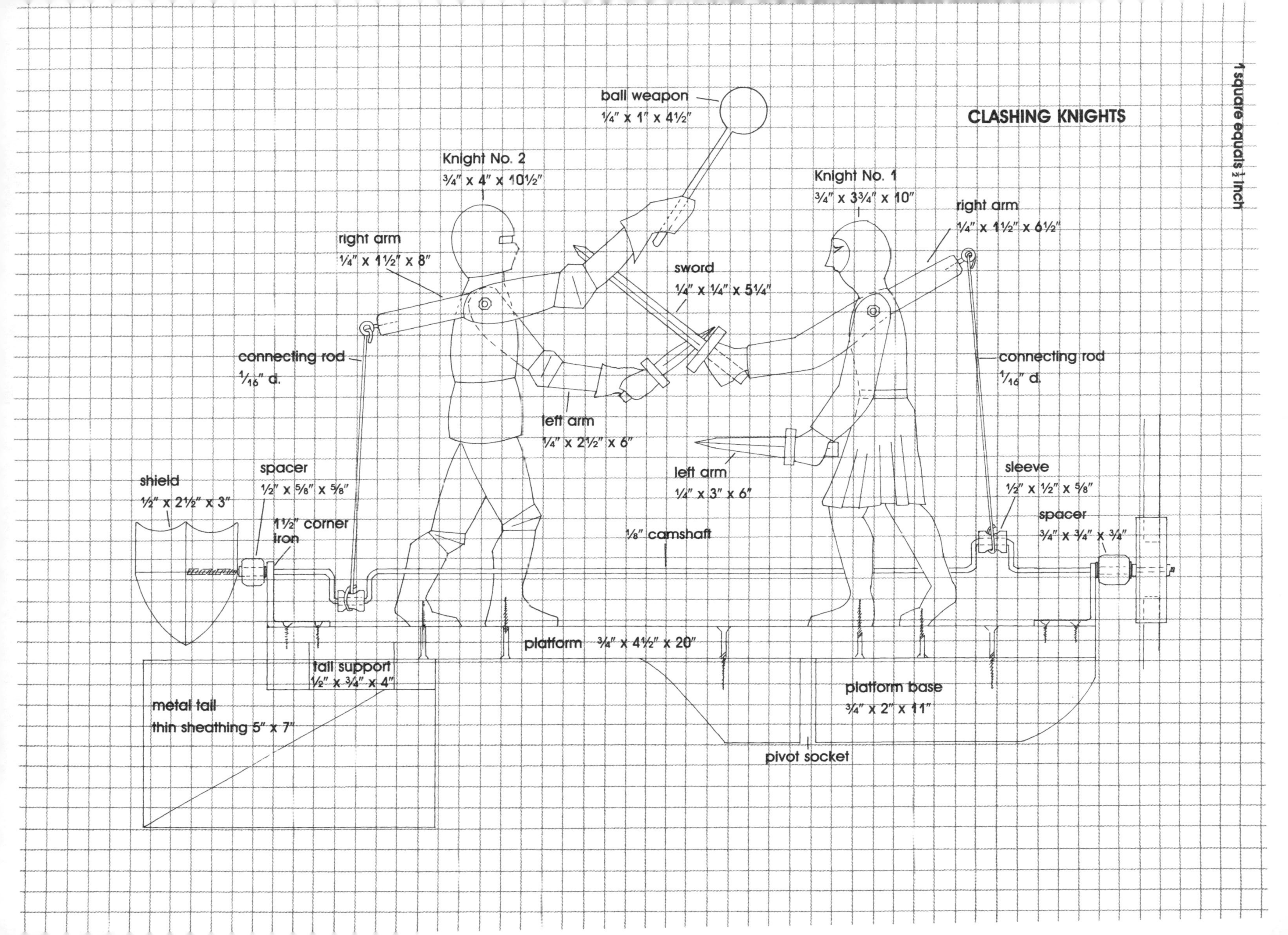
CLASHING KNIGHTS
1 square equals ½ inch
ball weapon
¼″ x 1″ x 4½″
Knight No. 2
¾″ x 4″ x 10½″
Knight No. 1
¾″ x 3¾″ x 10″
right arm
¼″ x 1½″ x 8″
right arm
¼″ x 1½″ x 6½″
sword
¼″ x ¼″ x 5¼″
connecting rod
1/16″ d.
connecting rod
1/16″ d.
left arm
¼″ x 2½″ x 6″
left arm
¼″ x 3″ x 6″
shield
½″ x 2½″ x 3″
spacer
½″ x 5/8″ x 5/8″
1½″ corner iron
sleeve
½″ x ½″ x 5/8″
spacer
¾″ x ¾″ x ¾″
1/8″ camshaft
platform ¾″ x 4½″ x 20″
tail support
½″ x ¾″ x 4″
metal tail
thin sheathing 5″ x 7″
platform base
¾″ x 2″ x 11″
pivot socket

Boone and the Bear, but the construction of the arms is more complicated. When one arm moves the other also moves. The illustrations will show how this is done. Also, the connecting rods are attached to the square cams on the drive shaft by means of wooden sleeves that prevent the rods from sliding off to the side. The propeller also is different from those used before—it is five-bladed, and the hub is a pentagon. The rudder is placed under the platform in order to have a clear view of the warrior's action.

Materials

Platform	$\frac{3}{4}$" × $4\frac{1}{2}$" × 20"
Platform base	$\frac{3}{4}$" × 2" × 11"
Pivot socket liner	$\frac{3}{8}$" tension pin, 2" long, with cap
Tail supports (2)	$\frac{1}{2}$" × $\frac{3}{4}$" × 4"
Tail or rudder	Thin sheathing, 5" × 7"
Corner irons (2)	$1\frac{1}{2}$" size
Decorative shield	$\frac{1}{2}$" × $2\frac{1}{2}$" × 3"
Knight No. 1	$\frac{3}{4}$" × $3\frac{3}{4}$" × 10"
Right arm	$\frac{1}{4}$" × $1\frac{1}{2}$" × $6\frac{1}{2}$"
Sword	$\frac{1}{4}$" × $\frac{1}{4}$" × $5\frac{1}{4}$"
Left arm (includes dagger)	$\frac{1}{4}$" × 3" × 6"
Knight No. 2	$\frac{3}{4}$" × 4" × $10\frac{1}{2}$"
Right arm	$\frac{1}{4}$" × $1\frac{1}{2}$" × 8"
Ball weapon	$\frac{1}{4}$" × 1" × $4\frac{1}{2}$"
Left arm (includes dagger)	$\frac{1}{4}$" × $2\frac{1}{2}$" × 6"
Axles (2)	$\frac{1}{8}$" brass rod, $2\frac{1}{4}$" long, threaded; with 4 machine nuts, washers
Camshaft	$\frac{1}{8}$" metal rod, 26" long
Front spacer	$\frac{3}{4}$" × $\frac{3}{4}$" wood block rounded
Back spacer	$\frac{1}{2}$" × $\frac{1}{2}$" wood block rounded
Camshaft sleeves	$\frac{1}{2}$" × $\frac{3}{4}$" lengthwise
Connecting rods (2)	$\frac{1}{16}$" brass rods or thin metal rods, cut as needed
Screw eyes (2)	$\frac{1}{2}$" size

Procedure

1. Cut out the *platform* and mark in pencil all the items that will be mounted on it: the corner irons, the center line of the camshaft, the position of the knights, and the holding screw holes. Underneath, mark the location of the platform base and the woodblocks that will hold the tail.

2. Cut out the *platform base*, trim it, and drill a pivot socket hole 7" from the front. Attach it with two holding screws and glue. Insert the socket liner with a metal cap. Put corner irons at the ends of the platform. Construct a stand to hold the whirligig as you work on it.

3. Make the figures of the *knights*, including some minor wood carving if you wish, and drill a $\frac{3}{16}$" hole through the shoulder for the axle as indicated. Cut out the arms and the weapons. Cut a slot in the right hand of Knight No. 1 and glue in his sword. Cut a slot in the right hand of Knight No. 2 and glue the handle of the ball weapon in it. To make sure you have the right angles, hold the arms next to the figures.

4. Make the *axles* for the knights' shoulders. They are identical. They require carefully threaded ends as shown in the drawing. You should constantly check the measurements as you go along. The arms are linked by the axle so that when the connecting rod moves one, the other also moves. The arms are held secure by $\frac{6}{32}$ machine nuts.

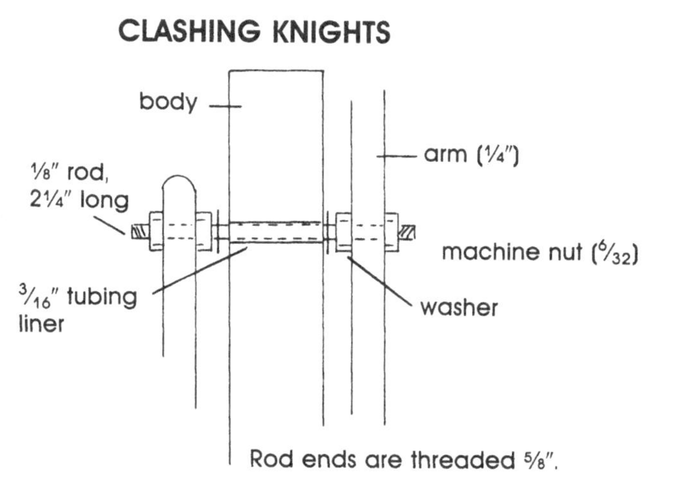

5. Put the arms aside for the moment. Screw/glue the knights in position on either side of the center line and angle them toward each other. When they are firmly in place, attach the arms with the screw eyes attached.

6. Make the *camshaft* as shown in the drawing. The first bend is 4" from the front end. A $\frac{3}{4}$" deep cam, 1" wide, is made there. There is a 14" space to the next bend, and that cam is made in the same way except that it should bend in the opposite direction; if the first one is down, the second one should be up. Place the camshaft in the corner irons to see that it fits. Then thread the ends 1" with a $\frac{6}{32}$ die. Make two wood sleeves for the cams as indicated.

7. Put the camshaft in place with the machine nuts, washers, and front and back spacers. Drill the spacers' centers with a $\frac{3}{16}$" bit and line them with tubing. Attach the $\frac{1}{16}$" connecting rods; the distance between the cam sleeves and the screw eye is about 7". Turn the crankshaft to see if the arms work prop-

Propeller for Clashing Knights

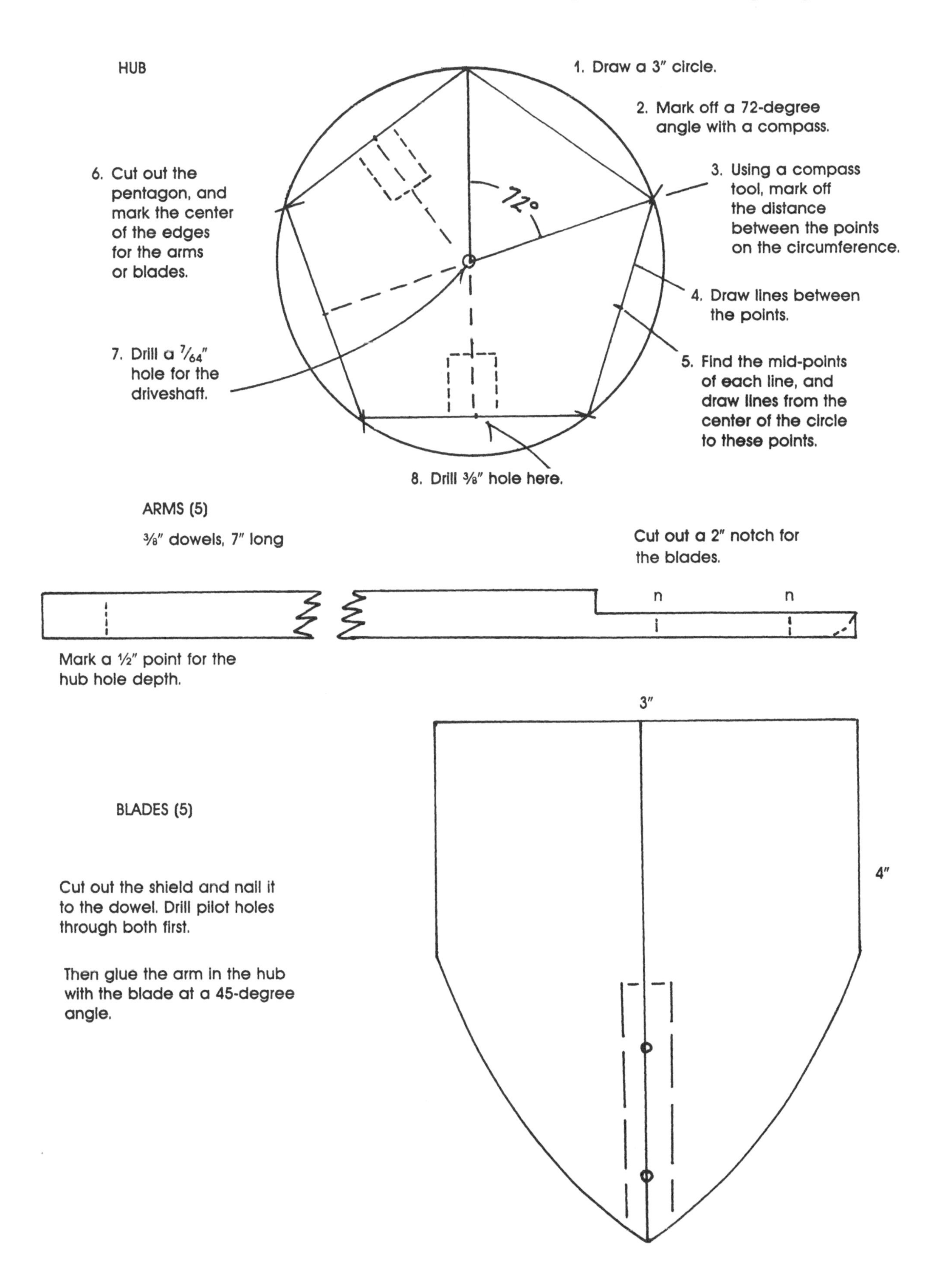

erly. You can adjust the arms by loosening and tightening the axle machine nuts.

8. Assemble all parts. Make a shield for the back end. Drill a $\frac{7}{64}$" hole in it and turn it on the threaded camshaft.
9. Make the propeller (directions follow) and turn it onto the threaded front end of the camshaft. Secure it with a machine nut.

Suggested Colors

Platform: green, Knight No. 1: silver with a red skirt, Knight No. 2: all gold armor, weapons: metal color or gold and silver. Note that the extensions of the right arms should be painted black so they do not appear to be part of the armor.

A Propeller for This Whirligig

Materials

Hub	a $\frac{3}{4}$" thick pentagon, 3" diameter
Arms (5)	$\frac{3}{8}$" dowel, 7" long
Blades (5)	$\frac{3}{8}$" × 3" × 4" (shaped as shields)

Procedure

1. Design and cut out a pentagon for the hub. Drill a $\frac{7}{64}$" hole in the center and $\frac{3}{8}$" holes in the centers of the sides $\frac{1}{2}$" deep.
2. Cut out the arms. With a coping saw cut 2" notches in one end for the blades. Put a $\frac{1}{2}$" mark on the other end.
3. Cut out the blades in a shield pattern and nail/glue them to the arms. First, drill small pilot holes for the nails to prevent splitting the wood.
4. Glue the arms in the side hub holes at a 45-degree angle. When dry, paint the shields in bright colors—your own heraldic colors if you have them.

Machine Lab

When the purpose or theme of a complex whirligig isn't easily apparent, give it any name that strikes your fancy. In this case I drew two figures to illustrate the double-cam mechanism and wondered what they should be doing. In an earlier whirligig I had them waving a flagpole; in another, they were moving a propeller. Here I decided to add a flywheel when it occurred to me that the people could be machinists or engineers in white coats testing different devices, and I thought of adding another wheel that looked like a gear. I decided to call it the Mechanical Laboratory and shortened it to Machine Lab. That's how creative ideas form once you begin to think of the possibilities of a project, even if you are only making whirligigs and not artistic masterpieces. The greatest difficulty with complex whirligigs is assembling them. To complete this whirligig you must assemble and disassemble it again and again to get it right. Detailed instructions show how the whirligig is constructed, put together, and also how it can be taken apart.

Materials

Platform	$\frac{3}{4}$" × 5" × $12\frac{1}{2}$"
Platform base	$\frac{3}{4}$" × 2" × 8"
Pillars (3)	1" × 1" × $4\frac{1}{2}$"
Flywheel	$\frac{3}{4}$" thick, 4" diameter
Machine wheel	$\frac{1}{4}$" thick, 10" diameter
Pivot socket liner	$\frac{3}{8}$" tension pin, or $\frac{1}{4}$" tubing, 2" long, and cap
Camshaft	$\frac{1}{8}$" brass rod, 20" long
Woman	
leg	$\frac{3}{4}$" × 1" × $3\frac{1}{2}$"
body	$1\frac{1}{4}$" × $1\frac{1}{4}$" × 5"
arms	$\frac{1}{4}$" × 1" × $2\frac{3}{4}$"
Man	
leg	$\frac{3}{4}$" × 1" × $3\frac{3}{4}$"
body	$1\frac{1}{4}$" × $1\frac{1}{4}$" × $5\frac{1}{2}$"
arms	$\frac{1}{4}$" × 1" × 3"
Axles (for both)	$\frac{3}{32}$" brass rods, cut to size
Screws for arms (4)	No. 4, $\frac{3}{4}$" long
Liners for leg holes	
Liners for pillars	

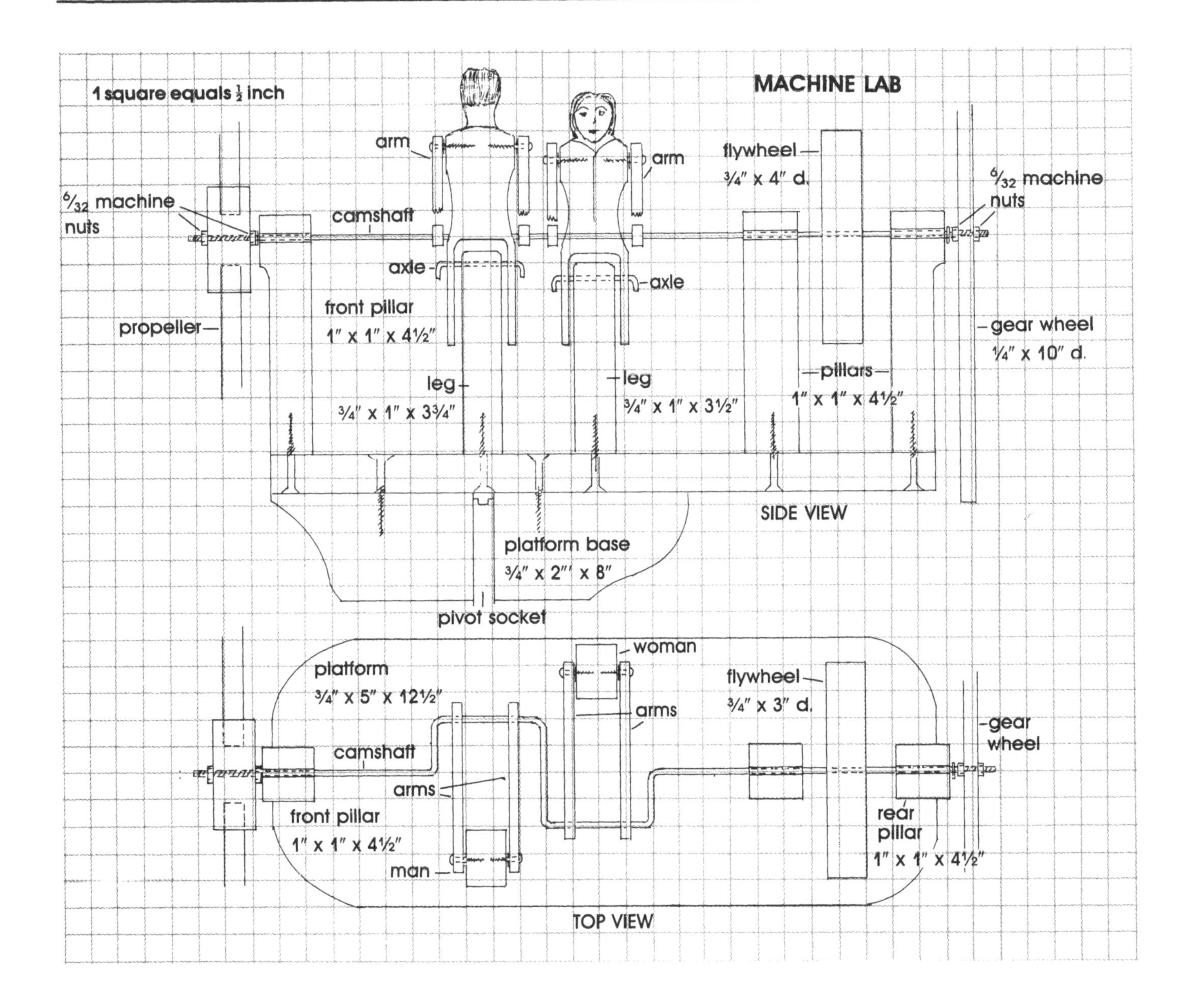

Procedure

1. Cut out the *platform* and mark the following on it with a pencil: center line, top and bottom; location of the platform base and screw holes; positions of the pillars and screw holes; placement of the legs of the man and woman, with screw holes. Drill all the holes—with the exception of those for the legs—and countersink them.

2. Cut out the *platform base* in a decorative shape. Drill the ⅜" or ¼" pivot socket 2" deep. Insert liner and cap. Cut out the three *pillars* and drill the pilot hole in the centers of their bases. Drill $\frac{3}{16}$" holes ½" from the top for the drive shaft. Trim two of the pillars for the front and back of the platform so they will have a ¼" projection at the top; line these with $\frac{3}{16}$" tubing. Do not put a liner in the third pillar. Put all the above parts aside for the moment.

3. Make the *camshaft* according to the detailed drawing. The first bend starts at 4½" from the front end, then make a second bend 1" further. Go over 2" more and make a third bend, and so on. The last stretch, after the double cams, will be over the approximately 6¼" needed for the length of the camshaft. Leave it for now unless it interferes with inserting the shaft through the pillars, then cut it no larger than necessary to permit this. Thread the front end 1¼" with a $\frac{6}{32}$ die. Do not thread the back end now.

4. Partially assemble the parts on the platform. First attach the front pillar loosely, and then the back

MACHINE LAB

Figures — Side View

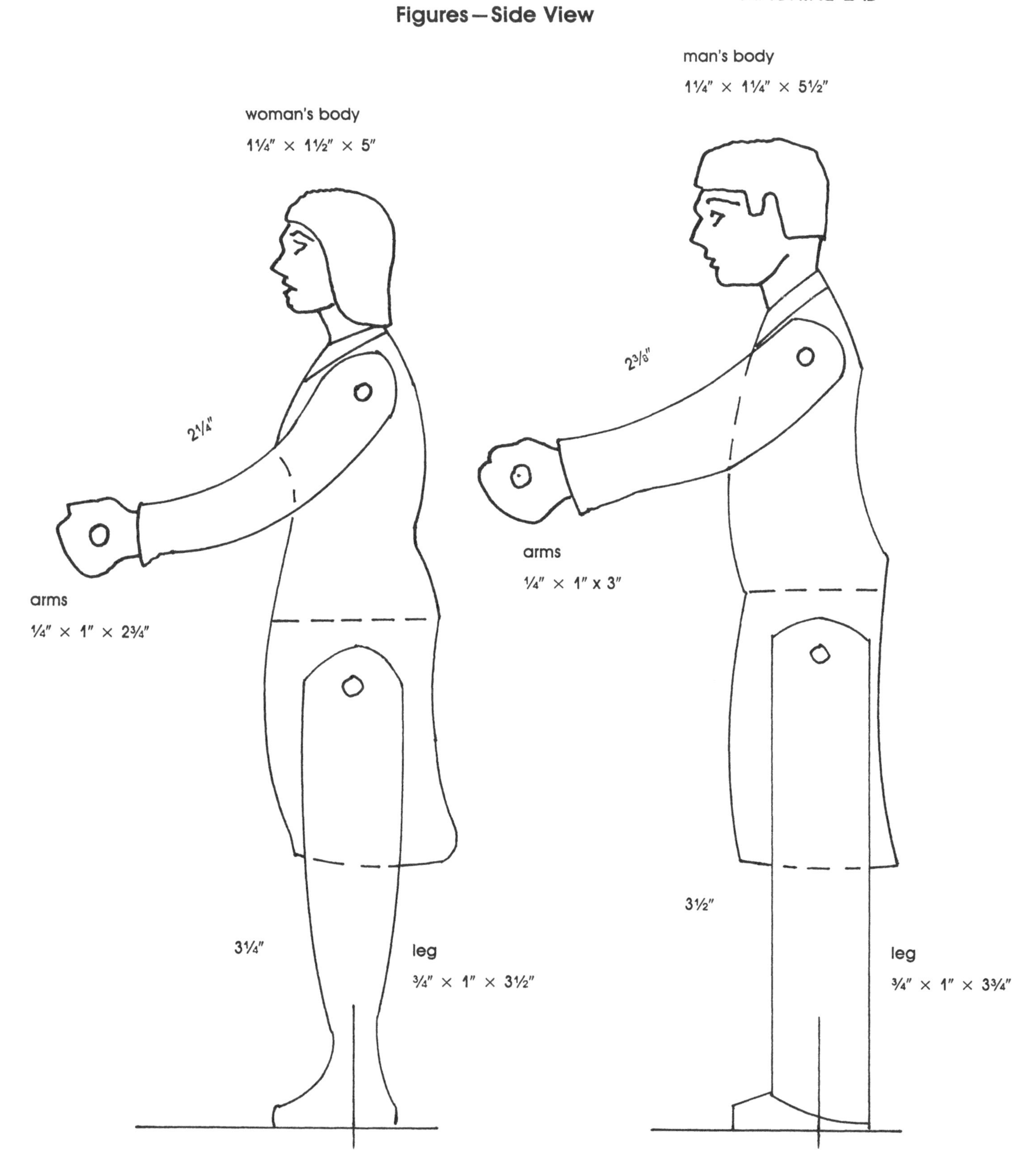

pillar. Put the camshaft in the pillar holes. If you first put the back end through the rear pillar, the front end of the shaft will fit easily into the front pillar. If not, you haven't cut enough off, as recommended previously. The camshaft should turn easily; you can twist the pillars so the holes do not bind the shaft. Try it with the third pillar in place; if this seems to stop the camshaft, drill a larger hole ($\frac{7}{32}$"). The camshaft must move fairly freely in the three holes. Now screw the front and back pillars in place with glue and check once again that they do not bind the movement of the shaft. Then attach the platform base to the bottom of the platform with screws and glue.

5. Insert the camshaft in position and place a $\frac{6}{32}$ machine nut and washer at the threaded front end. Always hold that nut against the pillar when making further tests and adjustments of the parts. Cut out the legs of the man and woman and drill $\frac{1}{8}$" holes $\frac{1}{2}$" from the top for the axles. Test their location in relation to the cams; their position should be in the center of the cams. If this is not the case, adjust the platform locations. Begin with the man's legs. Mark the location of the leg hole on the platform and in the side of the leg for accuracy. Drill the screw hole in the platform and a pivot hole in the bottom of the leg. Then check the location of the woman's leg, drill the screw hole in the right place, and attach the leg. The distance of the legs from the edge of the platform should be the same as in the illustration.

6. Cut out the upper bodies and arms of the man and woman. Shape the heads to the best of your ability. Drill small pilot holes in the shoulders for the arm screws. Drill a $\frac{3}{32}$" hole through the bottom part of the leg axles. Drill holes in the upper arms for the shoulder screws and $\frac{3}{16}$" holes in the hands. Disassemble the camshaft and place the hands on it; the hand holes are large enough to go around the bends.

7. Attach the bodies to the legs with the $\frac{3}{32}$" axles. Then attach the arms to the bodies with the arm screws. Turn the camshaft. The figures should move up and down without hindrance. If the camshaft strikes the bodies, see if the arms should be shortened or another hole drilled to lessen the distance between the holes. Also decide whether or not other axle holes should be drilled to move the body back. These types of adjustments are common with complex whirligigs, so be patient.

8. When the arms and bodies work smoothly, disassemble the camshaft mechanism, removing only the shoulder screws. Make the *flywheel* and drill a $\frac{7}{64}$" hole in the center. Slide the third pillar onto the rear of the shaft, followed by the flywheel. Then reassemble the mechanism. Screw the third pillar in place and turn the camshaft to see that everything works together. Check the back end of the camshaft. It should extend $\frac{3}{4}$" from the rear pillar, so cut it to that size. Mark a point $\frac{1}{4}$" from the pillar and thread the end of the shaft to that point.

9. Cut out the 10" *gear wheel* and drill a $\frac{7}{64}$" hole in the center. Turn it onto the camshaft and secure it with a nut. Turn the camshaft again to see that all works well.

10. Make the propeller (as in the following directions). Paint all the parts separately. When the parts are dry, go through the final assembly. Do not glue the

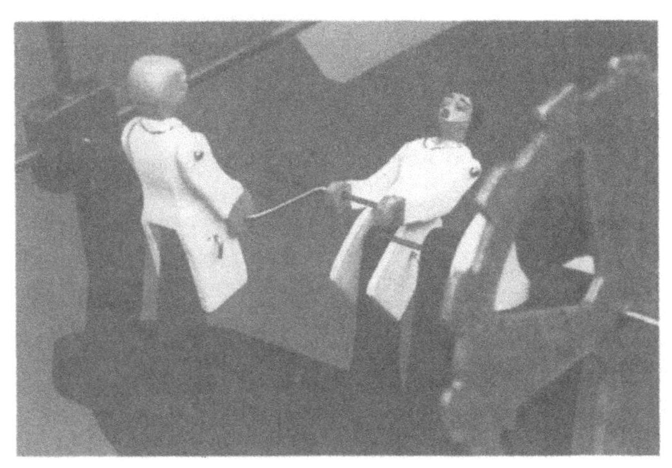

third pillar down. To disassemble the whirligig in the future, you will have to be able to unscrew that pillar first. If the flywheel is loose, put some glue on the camshaft, slide the wheel over it, and hold it with small wooden wedges.

Suggested Colors

Platform and base: red, coats: white, trousers: blue and green, flywheel: many circular colors, gear wheel: gold.

A Propeller for This Whirligig

See the Basic Propeller Design for Mechanical Whirligigs on p. 86.

Materials

Hub	$\frac{3}{4}$" × 3" diameter hexagon
Arms (6)	$\frac{3}{8}$" dowel, 8" long
Blades	Thin metal, 3" × 4"

Procedure

1. Cut out a six-sided hub piece and drill a $\frac{7}{64}$" hole in the center for the camshaft. In the middle of the six sides, drill $\frac{3}{8}$" holes for the arms $\frac{1}{2}$" deep.
2. Cut out the arms and in one end cut out 2" slots for the blades. Drill two pilot holes for the nails that will secure the blades. In the other end put a $\frac{1}{2}$" mark for guidance.
3. Cut out the blades and attach them to the arms with small nails.
4. Glue the arm/blades in the hub holes at a 45-degree angle.

If the breeze in your area is very strong, make a four-bladed propeller or cut down the size of the blades on this one.

Patriotic Drummer

This drummer uses one type of double cam that works similarly to the square type but is less complex. It does not need to have the connecting rods attached to special collars. The ends of the connecting rods are held in grooves filed into the camshaft. As the rods themselves are thin and the weight of the arms is negligible, this whirligig does not need a powerful propeller. It should operate in the slightest breeze. You can see why and perhaps invent other uses for the movement, or you can invent a whirligig with a triple cam or a quadruple cam!

Materials

Wood	
platform	$\frac{3}{4}$" × $2\frac{1}{4}$" × 17"
bass drum	$\frac{3}{4}$" × 3" diameter
drummer	$\frac{3}{4}$" × 2" × $8\frac{1}{2}$"
arms (2)	$\frac{1}{8}$" × 1" × $3\frac{1}{2}$"
drum stand	$\frac{5}{8}$" dowel, 4" long
flag	$\frac{1}{4}$" plywood, 6" × 7"
Metal	
camshaft	$\frac{1}{8}$" brass rod, 10" long
camshaft liner	$\frac{3}{16}$" brass tubing, 5" long
drum	Small tuna or meat can, $1\frac{1}{2}$" × $3\frac{1}{4}$" d.
drumsticks (2)	$\frac{1}{16}$" rods, 3" long
pivot socket liner	$\frac{3}{8}$" tension pin, or $\frac{1}{4}$" tubing, 2" long
cap	16d nail top, screw, or BB
screws (2)	No. 6 screws, $1\frac{1}{2}$" long
washers	as indicated
Propeller	
hub	$\frac{3}{4}$" × 2" × 2"
arms (4)	$\frac{3}{8}$" dowels, 6" long
blades (4)	Thin metal, 3" × 4"

Procedure

1. Cut out the *platform* and mark the locations of the holes and cuts: two holes for screws, one for the pivot point, one for the drum stand, and a slot for the rudder. Use a ruler and square to make the measurements exact and also to mark the opposite points on the top and bottom of the platform.
2. At the marks for the deep holes, drill holes halfway through the platform from top and bottom with a $\frac{1}{8}$" bit so the holes meet in the middle. These holes will act as guides for a larger bit and improve accuracy in drilling. Using a $\frac{3}{8}$" bit, redrill the holes from the bottom. The pivot socket will be 2" deep and the others will be $1\frac{3}{4}$" deep. With a $\frac{1}{2}$" bit, drill a hole $\frac{1}{2}$" deep in the top of the platform for the drum

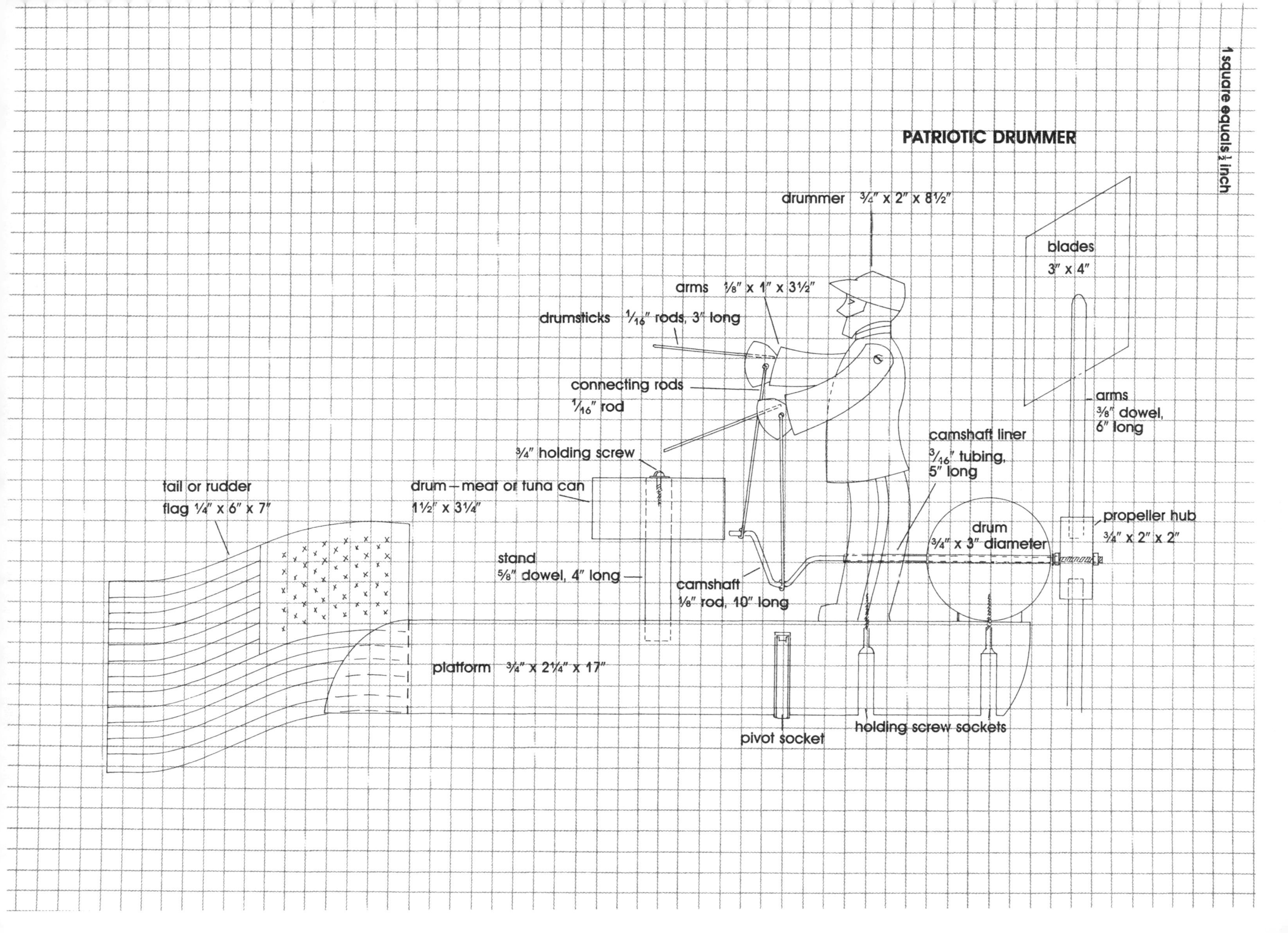
1 square equals ½ inch
PATRIOTIC DRUMMER
drummer ¾" x 2" x 8½"
blades
3" x 4"
arms ⅛" x 1" x 3½"
drumsticks 1/16" rods, 3" long
connecting rods
1/16" rod
arms
⅜" dowel,
6" long
camshaft liner
3/16" tubing,
5" long
¾" holding screw
tail or rudder
flag ¼" x 6" x 7"
drum – meat or tuna can
1½" x 3¼"
propeller hub
¾" x 2" x 2"
drum
¾" x 3" diameter
stand
⅝" dowel, 4" long
camshaft
⅛" rod, 10" long
platform ¾" x 2¼" x 17"
pivot socket
holding screw sockets

stand. Cut out a $\frac{1}{4}$" slot in the rear of the platform for the drum stand. Cut out a $\frac{1}{4}$" slot in the rear of the platform for the rudder. Cut a decorative pattern at the ends of the platform to make it look more interesting. Put the liner and cap in the pivot socket. This would be a good time to make a sturdy stand for the whirligig.

3. For the *bass drum,* cut out a piece of wood 3" square ($\frac{3}{4}$" × 3" × 3") or slightly larger. Find the center by drawing diagonal lines from the corners. Make a 3" circle with a compass. Designate the bottom of the drum, then draw a line across it through the middle of the circle ($1\frac{1}{2}$" from the base). Carry the lines around the sides and mark each center. Drill a $\frac{3}{16}$" hole through the drum halfway through from both sides. Do not cut out the circle yet.

4. Prepare the *drummer* block ($\frac{3}{4}$" × 2" × $8\frac{1}{2}$") and trace the figure on it. Before cutting out the figure, hold the block against the bass drum piece. With a $\frac{3}{16}$" bit or sharp point through the drum, mark the spot on the drummer where the hole will be. You can reverse the block and mark it the same way on the other side. Now you have two points by which to drill a $\frac{3}{16}$" hole through the legs; go halfway through from each side. The hole should correspond with that on the drum and be $1\frac{1}{2}$" from the bottom of the feet.

5. Now you can proceed to cut out the bass drum and the drummer. Leave a flat edge on the bottom of the drum, as shown in the illustration, to hold it firmly to the platform. To make sure you have the cross hole right, put a $\frac{3}{16}$" piece of tubing through the drum and drummer when they are upright. If there is some blockage or a mistake in measurement, you can make the adjustment now by redrilling. It will be hard to do once the pieces are firmly on the platform. When the objects are lined up with the tubing, mark the points where the screws will be located and drill a small pilot hole in the base of the drum and drummer. Fasten them with glue and screws to the platform, keeping the tubing in place.

6. Cut out the *flag* in any pattern. The drawings show a straight flag or a waving flag. The plywood flag measures 6" × 7". The blue field is $2\frac{1}{2}$" × $3\frac{1}{2}$"; the stripes are $\frac{3}{8}$" wide. To place the stars in the blue field (in the rows with six stars each), the rows follow the bottom lines of the stripes. Place the stars $\frac{1}{2}$" apart in each of these six lines, making thirty stars total. Locate these with a pencil and then, with a punch, put a small hole at each spot. These points will show up even when painted, and you can paint a small white cross there for stars. The other twenty stars are in four rows of five stars each, between the other stars. These will be easy to locate, mark, and paint. The flag should be completely painted before being attached to the platform.

7. Cut out the *arms.* Drill a hole for the connecting rod through the middle of each hand. Attach the arms to the body with small screws (like a No. 4 round-headed brass screw, $\frac{3}{4}$" long). A small No. 6 washer should be placed between each arm and the body.

8. Make the *camshaft* by bending a 10" piece of $\frac{1}{8}$" rod in a vise or with a pair of pliers. Make a full-size drawing and lay the rod on it. This will show you exactly where to make the bends. Make the first bend about $2\frac{1}{2}$" from the end of the rod and go on from there. With the end of a file, make grooves in the metal as shown. You may start with a three-corner file but will have to widen the grooves afterward. Thread the other end of the rod with a $\frac{6}{32}$ die to the length of 1" (thirty turns of the die). Put the camshaft in the $\frac{3}{16}$" liner and see if it turns easily. Turn a $\frac{6}{32}$ machine nut on the propeller end, with two washers between it and the whirligig.

9. Put the *drum* in position. Cut out a 4" piece of $\frac{5}{8}$" dowel for the drum stand. Drill a pilot hole in the top end. Put a hole in the center of a small meat or tuna can (about 3" in diameter). Attach the can to the drum stand with a small ($\frac{3}{4}$" No. 4 round-headed screw) and a small No. 6 washer. Then glue it in the $\frac{1}{2}$" deep hole. If it wiggles, put wedges in the hole.

10. Make the *connecting rods* of $\frac{1}{16}$" brass rods or thinner stiff rods. With a pair of pinch pliers, make a circle to fit close, but not tight, around the camshaft groove. Then hold the rod against the hand to see how high and low the arms will move. Cut the rod to size, leaving $\frac{3}{4}$" for the bend into the hands. Fit the rod into the hand holes and see how they work. The connecting rods should not hit the drum. If so, simply move the camshaft back and make adjustments on the propeller end, such as planning to add washers there.

You now have all the parts connected and working. Make a final attachment of the connecting rods and drumsticks. Paint the whirligig; attach the flag with glue and brads.

A Propeller for This Whirligig

The propeller that works well with this whirligig is the same in design as that for the Fisher in the Boat, except that the dimensions are slightly different.

Materials

Hub	$\frac{3}{4}''$ × 2″ × 2″
Arms (4)	$\frac{5}{8}''$ dowel, 6″ long
Blades (4)	Thin metal, 3″ × 4″

Procedure

1. Cut out the hub piece and drill a $\frac{7}{64}''$ hole in the center for the camshaft. Drill $\frac{5}{8}''$ holes $\frac{1}{2}''$ deep in the middle of the four sides.
2. Cut out the arms and, with a coping saw, cut thin slots 2″ long from one end of the dowels. Mark the two places where small $\frac{1}{2}''$ nails will go to attach the blades. A very small bit should be used to drill pilot holes for the nails.
3. Cut out the blades and attach them to the arms with the nails. Bend the ends of the nails over on the other side.
4. Glue the arms with blades into the four side holes on the hub at a 45-degree angle. If they are loose, insert small wooden wedges to hold them firm. When dry, turn the propeller on the whirligig and see how it works.

Winning Race Car

A lady whose son is a race car driver asked me to make a race car whirligig as a present to him. Old automobile whirligigs have been fashioned with wheels made of multibladed propellers, but I never have seen one in a racing setting. So I designed one that shows the driver getting the victory flag as he finishes the race. In this one you can design your own car and give it any color you like. Perhaps some day you will design an automobile whirligig with turning wheels!

Materials

Wood	
platform	$\frac{3}{4}''$ × $2\frac{1}{4}''$ × 20″
platform extension	$\frac{3}{4}''$ × $1\frac{5}{8}''$ × 3″
flag stand	$\frac{3}{4}''$ × 1″ × 6″
stand top	$\frac{1}{2}''$ × 1″ × $1\frac{1}{2}''$
flagger:	
legs (2)	$\frac{1}{4}''$ × $1\frac{1}{2}''$ × $3\frac{1}{2}''$
body	$\frac{3}{4}''$ × $2\frac{1}{2}''$ × $3\frac{1}{4}''$
auto	$\frac{3}{4}''$ × $2\frac{3}{4}''$ × 10″
wheels (4)	$1\frac{1}{2}''$ diameter
rudder exhaust (tail)	$\frac{1}{4}''$ plywood, 6″ × 8″
Metal	
camshaft	$\frac{1}{8}''$ brass rod, 6″ long
extension liner	$\frac{3}{16}''$ brass tubing, 3″ long
axle (for Flagger)	$\frac{3}{32}''$ brass rod, cut to size
body liner	$\frac{1}{8}''$ tubing
pivot socket liner	$\frac{3}{8}''$ tension pin, 2″ long, with cap
holding screws (4)	No. 6 flat-headed screws, $1\frac{1}{2}''$
screws for wheels	No. 4 round-headed brass, 1″
screw eye for body	$\frac{1}{2}''$ size
flag	$1\frac{1}{2}''$ square metal piece, attached to $\frac{1}{8}''$ dowel flagstick
machine nuts (4)	Size $\frac{6}{32}$
washers	No. 6 or No. 8 brass (as needed)

Procedure

1. Cut out the *platform*. With a pencil, ruler, and square, measure and mark the locations of the objects, holes, and cuts. Be sure to mark both the top and bottom of the platform. Then with a $\frac{3}{8}''$ bit, drill holes $1\frac{3}{4}''$ deep for the two screws holding the extension and the flag stand and a 2″ hole for the pivot socket. First, for all the holes, drill halfway through from top and bottom with a $\frac{1}{8}''$ bit. This will insure that you have a straight hole. Then widen the bottoms of the holes as needed with larger bits.

   Trim off the bottom of the platform to a 1″ width 6″ from the front end. At the same time, trim off the front to a pleasing curve. Cut out a 1″ slot in the rear, $\frac{1}{4}''$ wide, for the tail. Drill $\frac{5}{16}''$ holes for the car-holding screws; countersink these holes. Insert the socket liner with cap.
2. Prepare the *platform extension* by drilling a $\frac{3}{16}''$ hole through its length $1\frac{1}{4}''$ from the bottom. Drill in halfway from each end to guarantee a straight and level hole. Secure it with glue and a screw to the platform so that it extends 1″ beyond the platform.

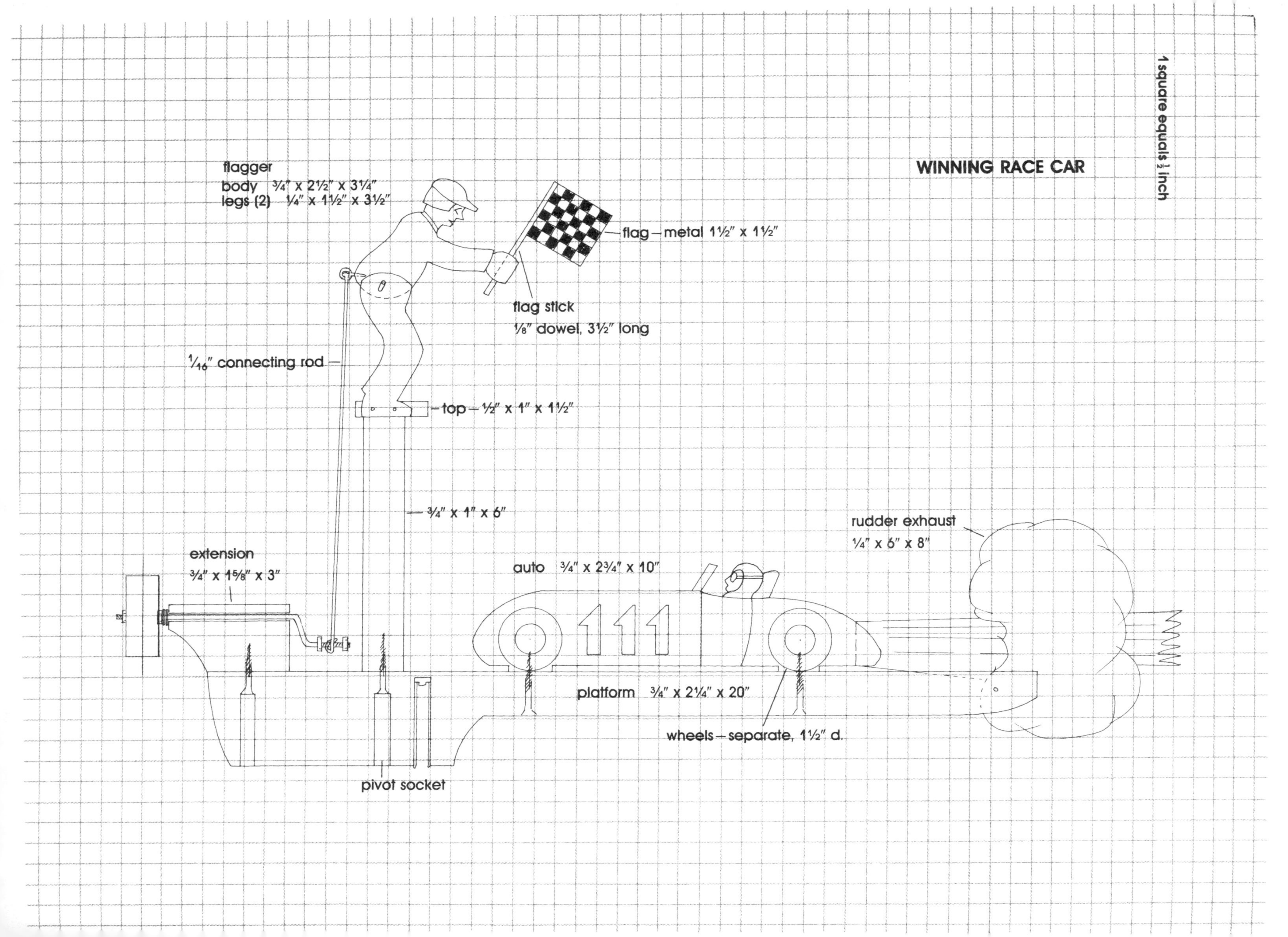
1 square equals ½ inch
WINNING RACE CAR
flagger
body ¾″ x 2½″ x 3¼″
legs (2) ¼″ x 1½″ x 3½″
flag—metal 1½″ x 1½″
flag stick
⅛″ dowel, 3½″ long
1/16″ connecting rod
top—½″ x 1″ x 1½″
¾″ x 1″ x 6″
extension
¾″ x 1⅝″ x 3″
auto ¾″ x 2¾″ x 10″
rudder exhaust
¼″ x 6″ x 8″
111
platform ¾″ x 2¼″ x 20″
wheels—separate, 1½″ d.
pivot socket

Line the hole with $\frac{3}{16}''$ tubing. Cut the front end, including the platform, to a pleasing curve.

3. Cut out the *flag stand* and the stand top. Nail the top to the stand with glue. Then, with glue and a screw, secure the stand to the platform.
4. Cut out the *race car* and cut out a 1" slot in the rear that is $\frac{1}{4}''$ wide. Smooth and round it off with sandpaper. Glue and screw it to the platform. The front end of the car is $6\frac{1}{4}''$ from the platform end, and the center of the front base is $7\frac{3}{4}''$ along the platform (the rear car base is centered at $14\frac{1}{4}''$).
5. Prepare the *rudder exhaust (tail)* piece. It should fit into the slot in the car and also the slot in the platform. Glue and nail it in place.
6. Prepare the camshaft by threading the propeller end 1" and the connecting rod end $\frac{3}{4}''$. Bend a $\frac{3}{4}''$ cam in it and put it in place with $\frac{6}{32}$ machine nuts and washers.
7. Cut out the legs and body of the *flagger*. Drill small pilot holes in the feet for the nails to hold him in place. Drill a $\frac{3}{32}''$ hole in one hip only. Nail and glue the legs to the stand. Then, holding the bit straight and level, put it through the hip hole and drill through the other hip. Drill a $\frac{1}{8}''$ hip hole in the body and line it with tubing. Mount it between the legs with the $\frac{3}{32}''$ axle in place. Put the screw eye in the best place. Drill a $\frac{1}{8}''$ hole through the hand for the flag stick. Make the flag and glue it in the hand.
8. Prepare the *connecting rod* and attach it to the camshaft and screw eye. Check the movement of the mechanism to make sure it works correctly. Attach the *car wheels* with No. 4 round-headed screws, and the piece is ready to be painted.

Suggested Colors

Platform (roadway): Dark gray; flag stand: white; race car: red with white numbers; exhaust: red below with white, red, and black streaked exhaust and white and light gray clouds.

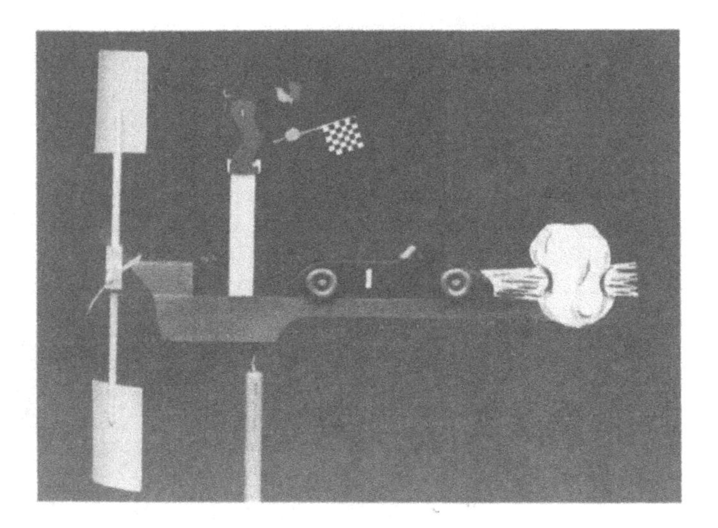

A Propeller for This Whirligig

See the Basic Propeller Design for Mechanical Whirligigs on p. 86.

Materials

Hub	2" square, $\frac{3}{4}'' \times 2'' \times 2''$
Arms (4)	$\frac{3}{8}''$, 7" long
Blades	thin metal, $3'' \times 4''$

Procedure

1. Drill the center of the hub with a $\frac{7}{64}''$ bit. Drill the center of the four sides $\frac{1}{2}''$ deep with a $\frac{3}{8}''$ bit.
2. Cut out the arms and cut 2" slots with a coping saw for the metal blades. Drill two small pilot holes in each one.
3. Cut out the four blades and nail them to the arms. Glue the arms in the hub holes with the blades at a 45-degree angle.

Daniel Boone and the Bear

Daniel Boone (1734–1820) grew up on a farm in Pennsylvania and later settled in North Carolina, the area he loved the most. He married there and his wilderness trail parties left from Hillsborough, at that time the westernmost town in the colonies. Pictures of him in a coonskin cap are incorrect; Daniel was a Quaker and most often wore a wide-brimmed black hat. He was friendly with the Indians and was adopted into at least one tribe. He fired his famous gun, Betsy, only when he needed food and in defense of his life. When he was young, he met up with a bear and carved into the bark of a tree, "D. Boone kild a bar." This whirligig commemorates that event.

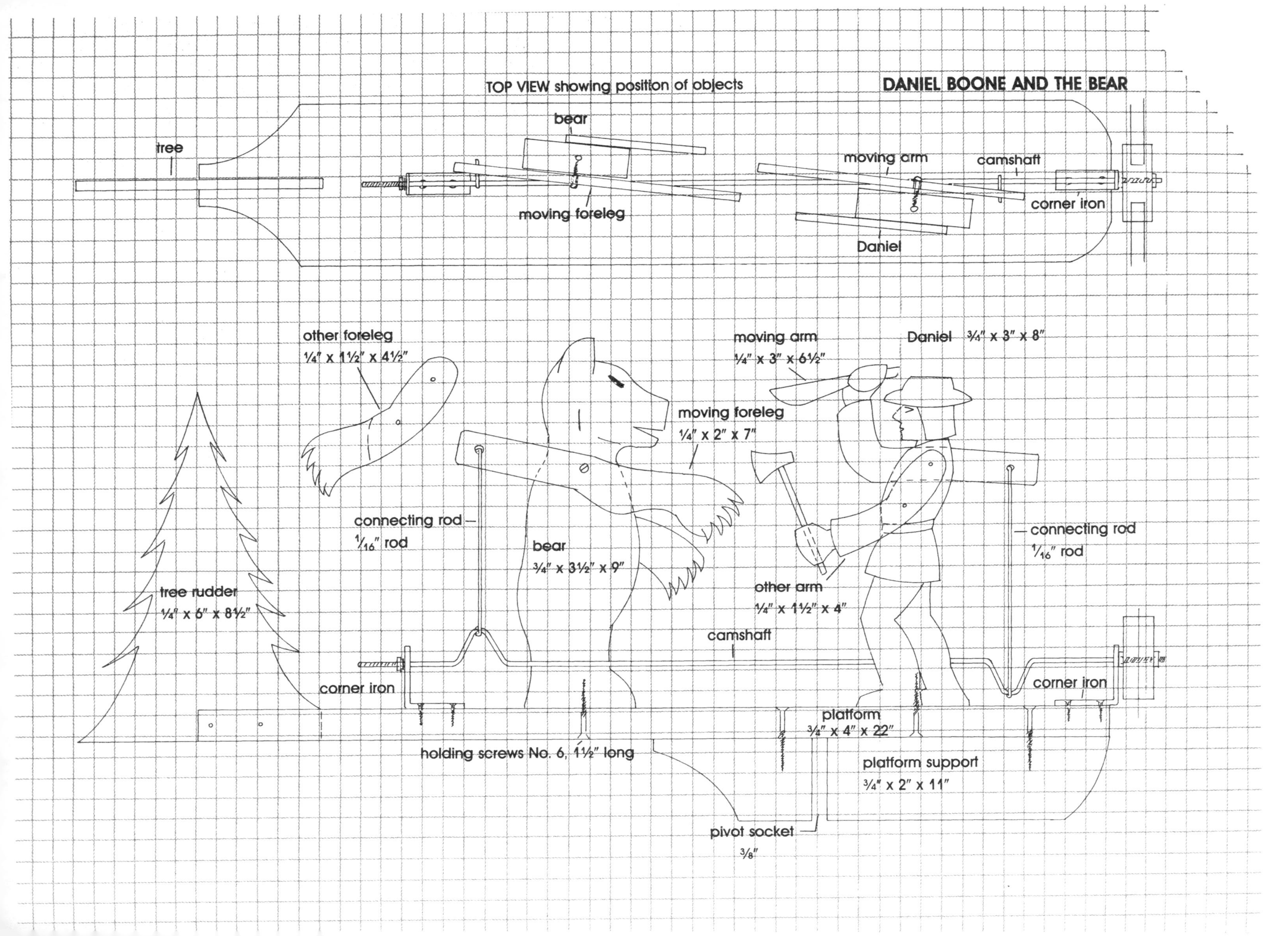
DANIEL BOONE AND THE BEAR
TOP VIEW showing position of objects
bear
tree
moving arm
camshaft
corner iron
moving foreleg
Daniel
other foreleg
1/4″ x 1 1/2″ x 4 1/2″
moving arm
1/4″ x 3″ x 6 1/2″
Daniel 3/4″ x 3″ x 8″
moving foreleg
1/4″ x 2″ x 7″
connecting rod —
1/16″ rod
bear
3/4″ x 3 1/2″ x 9″
— connecting rod
1/16″ rod
tree rudder
1/4″ x 6″ x 8 1/2″
other arm
1/4″ x 1 1/2″ x 4″
camshaft
corner iron
corner iron
platform
3/4″ x 4″ x 22″
holding screws No. 6, 1 1/2″ long
platform support
3/4″ x 2″ x 11″
pivot socket
3/8″

Materials

Wood	
platform	$\frac{3}{4}$" × 4" × 22"
platform support	$\frac{3}{4}$" × 2" × 11"
rudder (tree)	$\frac{1}{4}$" × 6" × $8\frac{1}{2}$"
Daniel	$\frac{3}{4}$" × 3" × 8"
moving arm	$\frac{1}{4}$" × 3" × $6\frac{1}{2}$"
other arm	$\frac{1}{4}$" × $1\frac{1}{2}$" × 4"
bear	$\frac{3}{4}$" × $3\frac{1}{2}$" × 9"
moving foreleg	$\frac{1}{4}$" × 2" × 7"
other foreleg	$\frac{1}{4}$" × $1\frac{1}{2}$" × $4\frac{1}{2}$"
Metal	
camshaft	$\frac{1}{8}$" brass rod, 22" long
corner irons (2)	$1\frac{1}{2}$" size
tension pin	$\frac{3}{8}$", 2" long, with cap
pivot socket liner	$\frac{3}{8}$" tension pin, 2" long, with cap
connecting rods (2)	$\frac{1}{16}$" brass rod, cut to size
arm and leg axles (2)	1" No. 6 round-headed screws
arm washers (2)	No. 6 or No. 8 brass washers
holding screws	No. 6 flat-headed, $1\frac{1}{2}$" long

Procedure

1. Cut out the *platform*. With a pencil draw a center line along the top and bottom and mark the location of all the objects that will be on it or under it, including the holes for the objects. Cut a 3" slot at the rear for the rudder. Drill the principal holes for the figures and the platform support. Trim the front and rear to make a pleasing appearance.

2. Cut out the *platform support* and drill a $\frac{3}{8}$" hole for the pivot socket 7" from the front. Trim the front and back to give the support piece a snappy look. Then glue and screw the platform to it and make sure it is in the center. Cut out the *tree rudder* and glue and nail it in place in the rudder slot. Insert the socket liner with cap. At this point you may wish to make a stand to hold the piece while you finish it.

3. Cut out the *figures* of Daniel and the Bear. Try placing them over the screw holes. Their feet will be angled toward each other on opposite sides of the camshaft, which will run down the middle of the platform. The very front of the feet should be about $\frac{1}{8}$" in front of the center line, no more. Screw the figures in position with glue.

4. Cut out the moving arm and foreleg of the figures. Drill the shoulder holes with a $\frac{3}{16}$" bit and line them with tubing. Then temporarily attach them to the figures.

5. Make a pilot hole and then screw the *corner irons* in position.

   Then make the *camshaft*. Thread the front end for a distance of 1" (the thread will be for the propeller). Put the camshaft between the corner irons and turn a $\frac{6}{32}$ machine nut on the thread. This will hold the camshaft in a proper position for working out measurements on the shaft. Starting from the front, make the first bend at $3\frac{1}{2}$" from the front and finish the first cam with two more bends. Put the rod over the drawing to check the angle and depth of the bend, which should be between $\frac{3}{4}$" and 1". Now, measuring again from the front, begin the second cam with a first bend at 16". Then check to see if the cam will be in proper position to move the bear's foreleg. Make the second cam bend in the opposite direction from the first cam. This will synchronize the movement and make the action easier. The bends can be done with a vise or with a pair of pliers. Brass is rather soft and easy to bend.

6. After bending, put the *camshaft* in a vise. With the edge of a file, cut shallow grooves around the top of each bend. You can start with a three-cornered file, but you will have to widen the groove with either the edge of a regular flat file or with a small round file. Don't cut too deep.

7. Place the camshaft in the corner irons with the front machine nut holding it steady as you work with the connecting rods. Cut out two pieces of $\frac{1}{16}$" brass rod (or smaller steel rod) for the connecting rods. Make a curve at one end and bend it over the camshaft groove. This may be tricky, but eventually it will work. Then, with the connecting rod against Daniel's arm extension, see how long it must be to get the movement you want. Check on the arm to see where the connecting rod should go, and drill a $\frac{1}{8}$" hole there. Bend the rod straight and put it through the hold to test it. Later, after the whirligig is finished and painted, you can make a second bend or hook to secure the rod in the arm. Do the same thing with the bear's foreleg. When you have finished, you may find that the camshaft is too long. I cut mine down to 1" beyond the rear corner iron and threaded the end part way, about $\frac{3}{4}$". When a washer and $\frac{6}{32}$ machine nut were put there, it kept the camshaft from wiggling back and forth.

8. Remove the camshaft, moving arm, and foreleg. Cut out the *other arm and leg*. These are curved and made to look realistic. They are placed even with the other shoulders and attached with glue and two small nails each. I drilled Daniel's hand with a $\frac{1}{8}$" bit and placed a tomahawk in it. This had a 3" long $\frac{1}{8}$" dowel for a handle; the axe was cut from a piece $\frac{1}{4}$" × 1" × 1" wood.

Suggested Colors

Platform: green or woodsy brown; tree: evergreen; Daniel: deerskin pants, tan shirt, and black hat; bear: dark brown with black markings, gray inside paws, and yellow claws. The arm and foreleg extensions (from the shoulders back) are painted black.

A Propeller for This Whirligig

See the Basic Propeller Design for Mechanical Whirligigs on p. 86.

Materials

Hub	$\frac{3}{4}'' \times 2'' \times 2''$
Arms (4)	$\frac{3}{8}''$ dowel, 6″ long
Blades (4)	aluminum, $3\frac{1}{2}'' \times 4\frac{1}{2}''$

Procedure

1. Cut out the *hub* and drill the center with a $\frac{7}{64}''$ bit. Drill the center of the sides $\frac{1}{2}''$ deep with a $\frac{3}{8}''$ bit.
2. Cut out the *arms*. With a coping saw, cut a blade slot 2″ long on each one. With a tiny bit, drill two nail holes through the slotted areas.
3. Cut out the *blades* and attach them to the arms in the slots with $\frac{3}{4}''$ small-headed nails. Bend the ends over to secure them. Glue the arms in the hub holes with the blades at a 45-degree angle. If they are loose, tighten them with wooden wedges.

Whirligigs as Sculpture

Whirligig sculpture is becoming popular. This creative art form, which is perhaps more wood sculpture than functional whirligig, is based on whirligig principles. The figures are carved in the round and are in settings that are unique in design and execution.

For the last few years I have designed some humorous whirligigs that resemble popular cartoons, poking fun at public personalities in ridiculous situations. I call these "The Whirligig of Politics" and "The Whirligigs of Religion," and they usually appear annually in the Christmas Snow for Collectors at the distinguished Somerhill Gallery in Chapel Hill, North Carolina. All of my whirligigs work in the wind although the sculptured ones are designed to be shown indoors. Some sculptors make ones that resemble whirligigs in appearance but not function. They are labelled "whirligigs" and have a propeller attached, but they have no moving parts.

Among the most unusual sculptural whirligigs are those made by Ann Wood and Dean Lucker of Minneapolis, Minnesota. Some years ago they found that real whirligigs are a wonderful sculptural medium and created a group of whimsical whirligigs for the St. Louis County Department of Parks and Recreation exhibition entitled "A Whirligig Garden." The exhibit was subsequently moved to the Laumeier Sculpture Park in St. Louis for permanent exhibition.

I mention this development in the art world because some of you may be interested in developing creative whirligigs of new and unusual designs. Whirligigs today are not only folk art, they also are modern art.

To demonstrate this new direction in the art world, I conclude the presentations in this book with a sculptured whirligig based on well-known America folk hero Johnny Appleseed. His real name was John Chapman, and he was born in Leominster, Massachusetts, in 1774. He was a dedicated professional nurseryman who hoped to make a living selling seeds and seedlings. He collected seeds from cider mills and distributed them to pioneer settlers from Pennsylvania to Ohio and beyond. His nursery was over 1,200 acres in size. He died in 1845 of exposure near Fort Wayne, Indiana. He lives on in the thousands of apple trees on many farms of the northern United States, the descendants of his original seeds.

In the whirligig I have tried to create the legendary Johnny Appleseed—not the weird-looking man with tin pan hat, bare feet, and old sad clothing as some of the mythical descriptions of him attest. He was, after all, a dedicated, intelligent, professional person.

Note: For those who are not adept at carving in the round and want to make this whirligig, the figure can be made flat ($\frac{3}{4}'' \times 4'' \times 9\frac{1}{2}''$). The arm mechanism will be the same as that in the Clashing Knights. The position of the figure on the platform can still be astride the center line at an angle and the holding screw holes should be drilled after the figure and arms are tested in place (see Step 8).

Johnny Appleseed

Materials

Platform	$\frac{3}{4}'' \times 6'' \times 26''$
Platform extension	$\frac{3}{4}'' \times 2'' \times 4''$
Platform base	$\frac{3}{4}'' \times 2'' \times 12''$
Camshaft	$\frac{1}{8}''$ brass rod, $7\frac{1}{4}''$ long, threaded both ends
Pivot socket liner	$\frac{3}{8}''$ tension pin, 2" long, or $\frac{1}{4}''$ brass tubing, with cap
Johnny	
figure	$2'' \times 4\frac{1}{2}'' \times 9\frac{1}{2}''$
arms (2)	$\frac{1}{2}'' \times 1\frac{1}{2}'' \times 4\frac{1}{2}''$
Arm mechanism	$\frac{1}{8}''$ rod, $3\frac{1}{2}''$ long, threaded $\frac{5}{8}''$ at ends
	4 $\frac{6}{32}$ machine nuts, and 2 No. 8 washers
Trees	
(A)	$\frac{1}{4}'' \times 8'' \times 11\frac{1}{2}''$
(B)	$\frac{1}{4}'' \times 6'' \times 8''$
(C)	$\frac{1}{4}'' \times 5'' \times 7''$
(D)	$\frac{1}{4}'' \times 3'' \times 5''$
	twigs as called for
Supports (2 ea):	
(A)	none
(B)	$\frac{1}{2}'' \times \frac{1}{2}'' \times 2''$
(C)	$\frac{1}{2}'' \times \frac{1}{2}'' \times 1\frac{1}{2}''$
(D)	$\frac{1}{2}'' \times \frac{1}{2}'' \times 1''$
Holding screws (5)	No. 6 flat-headed, $1\frac{1}{2}''$ long

Note: For this whirligig it is recommended that all parts be cut out first. This will make assembly easier. The procedure is the same in any case.

Procedure

1. Prepare the *platform* block ($\frac{3}{4}'' \times 6'' \times 26''$) and, with a pencil, mark the center line and the location of all objects on top and bottom. Then cut out the platform and smooth it down with a file and sandpaper. Cut out a $\frac{1}{4}''$ slot $3\frac{1}{2}''$ from the back for the large tree/rudder. Drill the hole for the screw to hold the platform extension and countersink it.
2. Cut out and shape the *platform extension.* Drill a $\frac{3}{16}''$ hole lengthwise $\frac{3}{8}''$ from the top. Drill halfway from both ends to make a level hole. Line it with $\frac{3}{16}''$ tubing. Glue/screw it to the platform.
3. Make the *camshaft.* With a $\frac{6}{32}$ die, thread one end 1" and the other end $\frac{3}{4}''$. Put a cam in the latter end $\frac{3}{4}''$ to 1" deep (and extending 1"), and pass the shaft through the extension. To hold it in place, add a washer and a $\frac{6}{32}$ machine nut at the propeller end.
4. Prepare the *platform base,* marking the areas to cut and drill. Drill the hole for the pivot socket and line it with tubing; put a cap at the bottom. Drill the two screw holes to hold the base to the platform. Attach the base to the platform with glue and screws. This is a good time to make a stand for the whirligig and paint the platform.
5. Trace the *figure* of Johnny on the block of wood in profile and then cut it out. Drill a $\frac{3}{16}''$ hole at the shoulder for the axle; line it with tubing. Note where the head and waist will be cut out and where the legs will be split into left (forward) and right (back). Saw the space between the legs first. Carve the figure out carefully, taking your time.
6. Make the *arms.* At $\frac{1}{2}''$ from the top, drill $\frac{7}{64}''$ shoulder holes and carve the arms as realistically as possible. The right arm scatters the seed and the left arm swings seedlings or cuttings. Turn a small screw eye into the bottom of the right hand.
7. Make the *arm mechanism* as shown in the drawing. This requires a $\frac{1}{8}''$ rod $3\frac{1}{2}''$ long and threaded $\frac{5}{8}''$ from each end. This makes for a close fit; you may wish to start with a longer rod. The main point is to have at least $2\frac{1}{4}''$ between the threads (and the nuts); otherwise the axle will not turn. Put the mechanism in the shoulder hole. Secure both arms to the axle with $\frac{6}{32}$ machine nuts and adjust their position.
8. The figure is more responsive to the cam and in a more dramatic position if it is placed at an approxi-

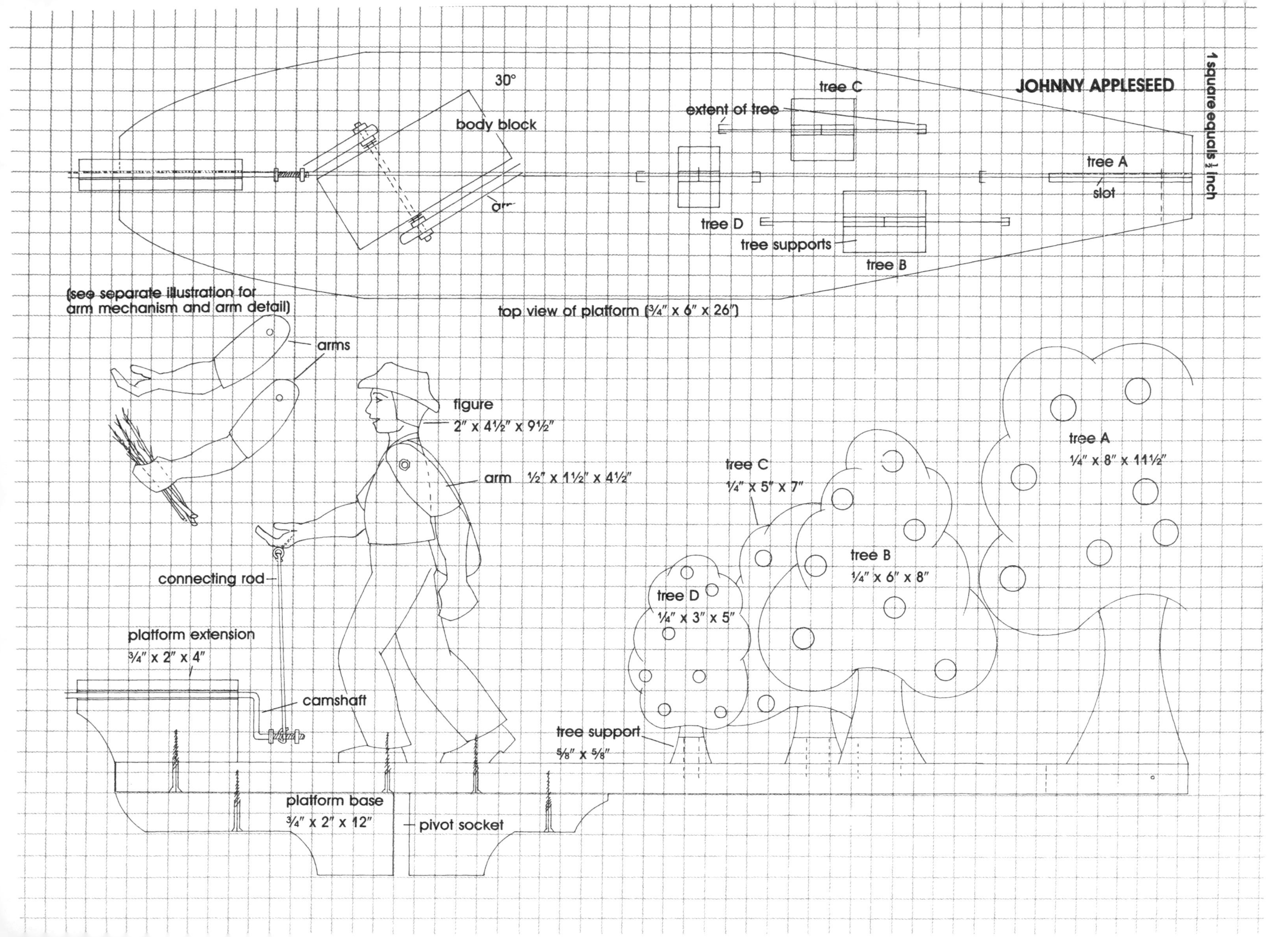

1 square equals ½ inch
JOHNNY APPLESEED
30°
body block
tree C
extent of tree
tree A
slot
tree D
tree supports
tree B
top view of platform (¾″ x 6″ x 26″)
(see separate illustration for
arm mechanism and arm detail)
arms
figure
2″ x 4½″ x 9½″
arm ½″ x 1½″ x 4½″
tree A
¼″ x 8″ x 11½″
tree C
¼″ x 5″ x 7″
tree B
¼″ x 6″ x 8″
tree D
¼″ x 3″ x 5″
connecting rod
platform extension
¾″ x 2″ x 4″
camshaft
tree support
⅝″ x ⅝″
platform base
¾″ x 2″ x 12″
pivot socket

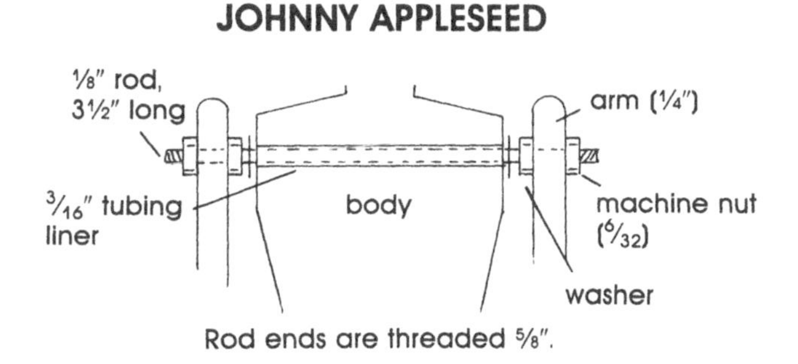

mately 30-degree angle across the center line of the platform. First, drill a hole for the forward left foot 6¾″ from the front and 1″ from the center line. Drill a pilot hole in the middle of the left foot and secure the figure to the platform with a screw. Turn the figure until the right hand, with the screw eye, is over the cam when swinging. With a temporary connecting rod, test the arm movement. When you have it right, mark the location of the right (rear) foot and drill the second holding screw hole there. Disassemble the figure and paint it.

9. Cut out the *trees* and the tree supports. Sand them well and attach the primary tree (A) on the rudder slot with glue and at least one nail. Drill a guide hole for this nail from the side of the platform. Glue and nail one of each tree supports in position. Drill pilot holes in the remaining supports, two for nails into the tree trunk and one for nailing to the platform. Nail and glue the supports to the base of these trees temporarily. They must be painted first because they overlap each other on the platform.
10. The final assembly now can take place. Begin with the trees; glue and nail them to the platform between the supports. Then glue/screw the figure in place. Attach the connecting rod and check the movement.

Suggested Colors

Platform: dark green with flowers and grasses along the side; trees: trunks—brown, foliage—various greens with lots of red apples; figure: shirt—white or homespun light brown, pants—blue, hat—brown, shoes—black.

A Propeller for This Whirligig

See the Basic Propeller Design for Mechanical Whirligigs on page 86 and the Propeller for the Clashing Knights on page 91.

Materials

Hub	a hexagon, 2½″ d.
Arms (6)	⅜″ dowels, 6″ long
Blades (6)	¼″ × 3″ × 3½″ apples

Procedure

1. Cut out the hexagonal hub. This is easily done by making a 2½″ circle and, using the radius, marking off six points on the circumference. To make it easier to drill holes, join these points with lines and find the centers of each line. Draw a line from the center of the circle to these midpoints. Cut out the hexagon and continue the lines over the edges. The midpoint of each side is the place to drill. Make ⅜″ holes ½″ deep. Then drill a $\frac{7}{64}$″ hole in the center of the circle.
2. Cut out the arms and put a ½″ mark on one end to show the hub depth. On the other end, cut a 2″ slit for metal blades and a 2″ slot/notch for wooden blades.
3. Cut out the blades in the shape of an apple. If the blades are metal, secure them in the slits with nails after drilling small pilot holes in the arms. If they are

wood, nail/glue them in the notches. Place them in the hub holes at a 45-degree angle.

If you are going to take the time to make a sculptured whirligig that people will enjoy, try to develop one around a traditional or familiar theme, story, or person. The Bible is full of wonderful themes of this sort, as are American history and American legends like that of Johnny Appleseed.

Other New Directions in Whirligig Construction

At a crafts show in Blowing Rock, North Carolina, some years ago, I met an old woodcarver who told me that his grandfather had made complicated whirligigs using wooden gears to move different parts. It took him all winter to carve one, he said, and that is why he had never gone into making whirligigs. Today, some whirligig makers use metal or plastic reduction gears that slow down the speed of the propeller shaft and keep figure action under control. In high and variable winds the propeller may spin fast but the action will not cause the whirligig to break up.

Jeff Crewe and Jane Corbus, who were trained as industrial designers, became fascinated with the potential of whirligigs both as machines and art forms. For the simple camshaft or crankshaft they developed mechanisms involving simple gears and the more complex worm gears, which, along with pushrods and levers, make for a smooth and controlled mechanical action. Their figures are made of colored industrial plastics, composite wood products, brass, and stainless steel that will last for decades. They produce their models at Amazing Wind Machines, P.O. Box 619, Littleton, MA 01460.

Jack Wiley (of Solipaz Publishing Company, P.O. Box 366, Lodi, CA 95241) is a product of the computer age. He designs whirligigs with the help of his computer, prints out the designs, tests them, and then publishes instruction materials and illustrations in book form—from the same computer and special printer. His books on wind toys and whirligigs indicate the possibilities of computer application to whirligig design production.

Sculptors, artists, designers, engineers, and computer operators are finding new ways to design and construct whirligigs. You may have special interests and talents that can be used to develop unexplored methods of creating whirligigs. But no matter what type of modern technology will be applied to whirligigs, they remain what they always have been: objects moved by the wind, made for pleasure, and enjoyed by all. I think I had it right in my first book, *Whirligigs: Design & Construction*, published a decade ago:

> *. . . there is something special about a whirligig. People like them not just because they are wind machines, although that is interesting in itself. The best ones fascinate us because they are droll, whimsical, humorous, unusual, startling, and aesthetic. They are rhythmical and graceful in motion. Because of the beauty of their design and movement, and their artistic integrity, a few belong to the category of kinetic sculpture. Perhaps you can create one of these, but remember, design comes first!*

We have come a long way from the simple propeller whirligigs of the fourteenth century.

Afterword

Designing Your Own Whirligigs

While making whirligigs from patterns is fun, making them from your own ideas and drawings is even *more* fun! Here are the steps I take in making a new whirligig of any type.

First, get the idea firmly fixed in your mind. Think about the type of whirligig you wish to make. Scribble some sketches on a piece of paper, look up objects in a library book, cut out photos from the newspaper, collect all the information you can so you can get the item or figure right as regards appearance or motion. Sometimes I think about a whirligig for days or weeks before I go to the next step.

Second, draw your idea full size on a sheet of paper and use a ruler to check your measurements. Try to make the measurements even for the sake of convenience and practical application. Make a figure an even 10″ tall, not $10\frac{5}{8}$″; make a platform 22″, not $22\frac{3}{16}$″. Put in all the details: where the holes will be drilled, how the arms will look and how long they will be, how big the propellers will be, where to put the pivot point, and so forth. When your drawing is complete, you will have a pattern by which to build. When you find something will not work, or changes have to be made, you can go back to the drawing, correct it, and have it for future reference. Always keep your original drawings; they will be valuable to you or someone else.

Third, list all the parts you will need to make the whirligig. This is important because you will have to get this material (wood, metal, screws, nails, brass rods, tubing, and other supplies) before you can begin. Over time you will accumulate odd pieces of wood and leftover items, and may have enough material on hand to do the job.

Fourth, check your tools to make sure you have the right ones for the job. If you do not, perhaps you can borrow them. If you need to have the lumberyard or a neighbor cut up some special sizes of lumber, you had better arrange for that before you begin.

Fifth, begin the work! You now should have everything in order and the plan laid out, so you can begin construction. Working with your hands gives a kind of satisfaction not obtained anywhere else. When the whirligig is finished and painted and placed outside in the wind, you will be a truly happy person, having experienced the joy of creating something of your own.

Adam and Eve.

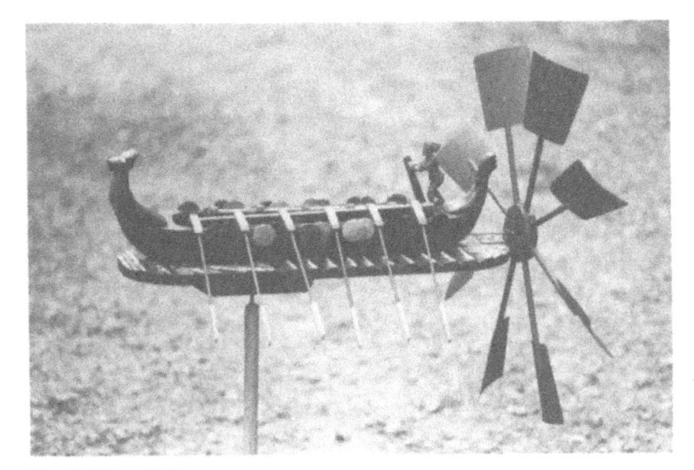

The Viking Ship.

A final word to young whirligig-makers: If you get stuck, ask for help. Someone will come to your rescue.

A final word to all whirligig-makers: Don't give up! Working with whirligigs, perhaps more than with any other wood craft, means learning patience, stick-to-it-iveness, and determination. Don't despair. It will all work out in the end.

The wind is waiting for your whirligig. The one you make will be the only one of its kind in the whole world. Remember that!

Index